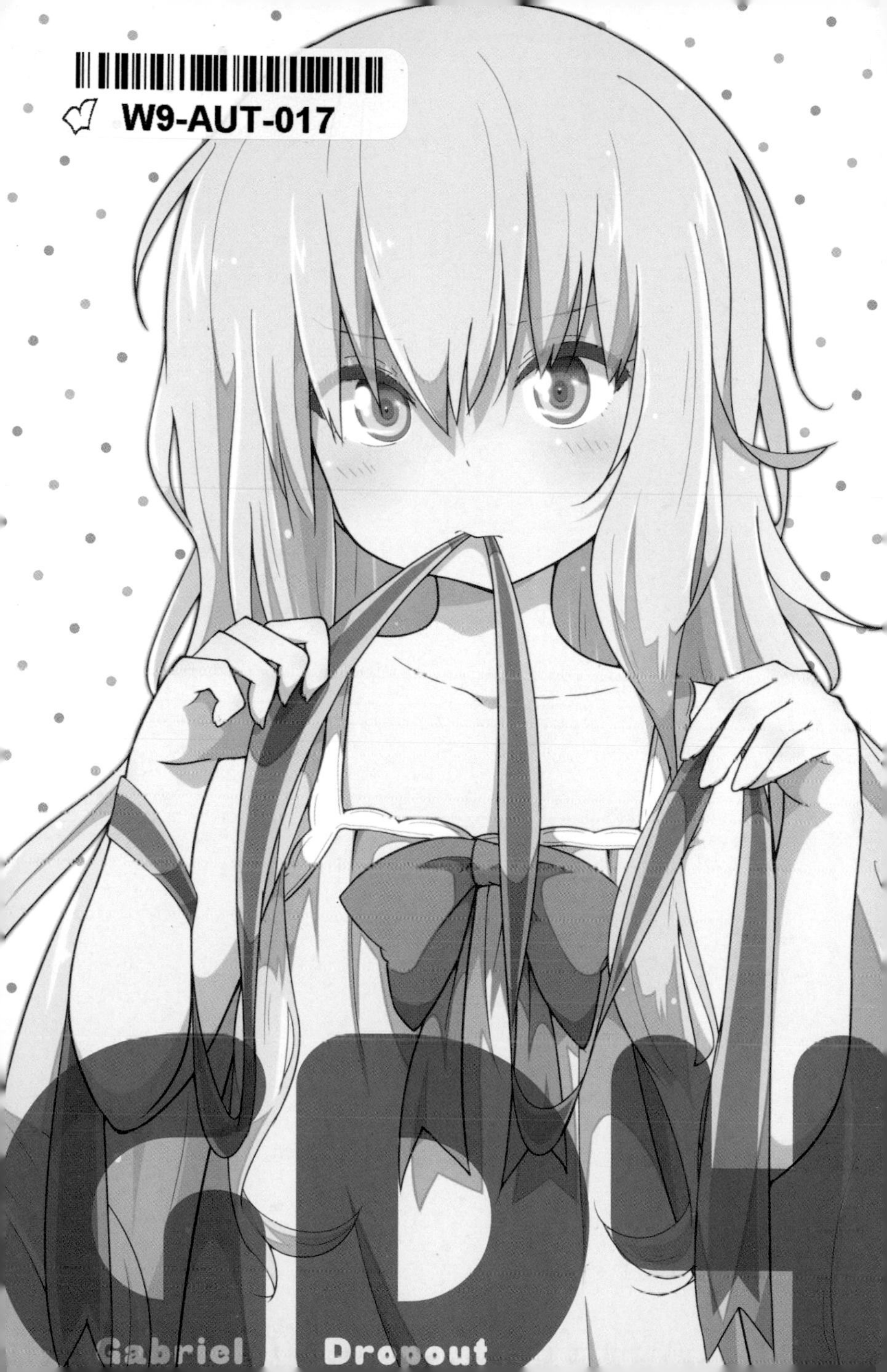
Gabriel Dropout

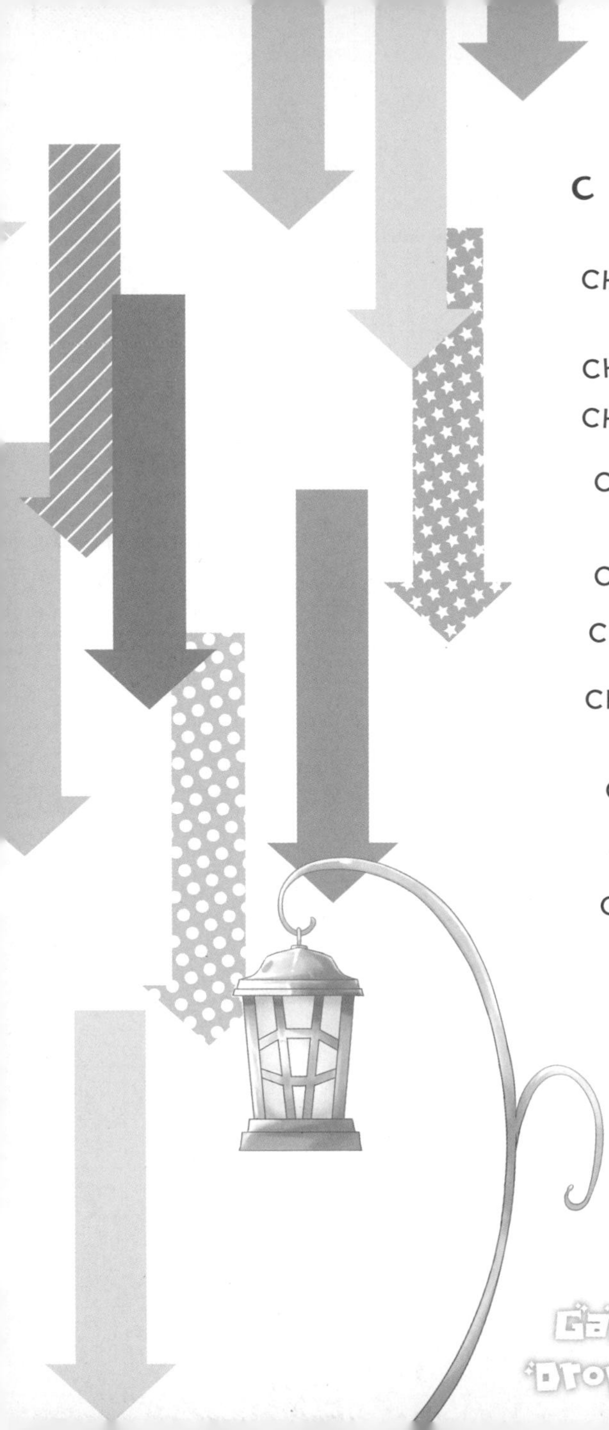

Contents

Gabriel Dropout 4

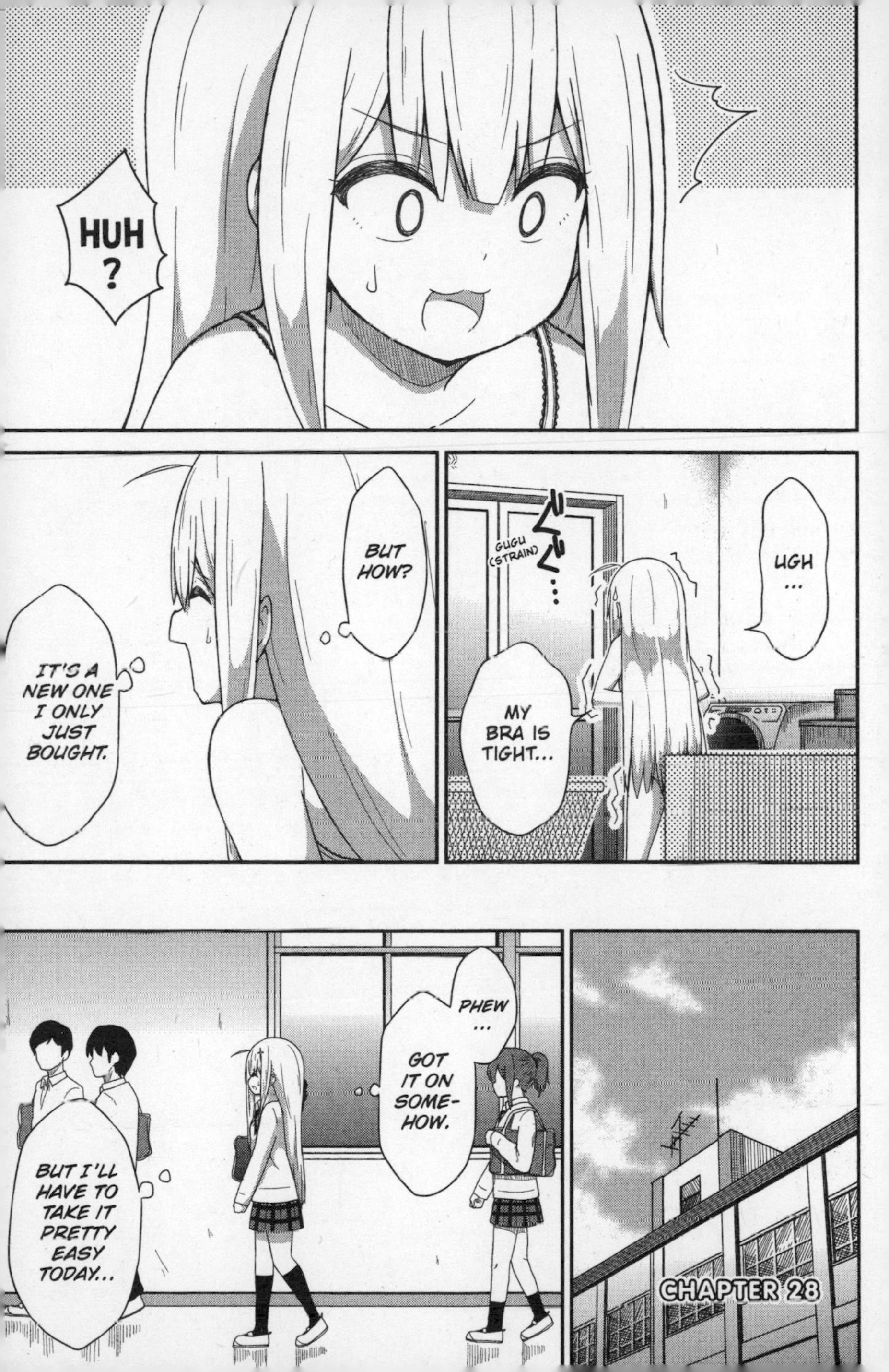
HUH?
UGH...
GUGU (STRAIN)
MY BRA IS TIGHT...
BUT HOW?
IT'S A NEW ONE I ONLY JUST BOUGHT.
CHAPTER 28
PHEW... GOT IT ON SOME-HOW.
BUT I'LL HAVE TO TAKE IT PRETTY EASY TODAY...

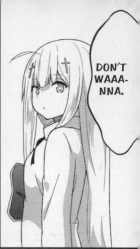

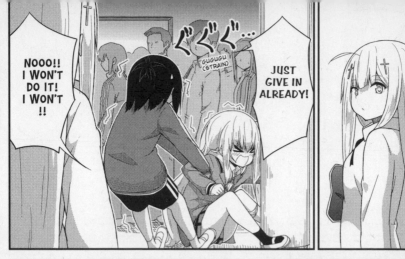

DON'T WAAANNA.
JUST GIVE IN ALREADY!
ぐぐぐ…
GUGUGU (STRAIN)
NOOO!! I WON'T DO IT! I WON'T !!
GOOD MORNING.
AH. MORNING, RAPHY.
WHAT ON EARTH IS THE MATTER?
OH? YOUR GYM OUTFIT?
I DIDN'T THINK WE HAD GYM TODAY?
NO, BUT TODAY IS...
TODAY'S OUR PHYSICAL FITNESS TESTS!! IT SUCKS !!
PHYSICAL FITNESS ...?
AH...

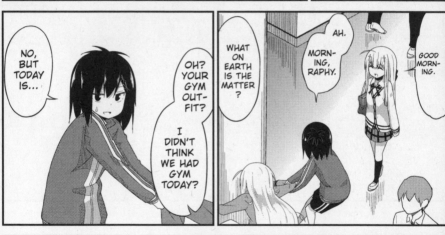

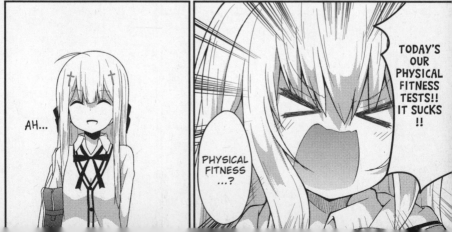

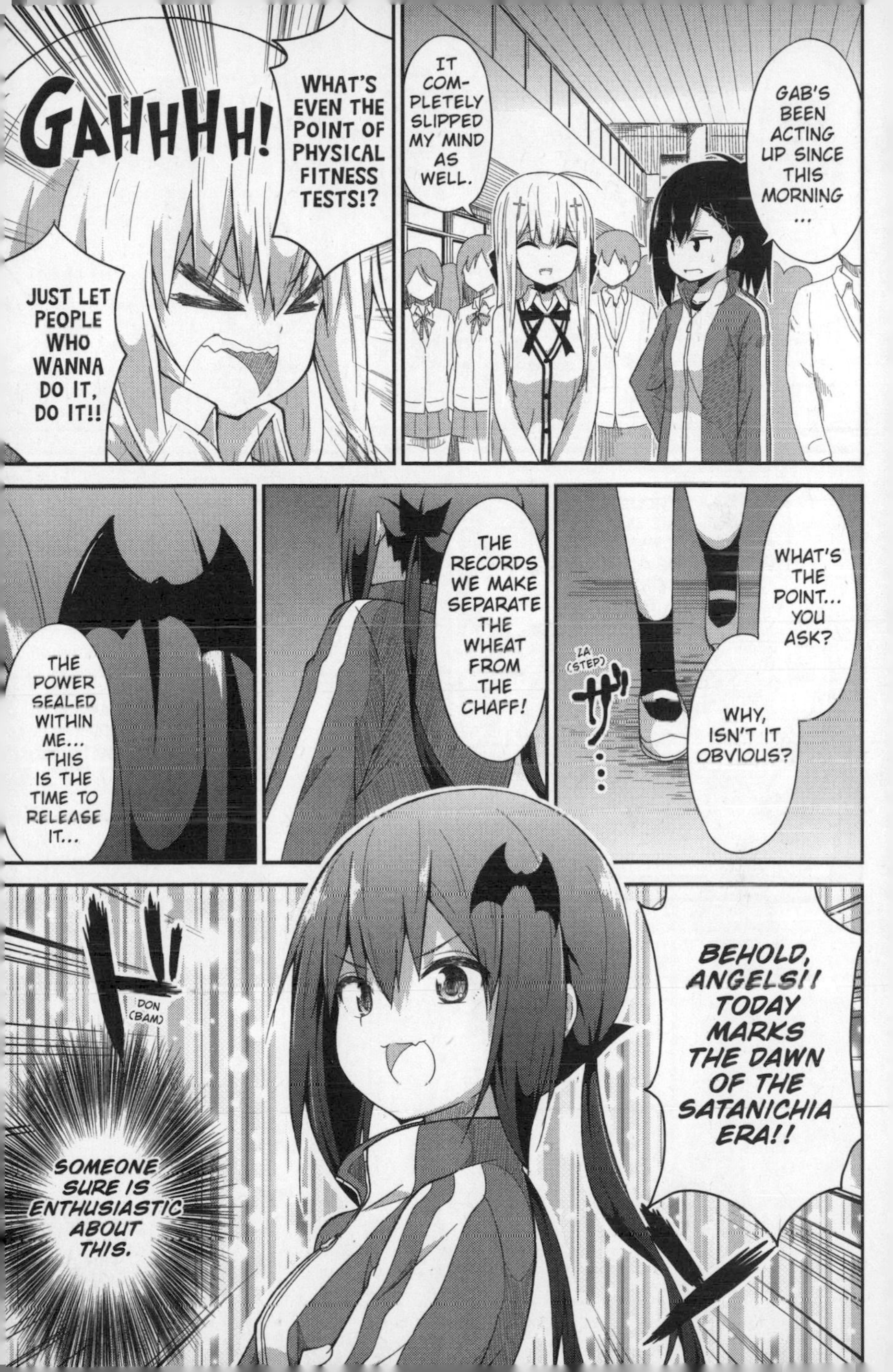
GAB'S BEEN ACTING UP SINCE THIS MORNING...
IT COMPLETELY SLIPPED MY MIND AS WELL.
WHAT'S EVEN THE POINT OF PHYSICAL FITNESS TESTS!?
GAHHHH!
JUST LET PEOPLE WHO WANNA DO IT, DO IT!!
WHAT'S THE POINT... YOU ASK?
WHY, ISN'T IT OBVIOUS?
ZA (STEP)
ザ...
THE RECORDS WE MAKE SEPARATE THE WHEAT FROM THE CHAFF!
THE POWER SEALED WITHIN ME... THIS IS THE TIME TO RELEASE IT...
BEHOLD, ANGELS!! TODAY MARKS THE DAWN OF THE SATANICHIA ERA!!
ド!!
DON (BAM)
SOMEONE SURE IS ENTHUSIASTIC ABOUT THIS.

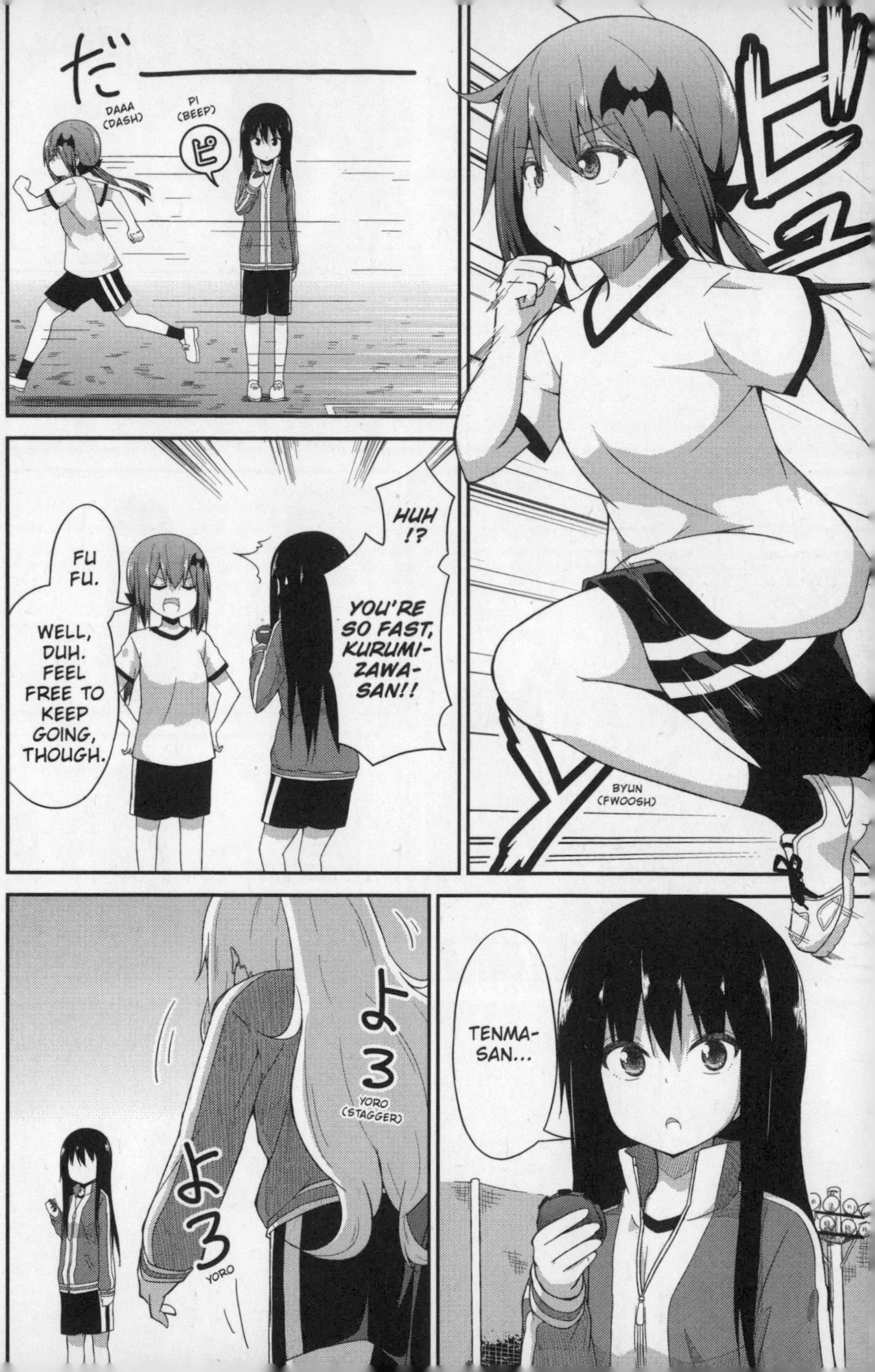
ビュ
BYUN (FWOOSH)
だー
DAAA (DASH)
PI (BEEP)
ピ
HUH!?
YOU'RE SO FAST, KURUMIZAWA-SAN!!
FU FU.
WELL, DUH. FEEL FREE TO KEEP GOING, THOUGH.
TENMA-SAN...
よろ
YORO (STAGGER)
よろ
YORO

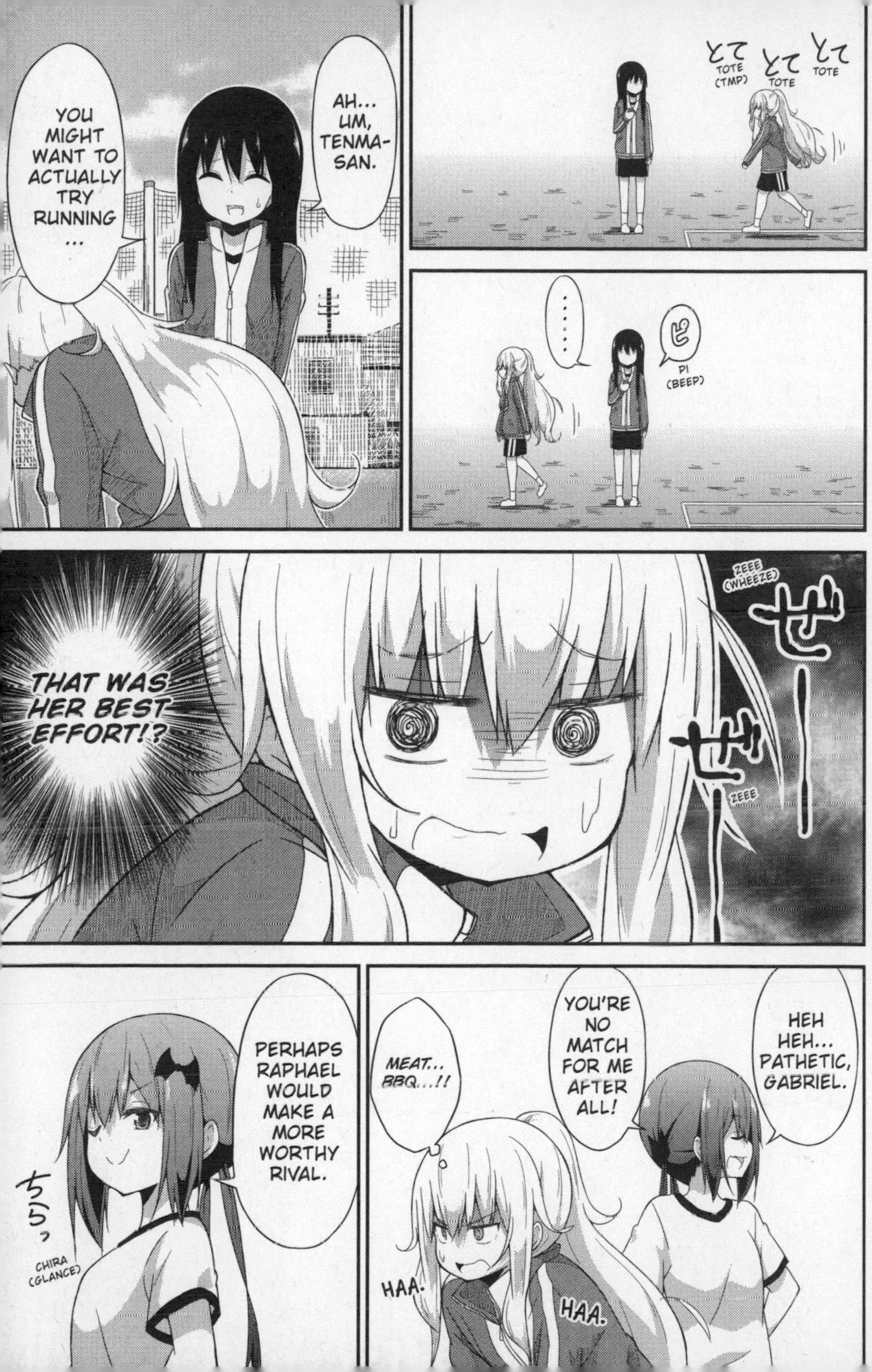
とて
TOTE
とて
TOTE
とて
TOTE (TMP)
ピ
PI (BEEP)
......
AH... UM, TENMA-SAN.
YOU MIGHT WANT TO ACTUALLY TRY RUNNING ...
ぜー
ZEEE (WHEEZE)
ぜー
ZEEE
THAT WAS HER BEST EFFORT!?
HEH HEH... PATHETIC, GABRIEL.
YOU'RE NO MATCH FOR ME AFTER ALL!
MEAT... BBQ...!!
HAA.
HAA.
PERHAPS RAPHAEL WOULD MAKE A MORE WORTHY RIVAL.
ちらっ
CHIRA (GLANCE)

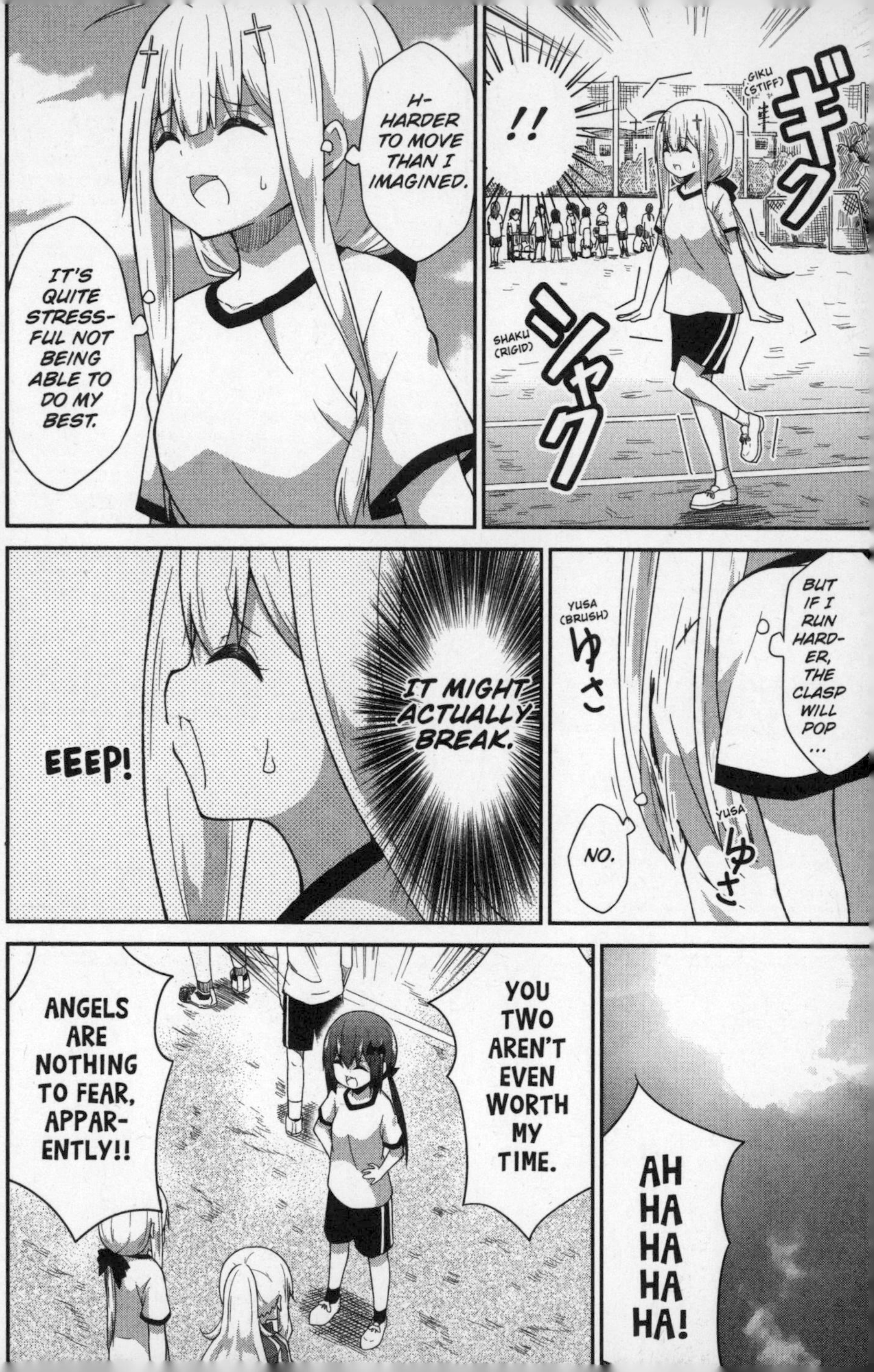
GIKU (STIFF)
ギク
!!
SHAKU (RIGID)
シャク
H-HARDER TO MOVE THAN I IMAGINED.
IT'S QUITE STRESSFUL NOT BEING ABLE TO DO MY BEST.
BUT IF I RUN HARDER, THE CLASP WILL POP...
YUSA (BRUSH)
ゆさ
YUSA
ゆさ
NO.
IT MIGHT ACTUALLY BREAK.
EEEP!
AH HA HA HA HA!
YOU TWO AREN'T EVEN WORTH MY TIME.
ANGELS ARE NOTHING TO FEAR, APPARENTLY!!

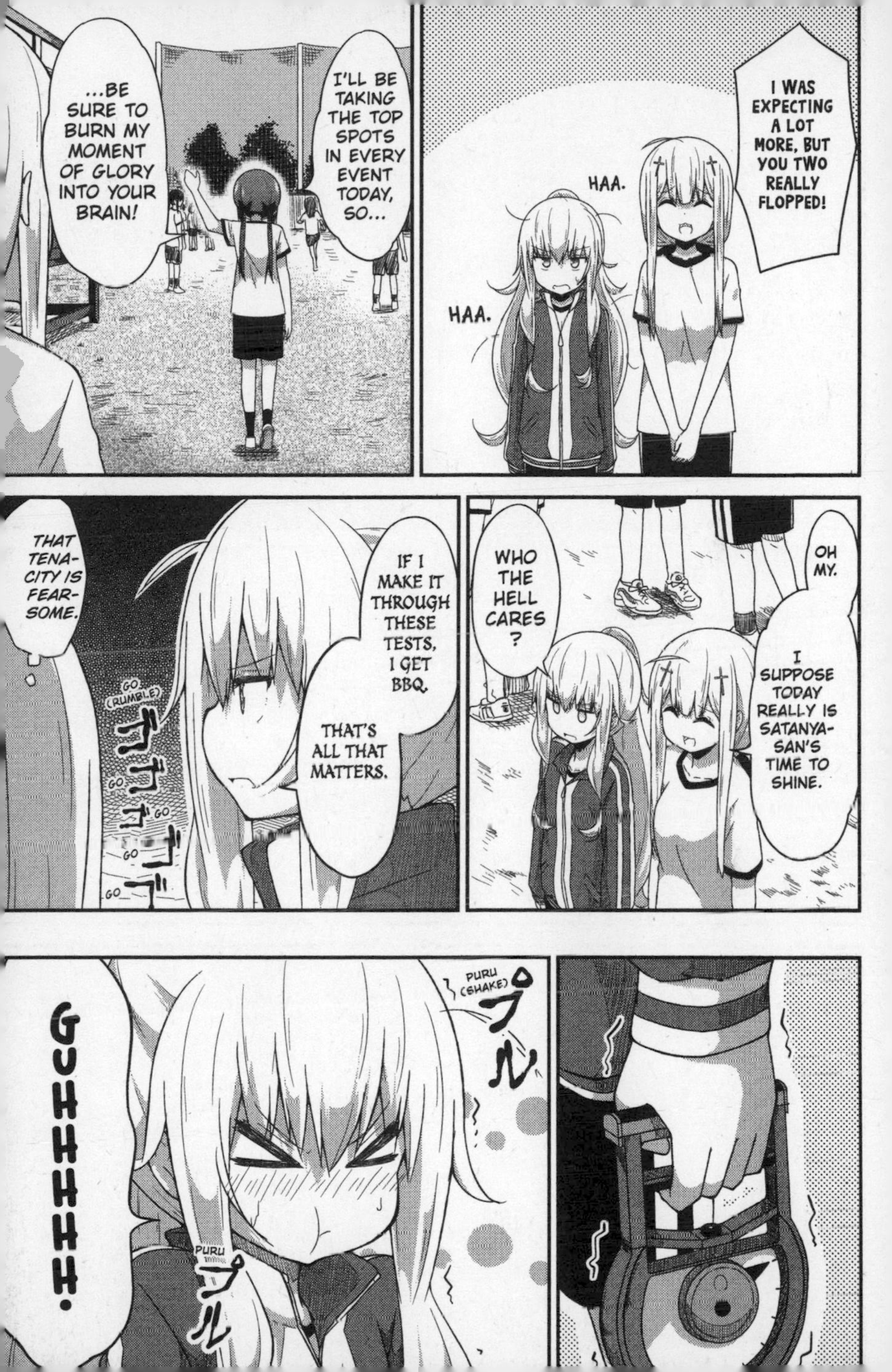
I WAS EXPECTING A LOT MORE, BUT YOU TWO REALLY FLOPPED!
HAA.
HAA.
I'LL BE TAKING THE TOP SPOTS IN EVERY EVENT TODAY, SO...
...BE SURE TO BURN MY MOMENT OF GLORY INTO YOUR BRAIN!
OH MY.
I SUPPOSE TODAY REALLY IS SATANYA-SAN'S TIME TO SHINE.
WHO THE HELL CARES?
IF I MAKE IT THROUGH THESE TESTS, I GET BBQ.
THAT'S ALL THAT MATTERS.
THAT TENACITY IS FEARSOME.
GO (RUMBLE)
GO
GO
GO
GO
PURU (SHAKE)
GUHHHHHH!
PURU

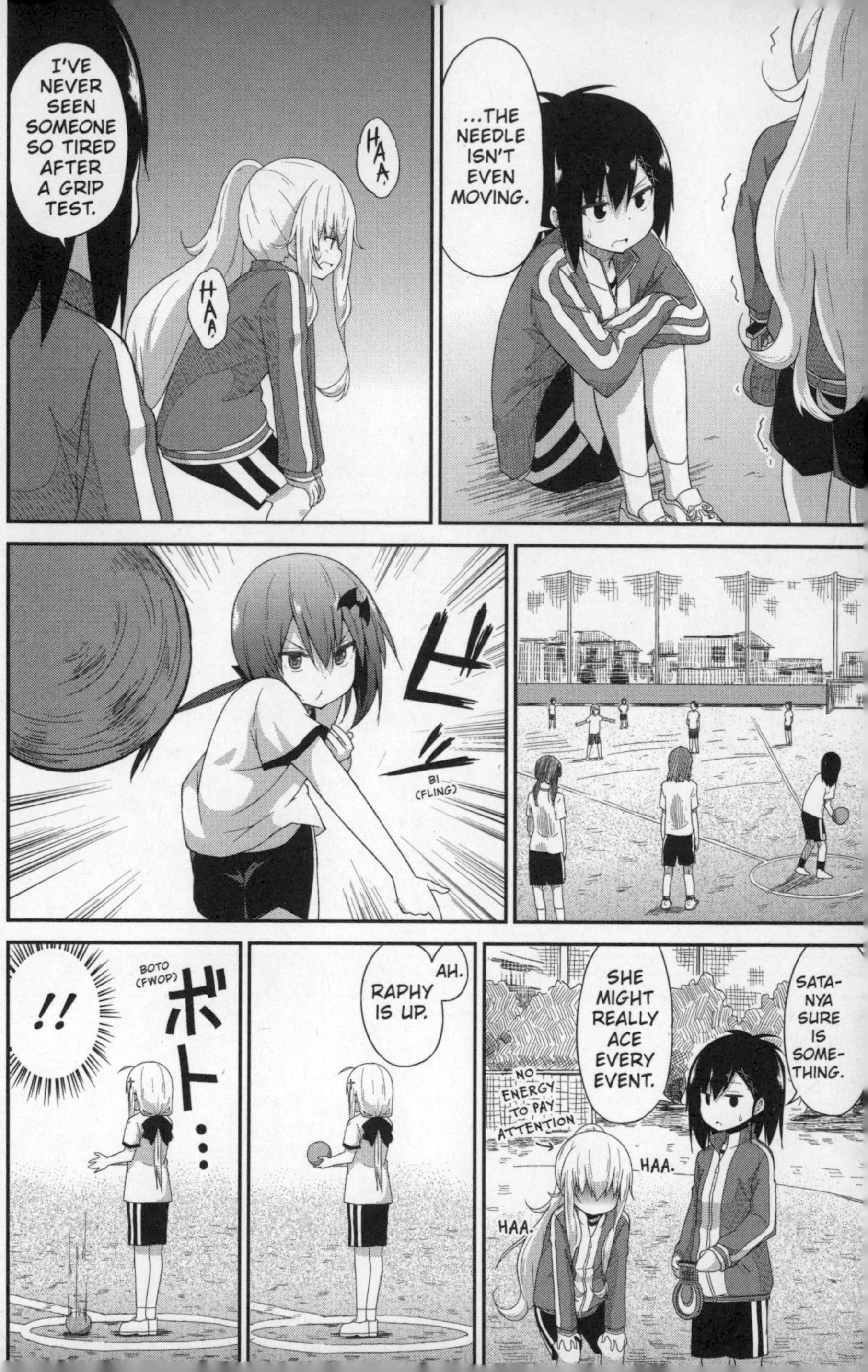
...THE NEEDLE ISN'T EVEN MOVING.
HAA.
I'VE NEVER SEEN SOMEONE SO TIRED AFTER A GRIP TEST.
HAA.
ビ
BI (FLING)
SATA-NYA SURE IS SOME-THING.
SHE MIGHT REALLY ACE EVERY EVENT.
HAA.
NO ENERGY TO PAY ATTENTION
HAA.
AH. RAPHY IS UP.
!!
ボト…
BOTO (FWOP)

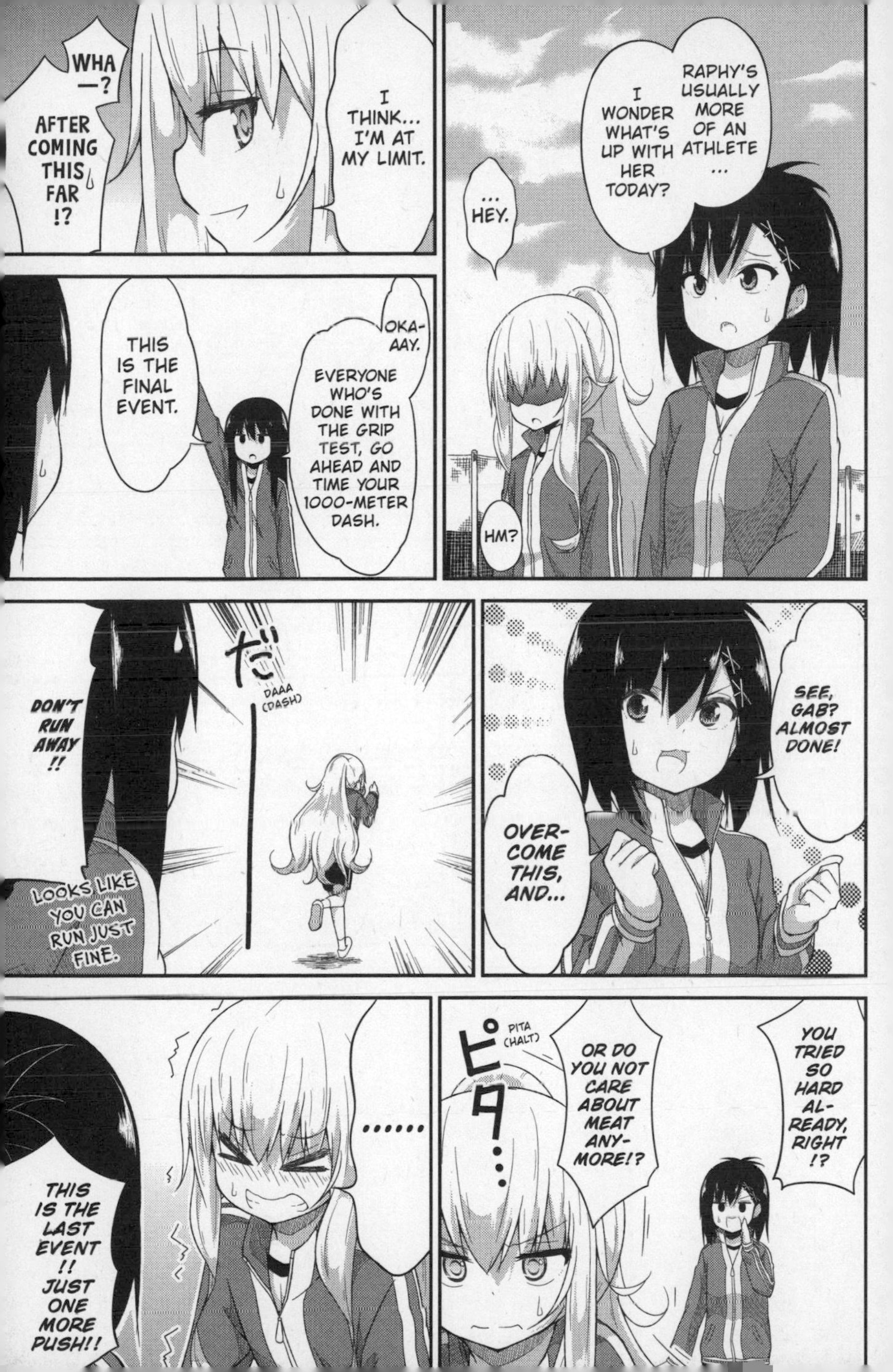
RAPHY'S USUALLY MORE OF AN ATHLETE...
I WONDER WHAT'S UP WITH HER TODAY?
...HEY.
HM?
I THINK... I'M AT MY LIMIT.
WHA—? AFTER COMING THIS FAR!?
OKA-AAY.
EVERYONE WHO'S DONE WITH THE GRIP TEST, GO AHEAD AND TIME YOUR 1000-METER DASH.
THIS IS THE FINAL EVENT.
SEE, GAB? ALMOST DONE!
OVER-COME THIS, AND...
だ
DAAA (DASH)
DON'T RUN AWAY!!
LOOKS LIKE YOU CAN RUN JUST FINE.
YOU TRIED SO HARD AL-READY, RIGHT!?
OR DO YOU NOT CARE ABOUT MEAT ANY-MORE!?
ピタ...
PITA (HALT)
......
THIS IS THE LAST EVENT!! JUST ONE MORE PUSH!!

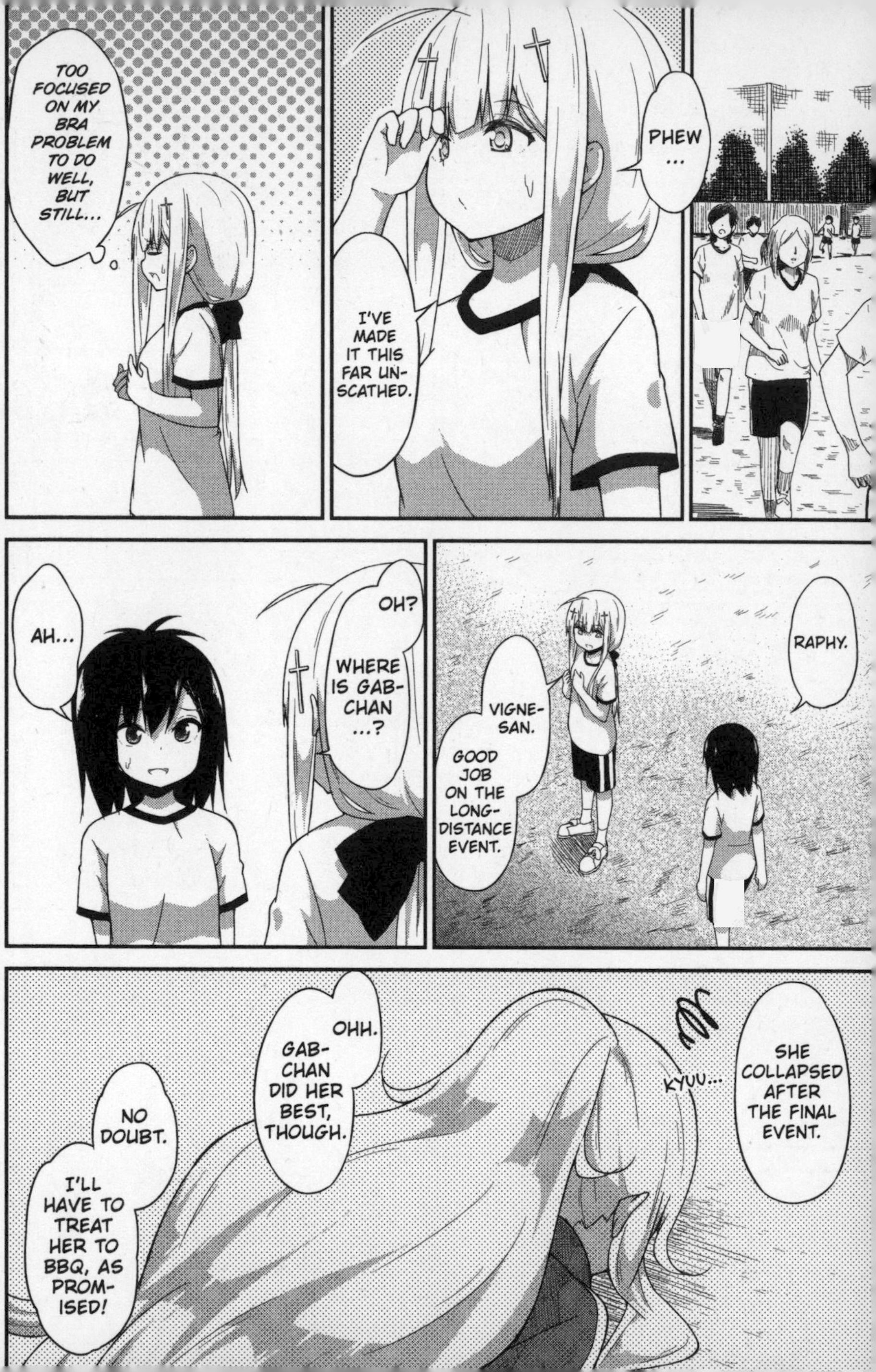
PHEW...
I'VE MADE IT THIS FAR UNSCATHED.
TOO FOCUSED ON MY BRA PROBLEM TO DO WELL, BUT STILL...
RAPHY.
VIGNE-SAN.
GOOD JOB ON THE LONG-DISTANCE EVENT.
OH?
WHERE IS GAB-CHAN...?
AH...
SHE COLLAPSED AFTER THE FINAL EVENT.
KYUU...
OHH.
GAB-CHAN DID HER BEST, THOUGH.
NO DOUBT.
I'LL HAVE TO TREAT HER TO BBQ, AS PROMISED!

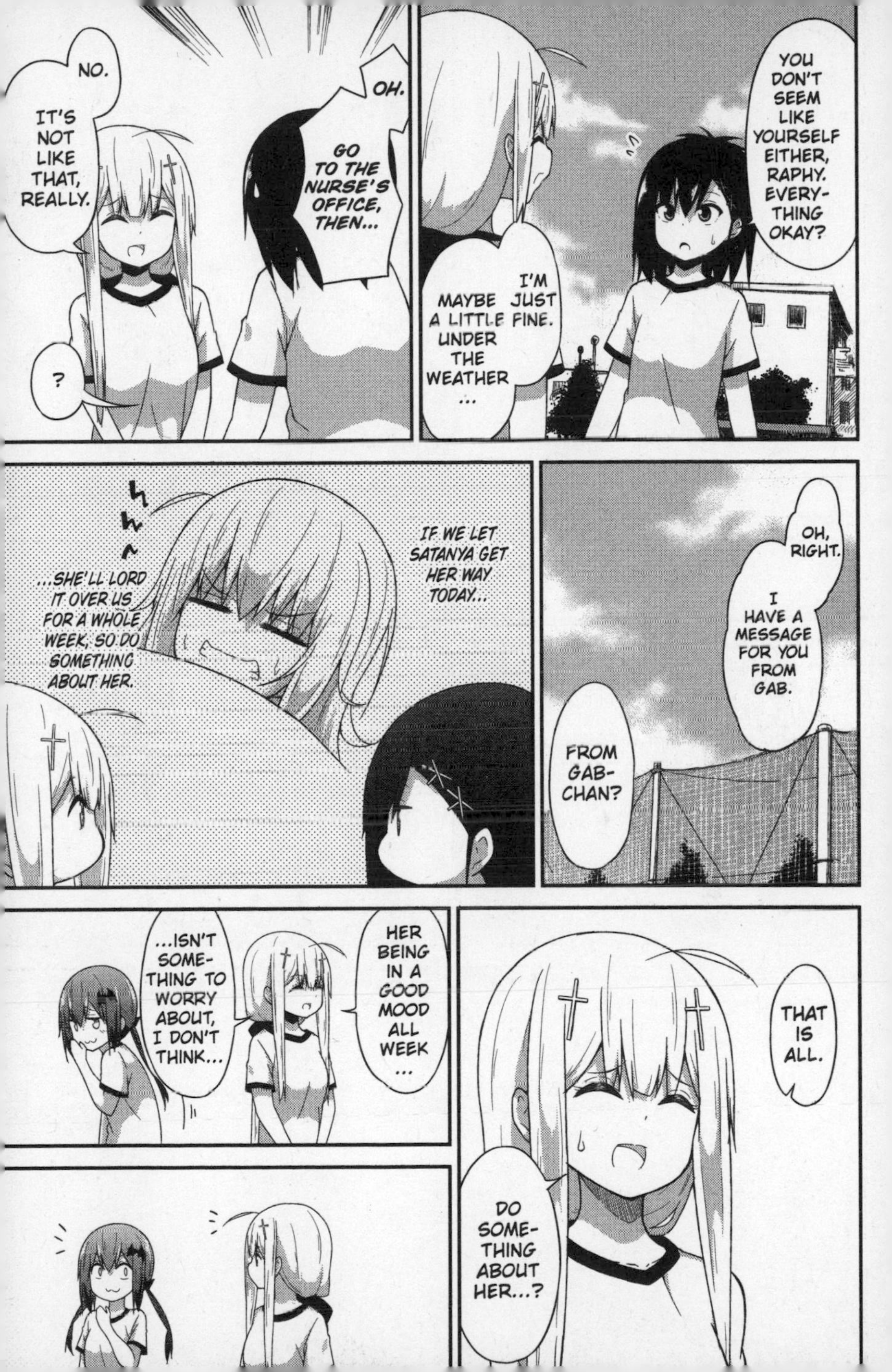
YOU DON'T SEEM LIKE YOURSELF EITHER, RAPHY. EVERYTHING OKAY?
I'M JUST FINE.
MAYBE A LITTLE UNDER THE WEATHER...
OH.
GO TO THE NURSE'S OFFICE, THEN...
NO.
IT'S NOT LIKE THAT, REALLY.
?
OH, RIGHT.
I HAVE A MESSAGE FOR YOU FROM GAB.
FROM GAB-CHAN?
IF WE LET SATANYA GET HER WAY TODAY...
...SHE'LL LORD IT OVER US FOR A WHOLE WEEK, SO DO SOMETHING ABOUT HER.
THAT IS ALL.
DO SOMETHING ABOUT HER...?
HER BEING IN A GOOD MOOD ALL WEEK...
...ISN'T SOMETHING TO WORRY ABOUT, I DON'T THINK...

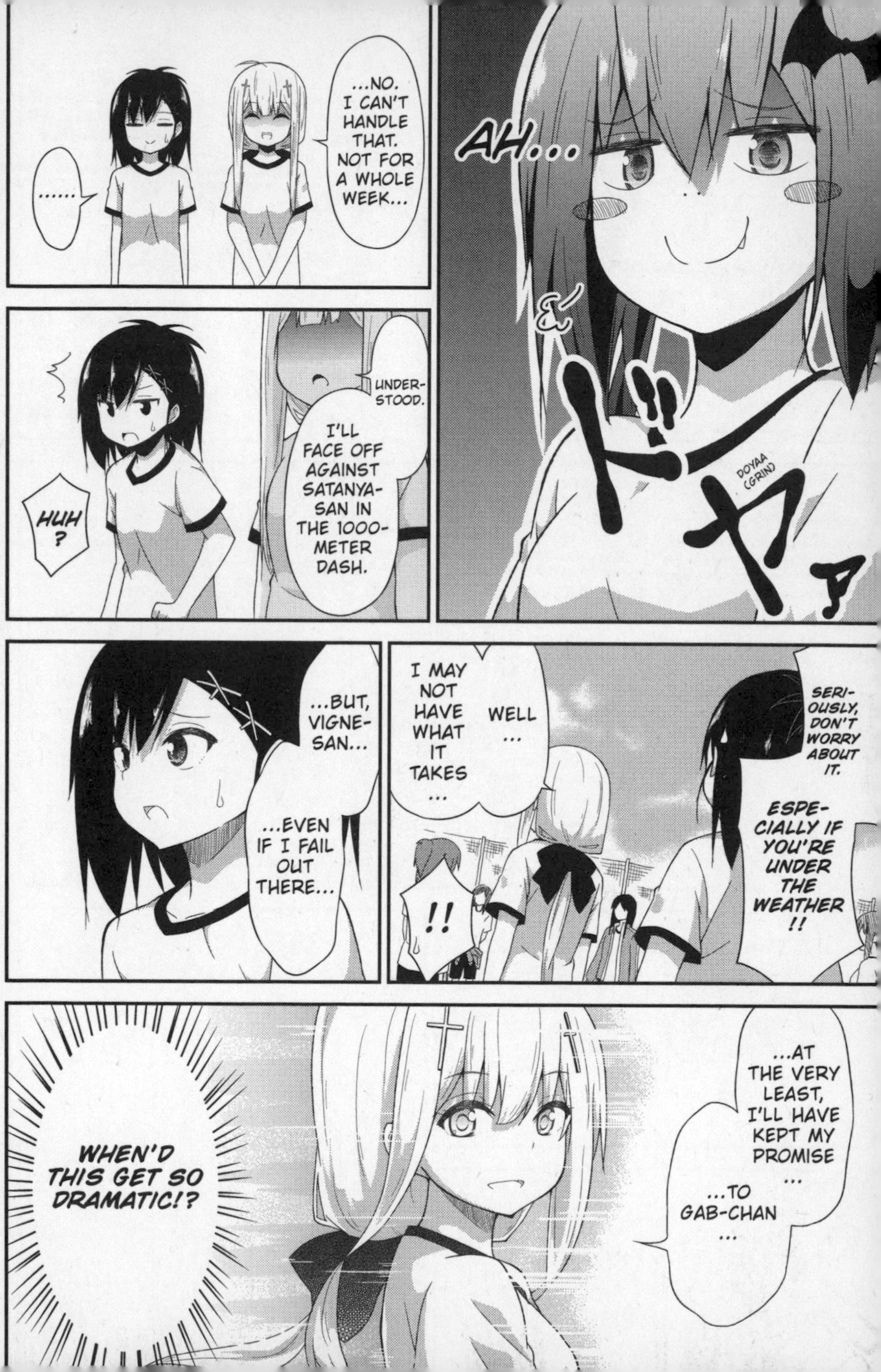
AH...
ドヤァ
DOYAA (GRIND)
...NO. I CAN'T HANDLE THAT. NOT FOR A WHOLE WEEK...
......
UNDERSTOOD.
I'LL FACE OFF AGAINST SATANYA-SAN IN THE 1000-METER DASH.
HUH?
SERIOUSLY, DON'T WORRY ABOUT IT.
ESPECIALLY IF YOU'RE UNDER THE WEATHER!!
WELL...
I MAY NOT HAVE WHAT IT TAKES...
!!
...BUT, VIGNE-SAN...
...EVEN IF I FAIL OUT THERE...
...AT THE VERY LEAST, I'LL HAVE KEPT MY PROMISE...
...TO GAB-CHAN...
WHEN'D THIS GET SO DRAMATIC!?

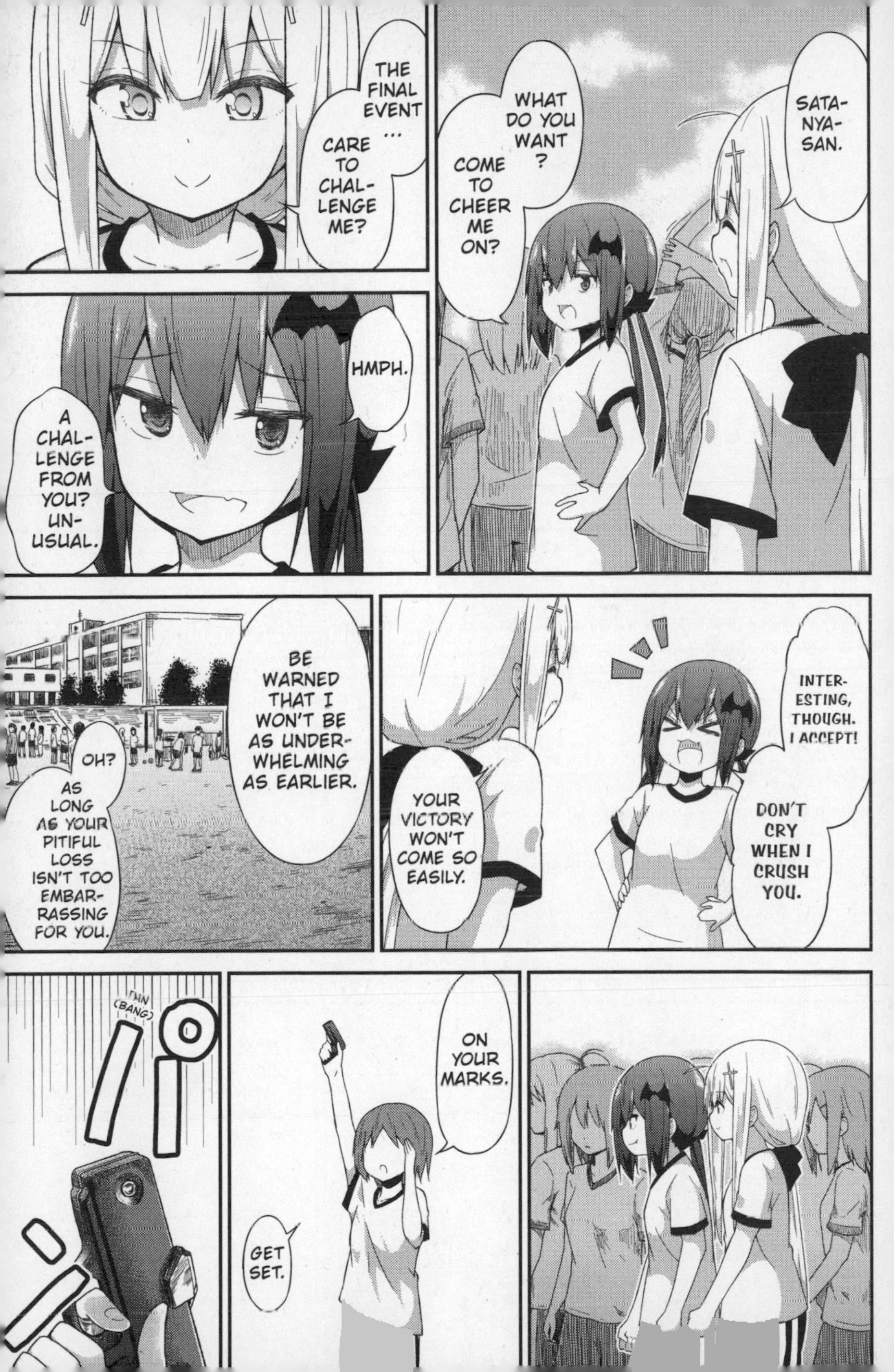
SATA-NYA-SAN.
WHAT DO YOU WANT?
COME TO CHEER ME ON?
THE FINAL EVENT...
CARE TO CHALLENGE ME?
HMPH.
A CHALLENGE FROM YOU? UNUSUAL.
INTERESTING, THOUGH. I ACCEPT!
DON'T CRY WHEN I CRUSH YOU.
YOUR VICTORY WON'T COME SO EASILY.
BE WARNED THAT I WON'T BE AS UNDERWHELMING AS EARLIER.
OH?
AS LONG AS YOUR PITIFUL LOSS ISN'T TOO EMBARRASSING FOR YOU.
ON YOUR MARKS.
GET SET.
(BANG)

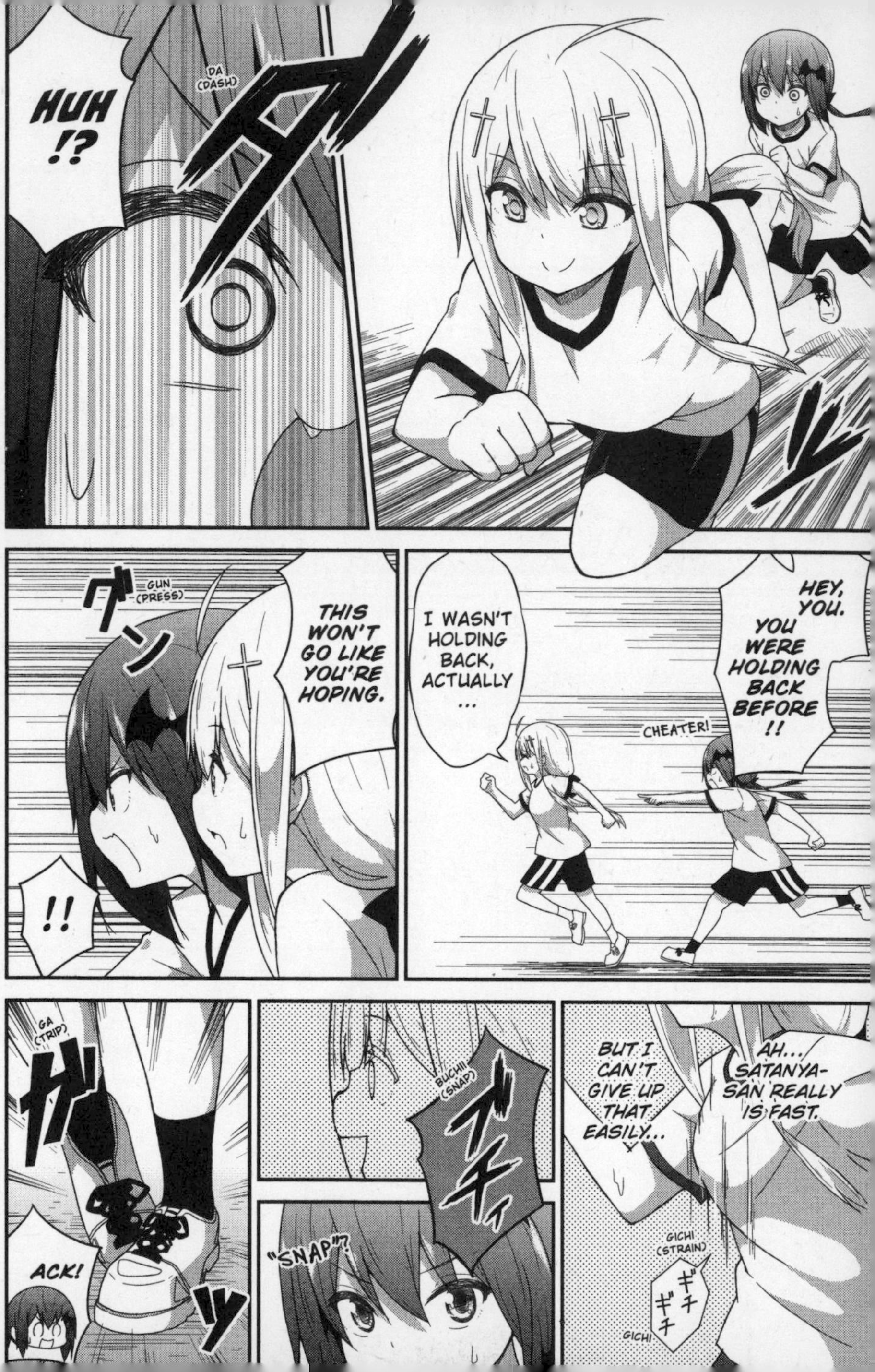
DA (DASH)
HUH!?
HEY, YOU. YOU WERE HOLDING BACK BEFORE!!
CHEATER!
I WASN'T HOLDING BACK, ACTUALLY...
GUN (PRESS)
THIS WON'T GO LIKE YOU'RE HOPING.
!!
AH... SATANYA-SAN REALLY IS FAST.
BUT I CAN'T GIVE UP THAT EASILY...
GICHI (STRAIN)
GICHI
BUCHII (SNAP)
"SNAP"?
GA (TRIP)
ACK!

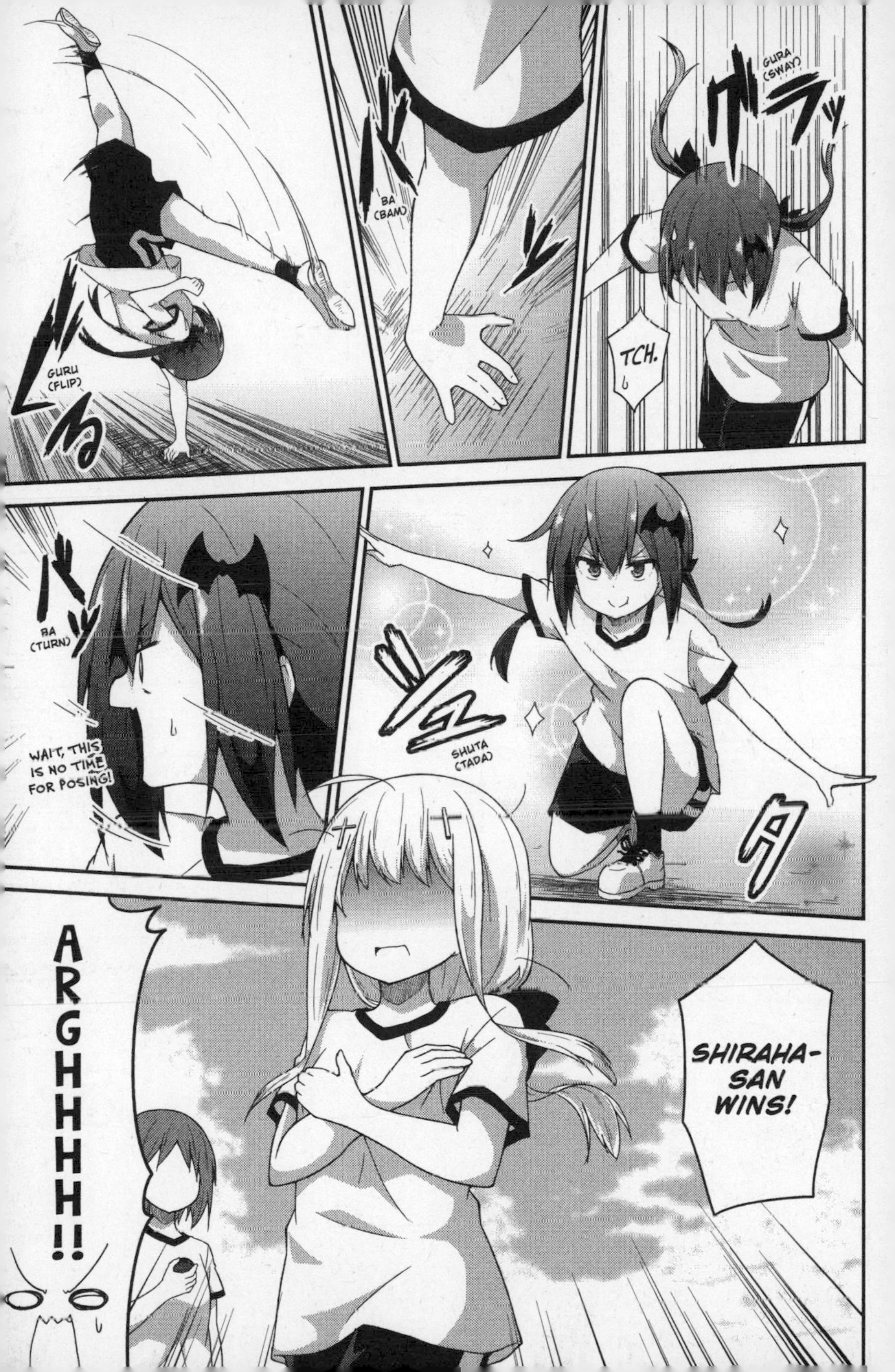
GURA (SWAY)
TCH.
BA (BAM)
GURU (FLIP)
SHUTA (TADA)
BA (TURN)
WAIT, THIS IS NO TIME FOR POSING!
SHIRAHA-SAN WINS!
ARGHHHH!!

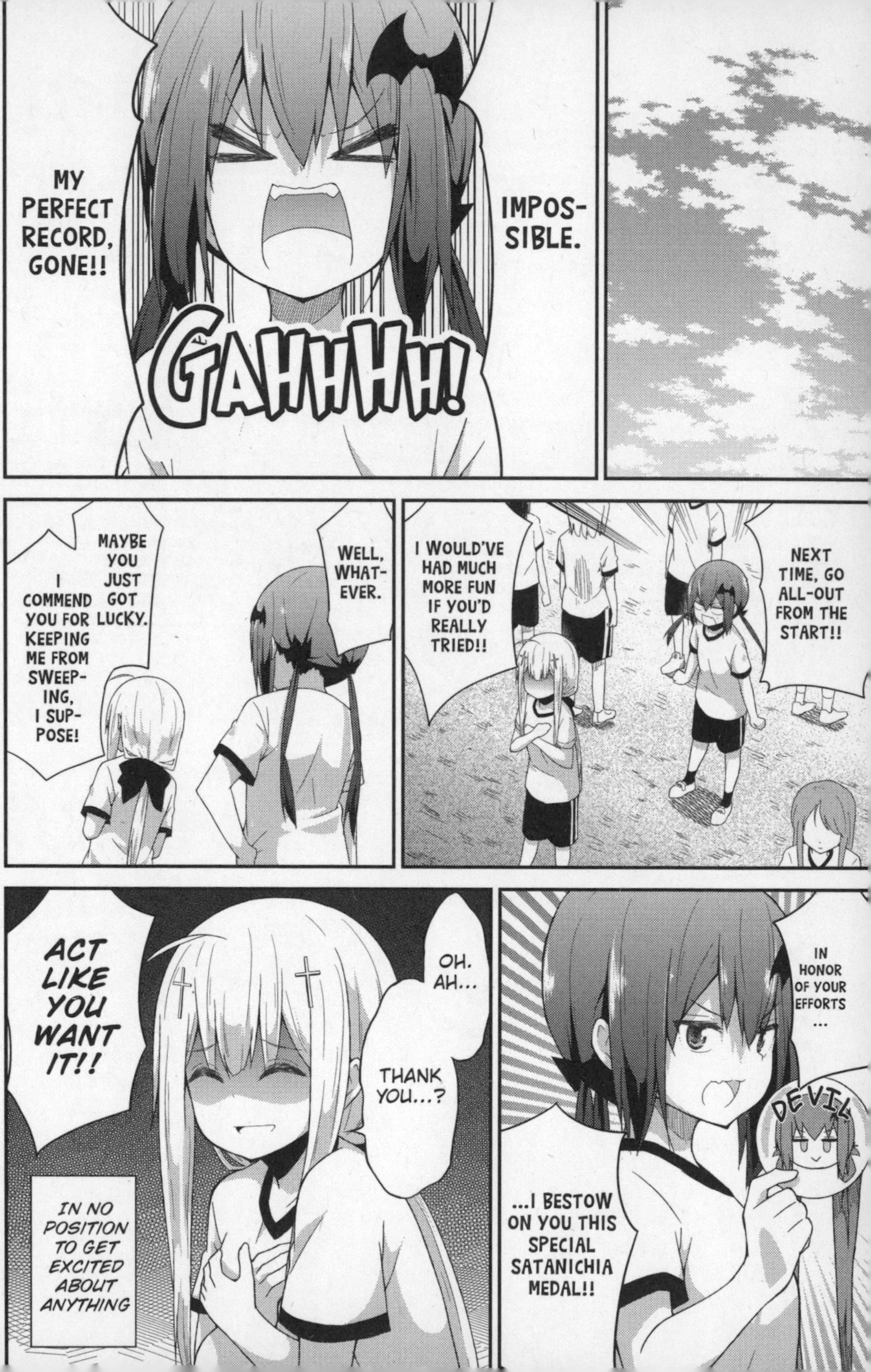
IMPOSSIBLE.
MY PERFECT RECORD, GONE!!
GAHHHH!
NEXT TIME, GO ALL-OUT FROM THE START!!
I WOULD'VE HAD MUCH MORE FUN IF YOU'D REALLY TRIED!!
WELL, WHATEVER.
MAYBE YOU JUST GOT LUCKY.
I COMMEND YOU FOR KEEPING ME FROM SWEEPING, I SUPPOSE!
IN HONOR OF YOUR EFFORTS ...
DEVIL
...I BESTOW ON YOU THIS SPECIAL SATANICHIA MEDAL!!
OH. AH...
THANK YOU...?
ACT LIKE YOU WANT IT!!
IN NO POSITION TO GET EXCITED ABOUT ANYTHING

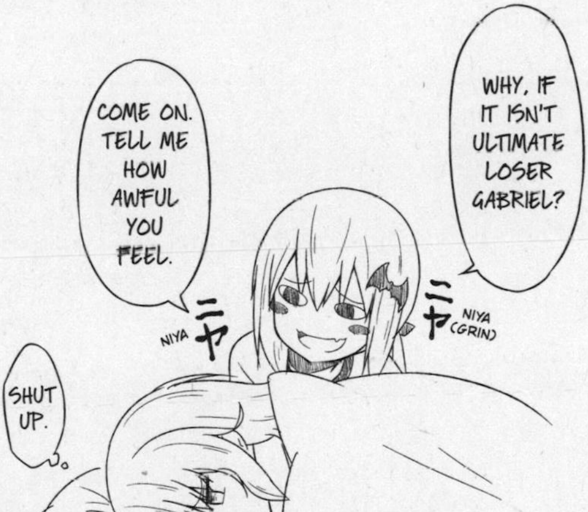
WHY, IF IT ISN'T ULTIMATE LOSER GABRIEL?
ニヤ NIYA (GRIN)
COME ON. TELL ME HOW AWFUL YOU FEEL.
ニヤ NIYA
SHUT UP.

Gabriel Dropout

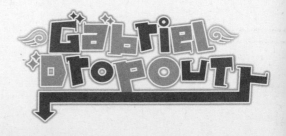

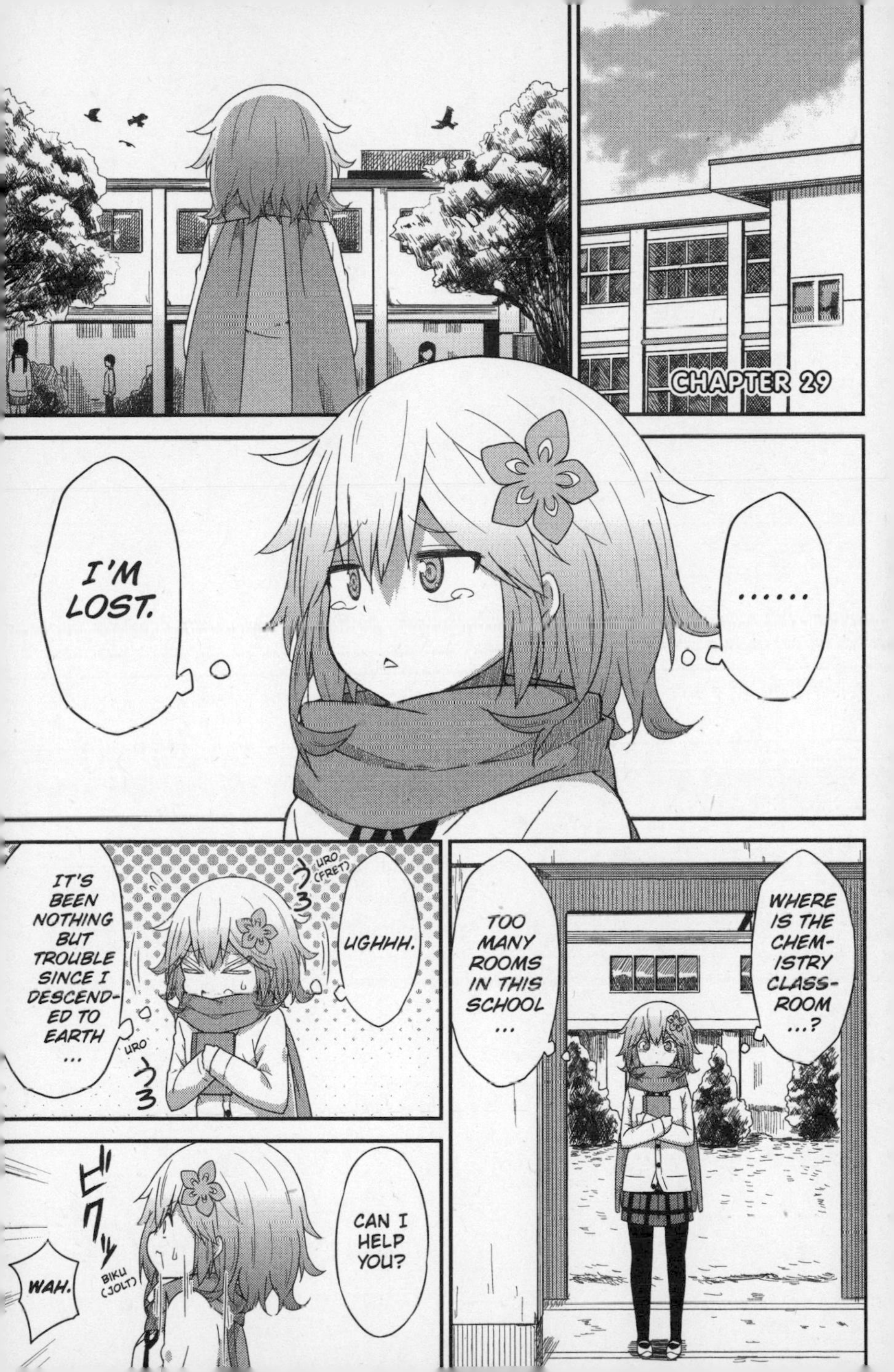
CHAPTER 29
......
I'M LOST.
WHERE IS THE CHEM-ISTRY CLASS-ROOM ...?
TOO MANY ROOMS IN THIS SCHOOL ...
URO (FRET)
UGHHH.
IT'S BEEN NOTHING BUT TROUBLE SINCE I DESCEND-ED TO EARTH ...
URO
CAN I HELP YOU?
BIKU (JOLT)
WAH.

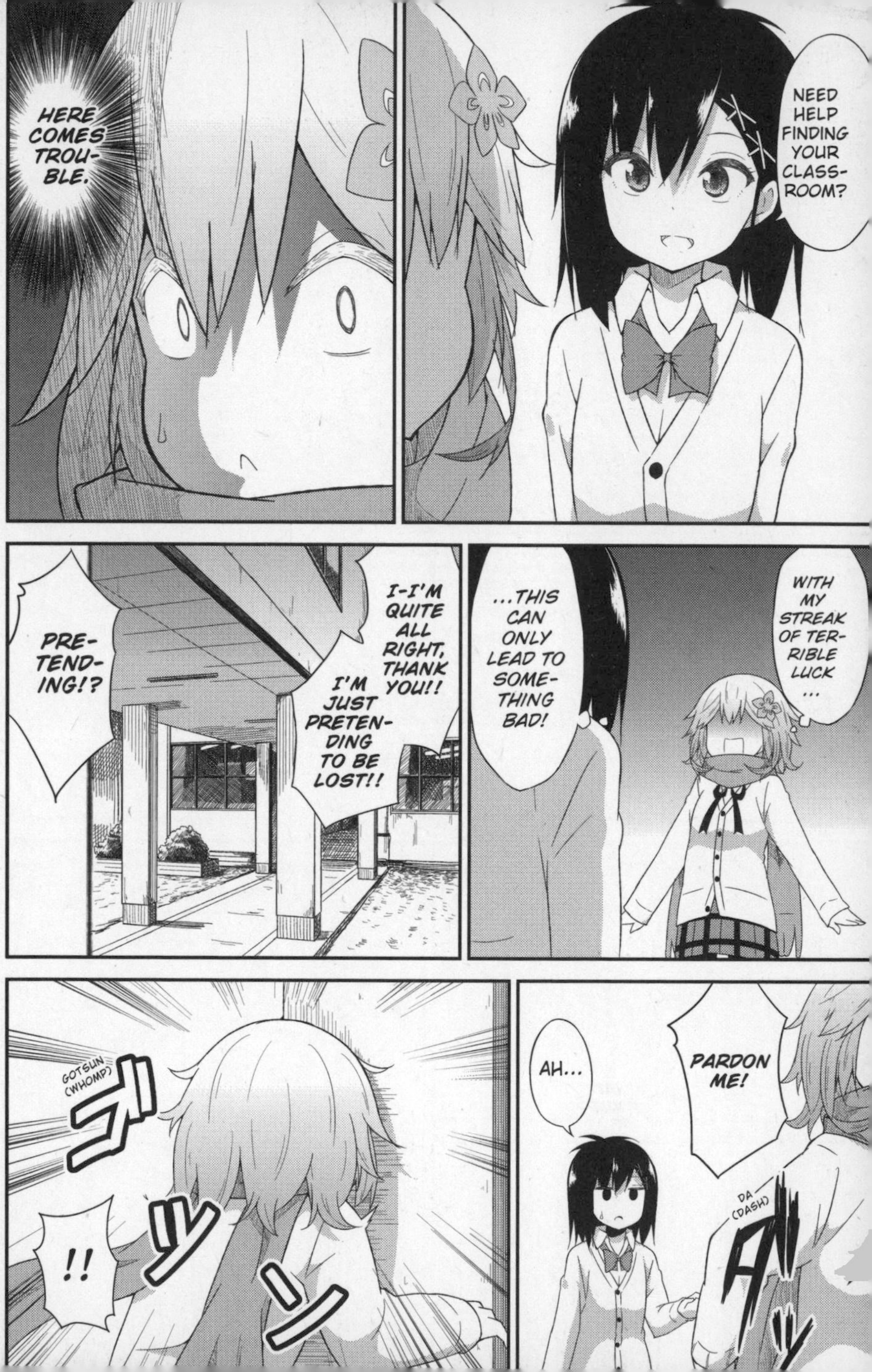
NEED HELP FINDING YOUR CLASS-ROOM?
HERE COMES TROU-BLE.
WITH MY STREAK OF TER-RIBLE LUCK...
...THIS CAN ONLY LEAD TO SOME-THING BAD!
I-I'M QUITE ALL RIGHT, THANK YOU!!
I'M JUST PRETEN-DING TO BE LOST!!
PRE-TEND-ING!?
PARDON ME!
DA (DASH)
AH...
GOTSUN (WHOMP)
!!

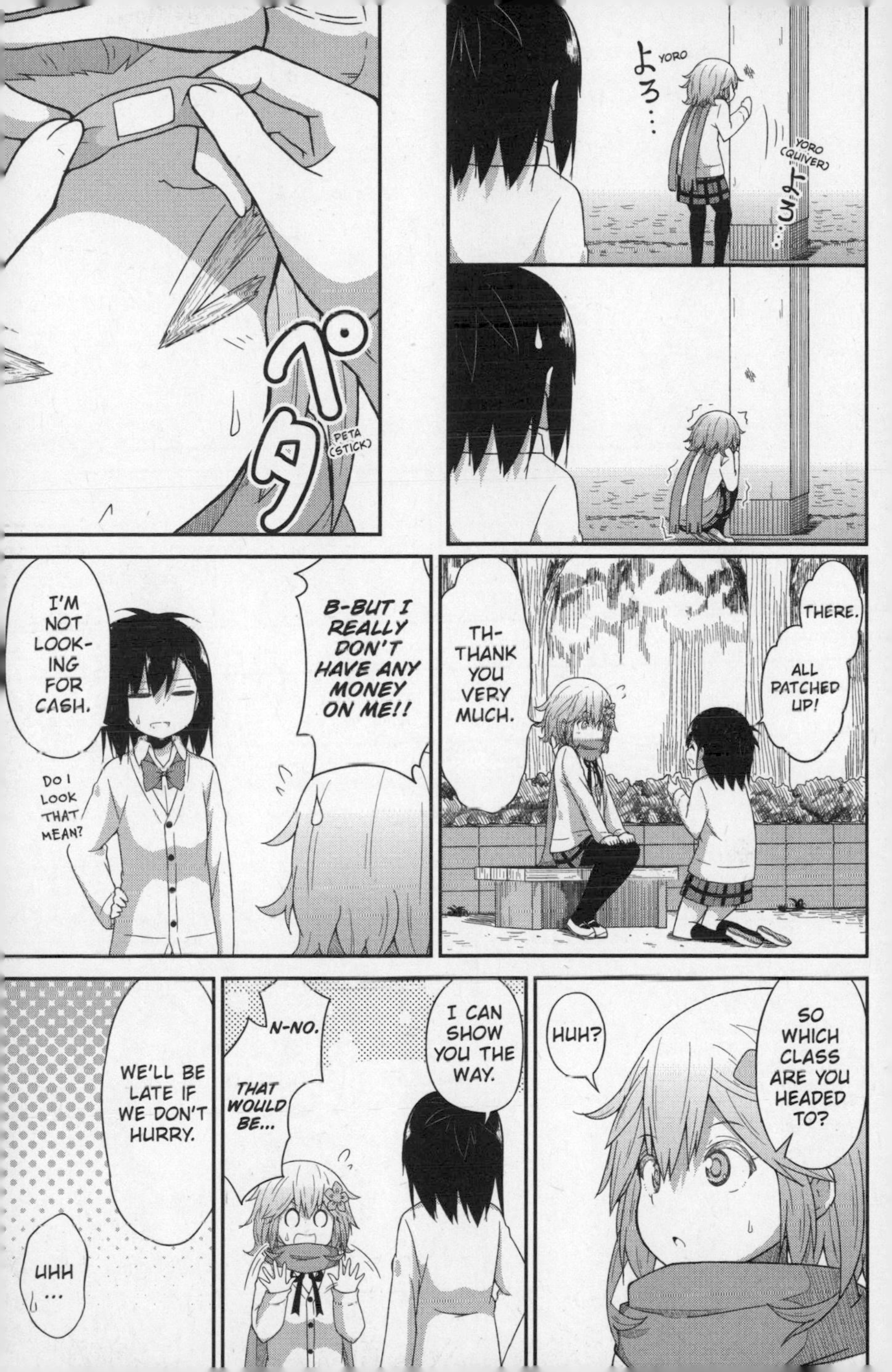
よろ…
YORO
YORO (QUIVER)
よろ…
ペタ
PETA (STICK)
THERE.
ALL PATCHED UP!
TH-THANK YOU VERY MUCH.
B-BUT I REALLY DON'T HAVE ANY MONEY ON ME!!
I'M NOT LOOKING FOR CASH.
DO I LOOK THAT MEAN?
SO WHICH CLASS ARE YOU HEADED TO?
HUH?
I CAN SHOW YOU THE WAY.
N-NO.
THAT WOULD BE...
WE'LL BE LATE IF WE DON'T HURRY.
UHH...

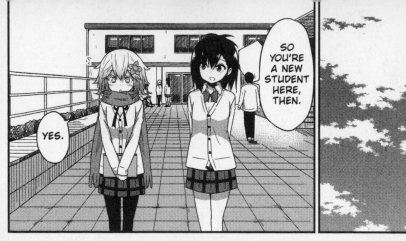

SO YOU'RE A NEW STUDENT HERE, THEN.
YES.
THIS SCHOOL IS HARD TO GET A HANDLE ON AT FIRST.
I'M SORRY ...
...FOR GETTING LOST AND TROUBLING YOU...
NO TROUBLE AT ALL. YOU'RE FINE.
DON'T WORRY ABOUT IT.
... WHAT IS THIS?
THIS PERSON...
I CAN FEEL AN AURA OF KINDNESS RADIATING FROM HER.
ぱあぁああ
PAAAAA (GLOW)
IT'S AS IF SHE'S THE VERY EMBODIMENT OF COMPASSION AND UNDERSTANDING!
OHHH.

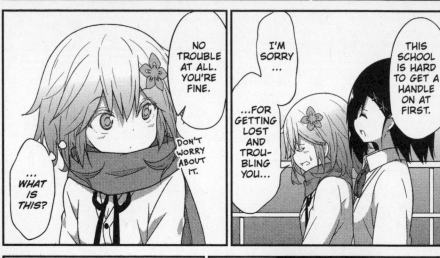

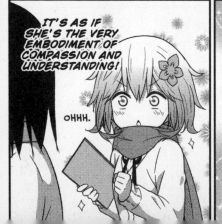

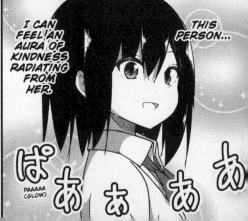

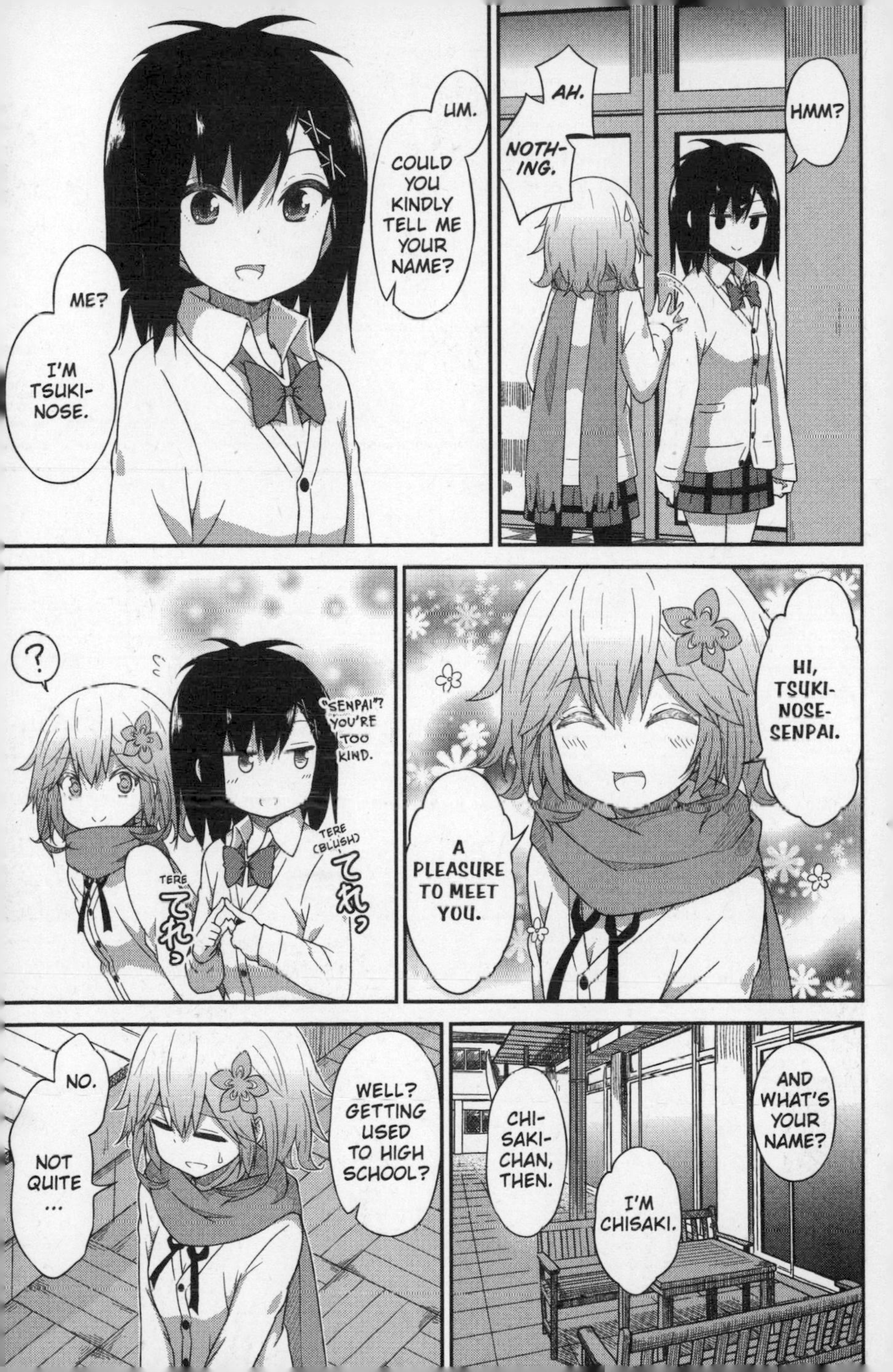
HMM?
AH.
NOTH-ING.
UM.
COULD YOU KINDLY TELL ME YOUR NAME?
ME?
I'M TSUKI-NOSE.
HI, TSUKI-NOSE-SENPAI.
A PLEASURE TO MEET YOU.
"SENPAI"? YOU'RE TOO KIND.
TERE (BLUSH)
てれっ
TERE
てれっ
?
AND WHAT'S YOUR NAME?
I'M CHISAKI.
CHI-SAKI-CHAN, THEN.
WELL? GETTING USED TO HIGH SCHOOL?
NO.
NOT QUITE ...

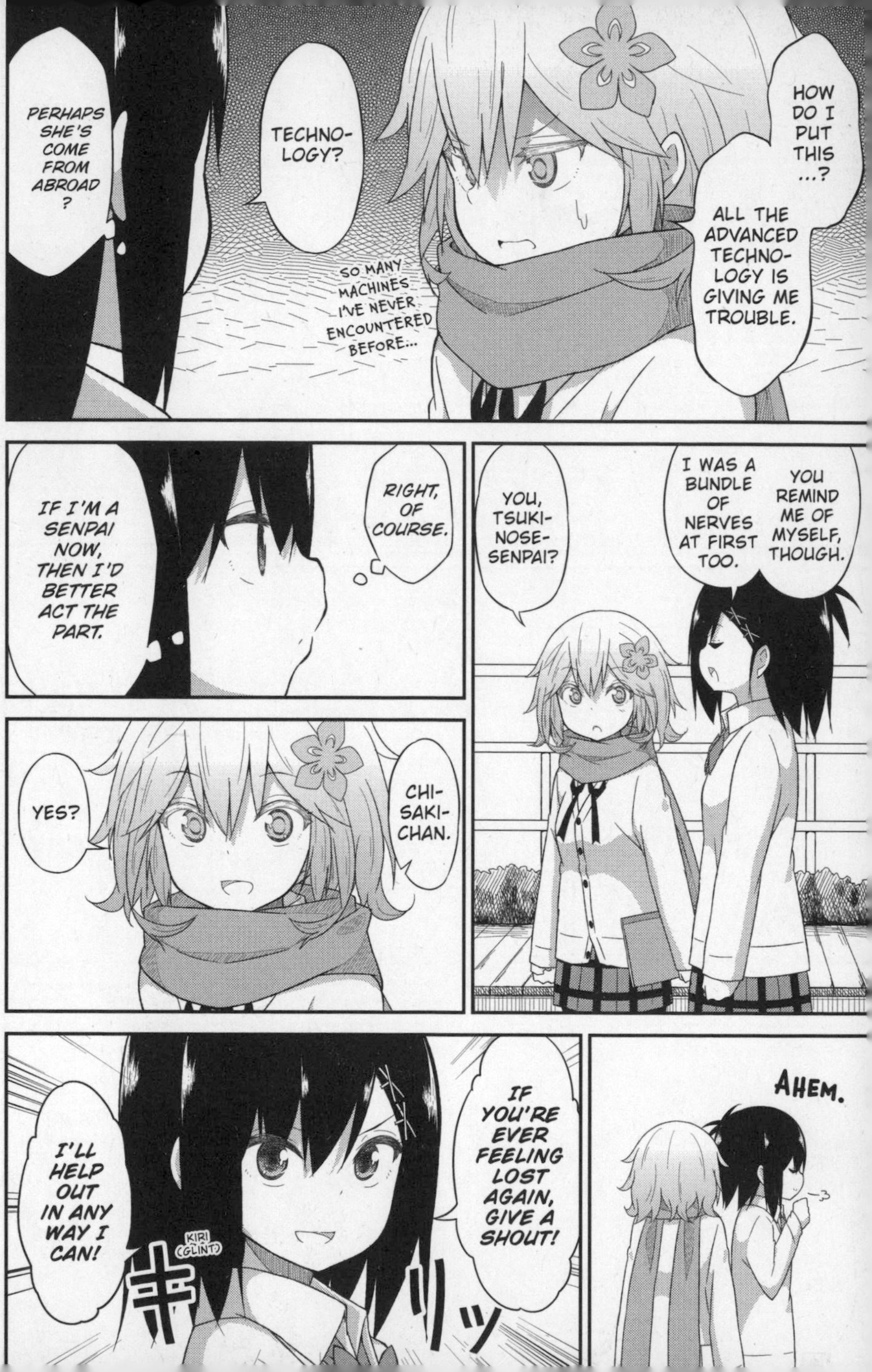
HOW DO I PUT THIS ...?
ALL THE ADVANCED TECHNO-LOGY IS GIVING ME TROUBLE.
SO MANY MACHINES I'VE NEVER ENCOUNTERED BEFORE...
TECHNO-LOGY?
PERHAPS SHE'S COME FROM ABROAD ?
YOU REMIND ME OF MYSELF, THOUGH.
I WAS A BUNDLE OF NERVES AT FIRST TOO.
YOU, TSUKI-NOSE-SENPAI?
RIGHT, OF COURSE.
IF I'M A SENPAI NOW, THEN I'D BETTER ACT THE PART.
CHI-SAKI-CHAN.
YES?
AHEM.
IF YOU'RE EVER FEELING LOST AGAIN, GIVE A SHOUT!
KIRI (GLINT)
I'LL HELP OUT IN ANY WAY I CAN!

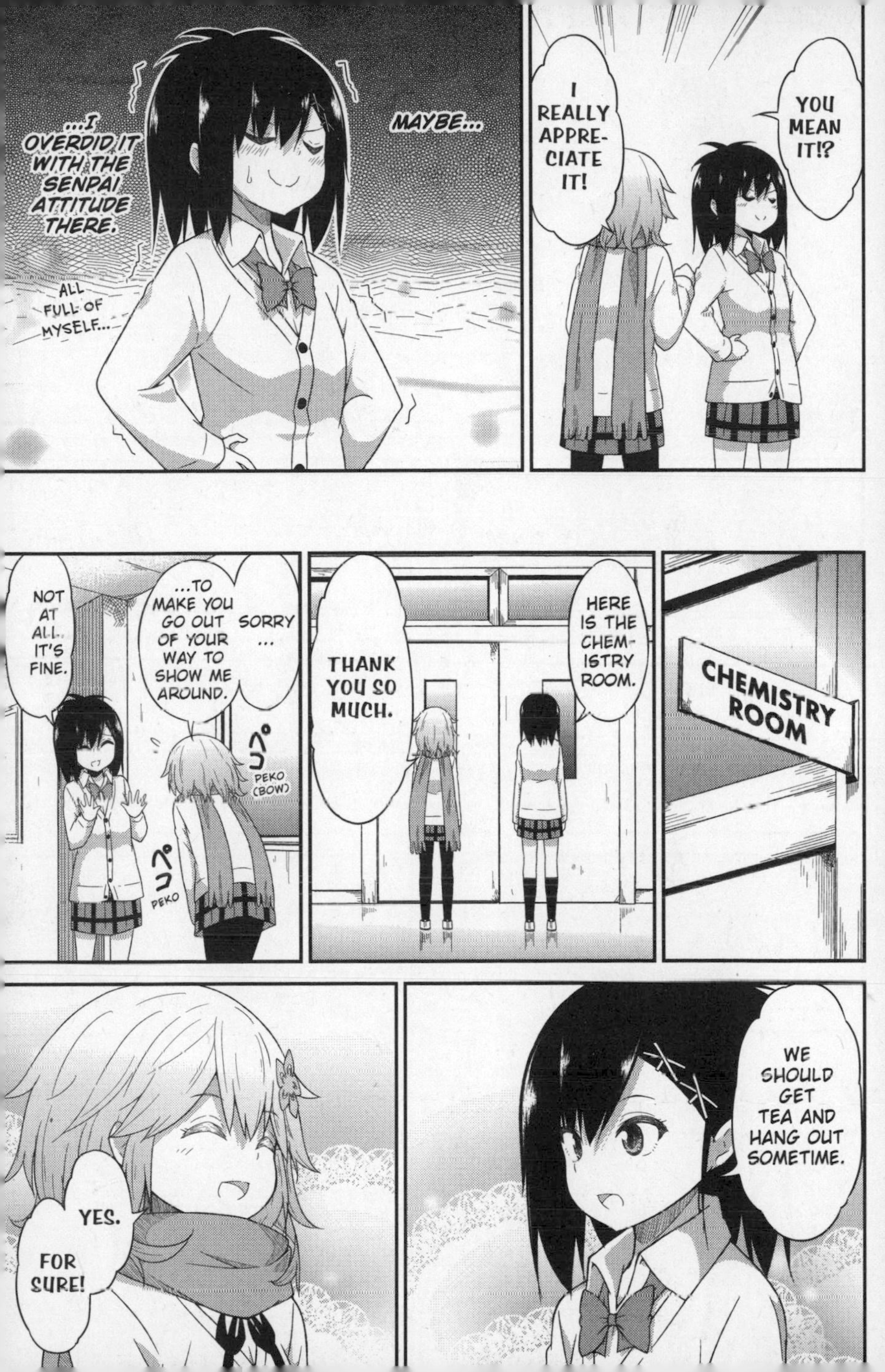

YOU MEAN IT!?
I REALLY APPRECIATE IT!
MAYBE...
...I OVERDID IT WITH THE SENPAI ATTITUDE THERE.
ALL FULL OF MYSELF...
CHEMISTRY ROOM
HERE IS THE CHEMISTRY ROOM.
THANK YOU SO MUCH.
SORRY...
...TO MAKE YOU GO OUT OF YOUR WAY TO SHOW ME AROUND.
ペコ PEKO (BOW)
ペコ PEKO
NOT AT ALL. IT'S FINE.
WE SHOULD GET TEA AND HANG OUT SOMETIME.
YES.
FOR SURE!

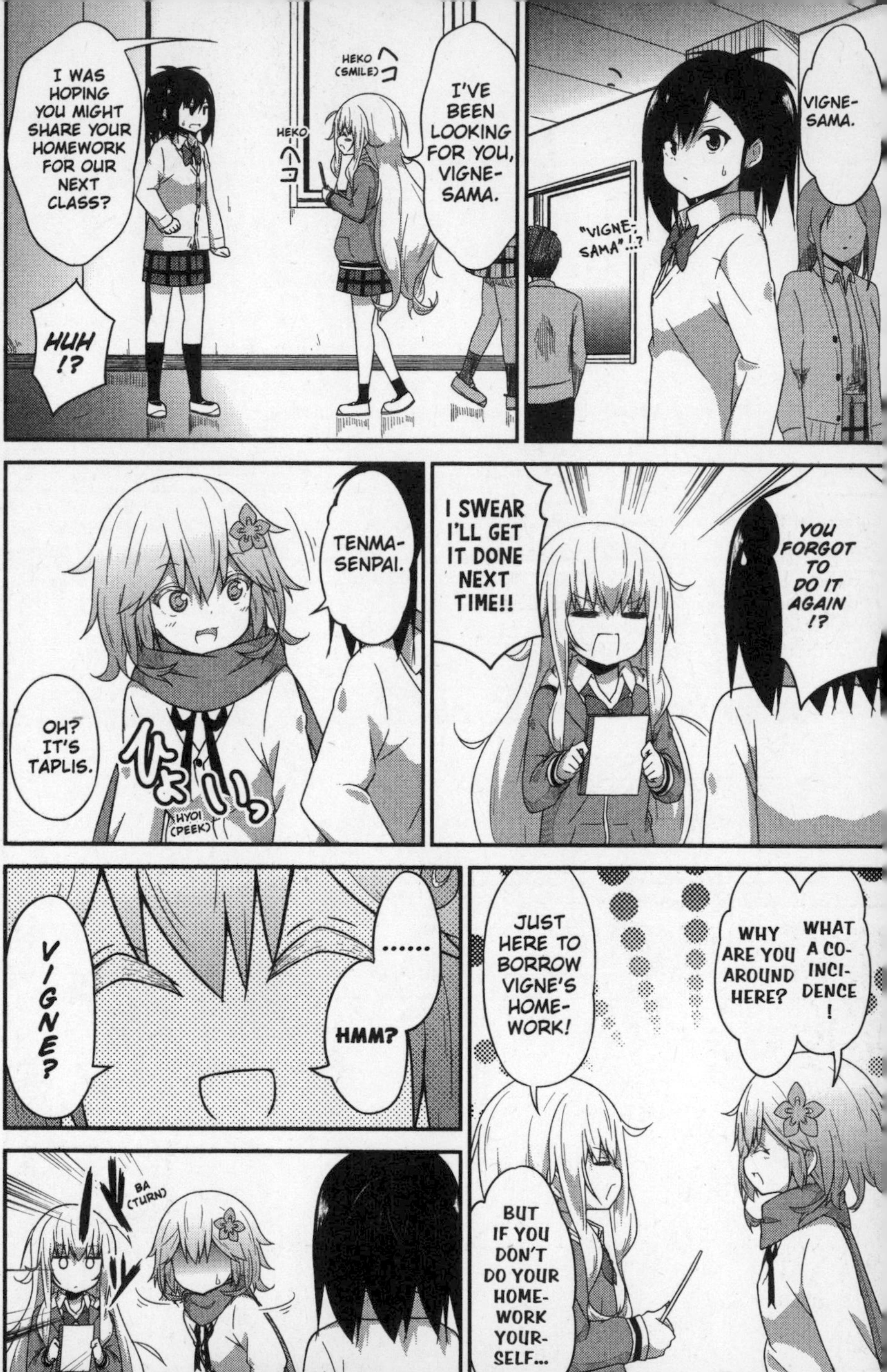
VIGNE-SAMA.
"VIGNE-SAMA"!?
I'VE BEEN LOOKING FOR YOU, VIGNE-SAMA.
HEKO (SMILE)
HEKO
I WAS HOPING YOU MIGHT SHARE YOUR HOMEWORK FOR OUR NEXT CLASS?
HUH!?
YOU FORGOT TO DO IT AGAIN!?
I SWEAR I'LL GET IT DONE NEXT TIME!!
TENMA-SENPAI.
OH? IT'S TAPLIS.
HYOI (PEEK)
WHAT A CO-INCI-DENCE!
WHY ARE YOU AROUND HERE?
JUST HERE TO BORROW VIGNE'S HOME-WORK!
BUT IF YOU DON'T DO YOUR HOME-WORK YOUR-SELF...
......
HMM?
VIGNE?
BA (TURN)

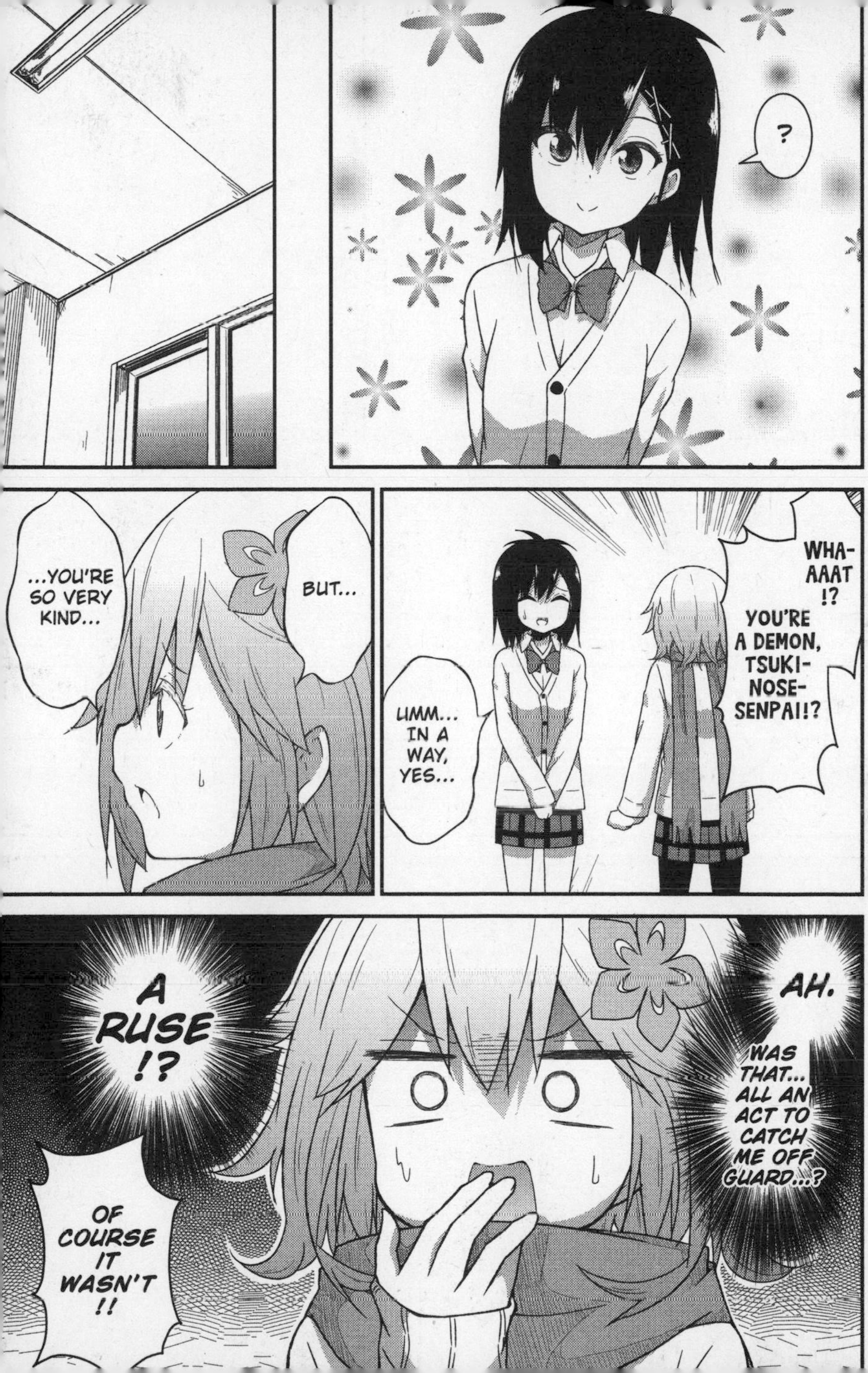
?
WHA-AAAT!? YOU'RE A DEMON, TSUKI-NOSE-SENPAI!?
UMM... IN A WAY, YES...
BUT...
...YOU'RE SO VERY KIND...
AH.
WAS THAT... ALL AN ACT TO CATCH ME OFF GUARD...?
A RUSE!?
OF COURSE IT WASN'T!!

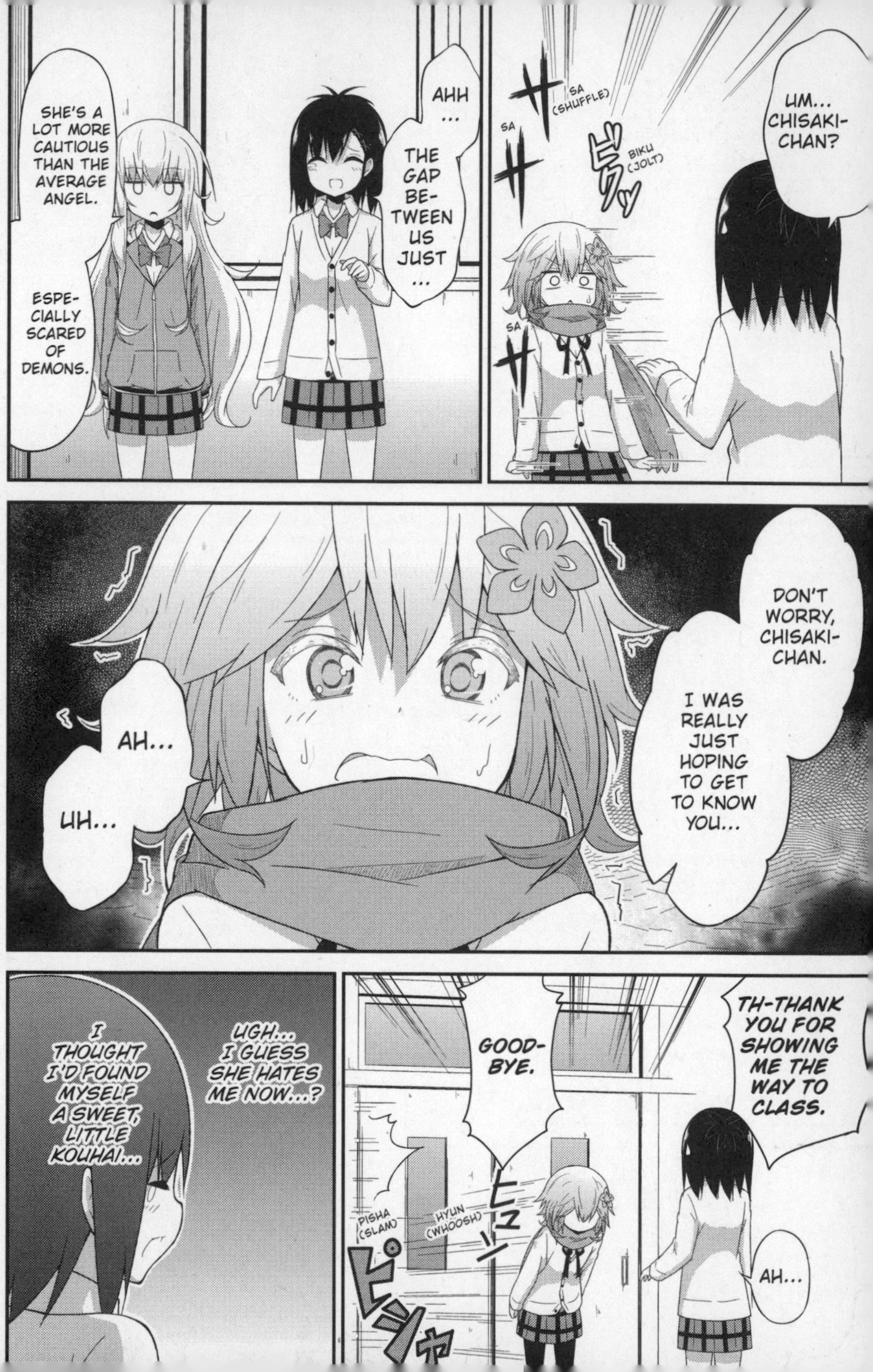
UM... CHISAKI-CHAN?
SA (SHUFFLE)
SA
BIKU (JOLT)
SA
AHH ...
THE GAP BE-TWEEN US JUST ...
SHE'S A LOT MORE CAUTIOUS THAN THE AVERAGE ANGEL.
ESPE-CIALLY SCARED OF DEMONS.
DON'T WORRY, CHISAKI-CHAN.
I WAS REALLY JUST HOPING TO GET TO KNOW YOU...
AH...
UH...
TH-THANK YOU FOR SHOWING ME THE WAY TO CLASS.
AH...
GOOD-BYE.
HYUN (WHOOSH)
PISHA (SLAM)
UGH... I GUESS SHE HATES ME NOW...?
I THOUGHT I'D FOUND MYSELF A SWEET, LITTLE KOUHAI...

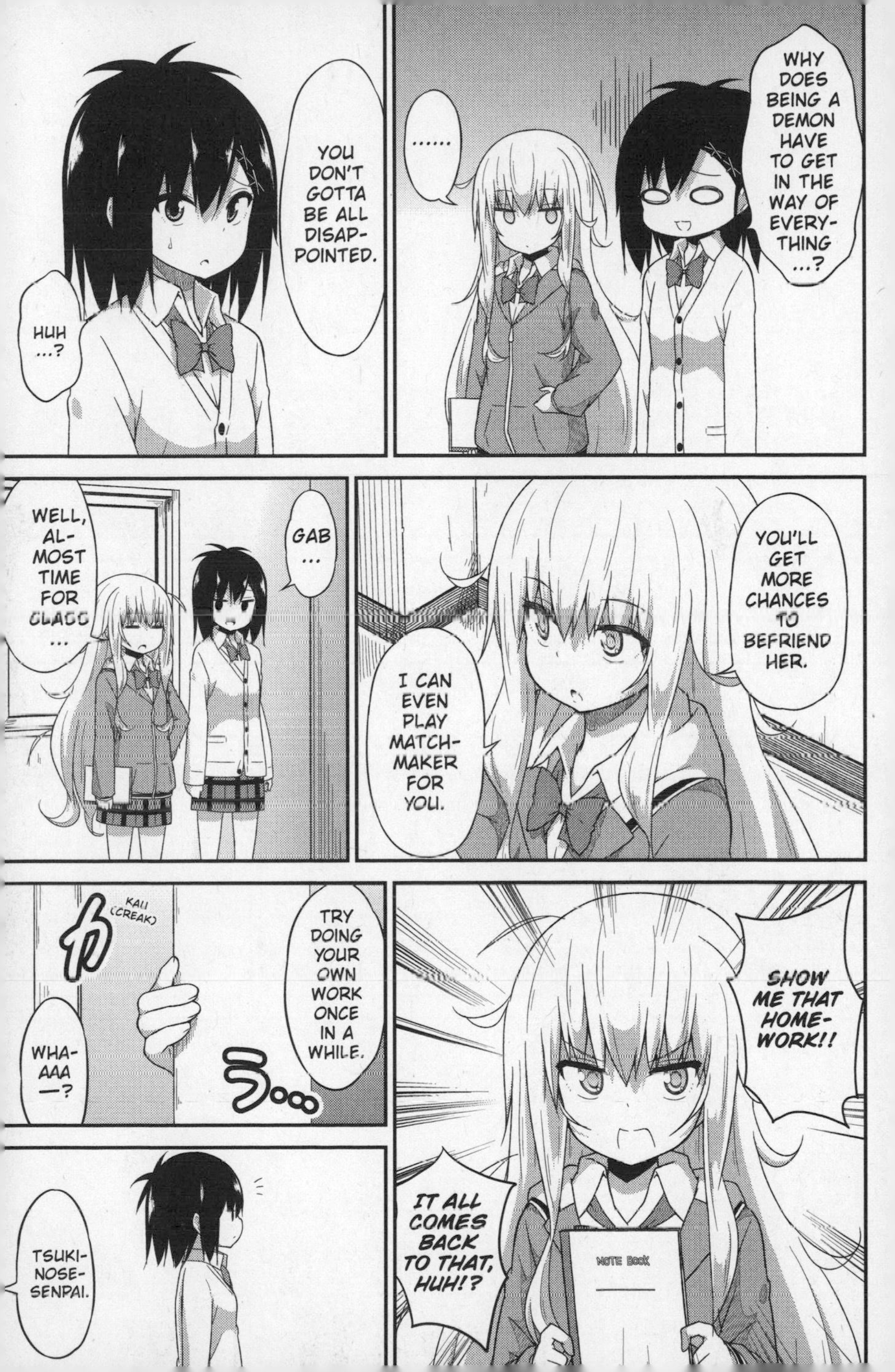

WHY DOES BEING A DEMON HAVE TO GET IN THE WAY OF EVERYTHING...?
......
YOU DON'T GOTTA BE ALL DISAPPOINTED.
HUH...?
YOU'LL GET MORE CHANCES TO BEFRIEND HER.
I CAN EVEN PLAY MATCHMAKER FOR YOU.
GAB...
WELL, ALMOST TIME FOR CLASS...
SHOW ME THAT HOMEWORK!!
NOTE BOOK
IT ALL COMES BACK TO THAT, HUH!?
TRY DOING YOUR OWN WORK ONCE IN A WHILE.
KALI (CREAK)
WHA-AAA—?
TSUKINOSE-SENPAI.

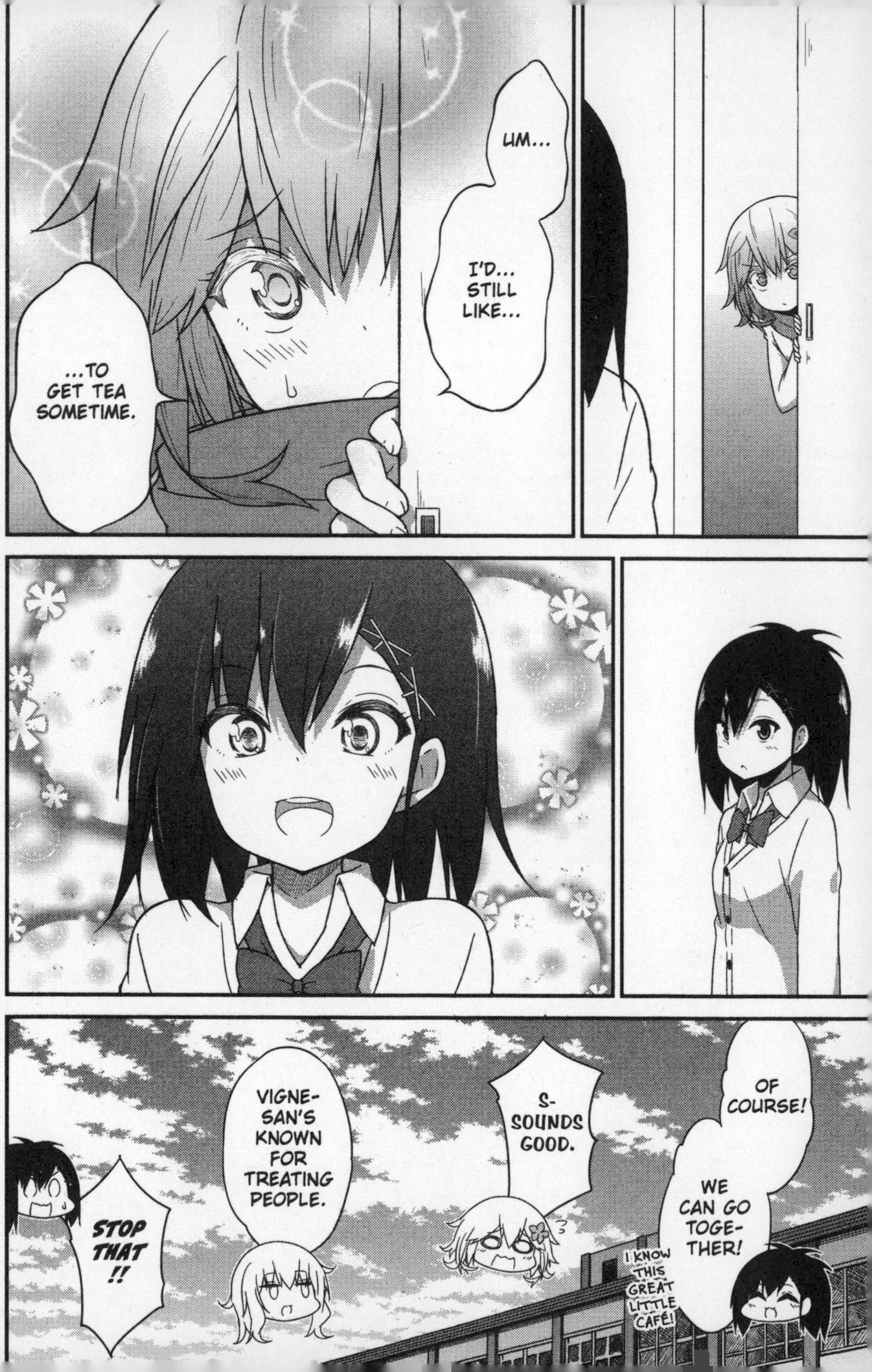
UM...
I'D... STILL LIKE...
...TO GET TEA SOMETIME.
OF COURSE!
WE CAN GO TOGE-THER!
I KNOW THIS GREAT LITTLE CAFÉ!
S-SOUNDS GOOD.
VIGNE-SAN'S KNOWN FOR TREATING PEOPLE.
STOP THAT!!

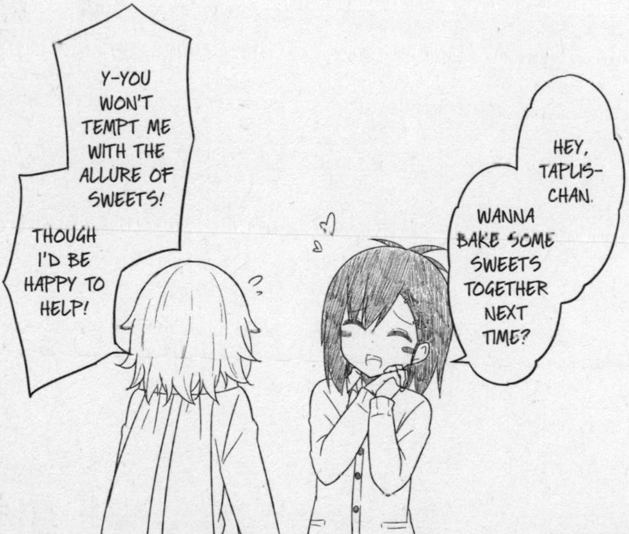
HEY, TAPLIS-CHAN.
WANNA BAKE SOME SWEETS TOGETHER NEXT TIME?
Y-YOU WON'T TEMPT ME WITH THE ALLURE OF SWEETS!
THOUGH I'D BE HAPPY TO HELP!

Gabriel DropOut

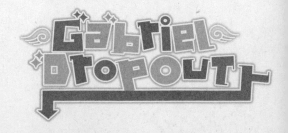

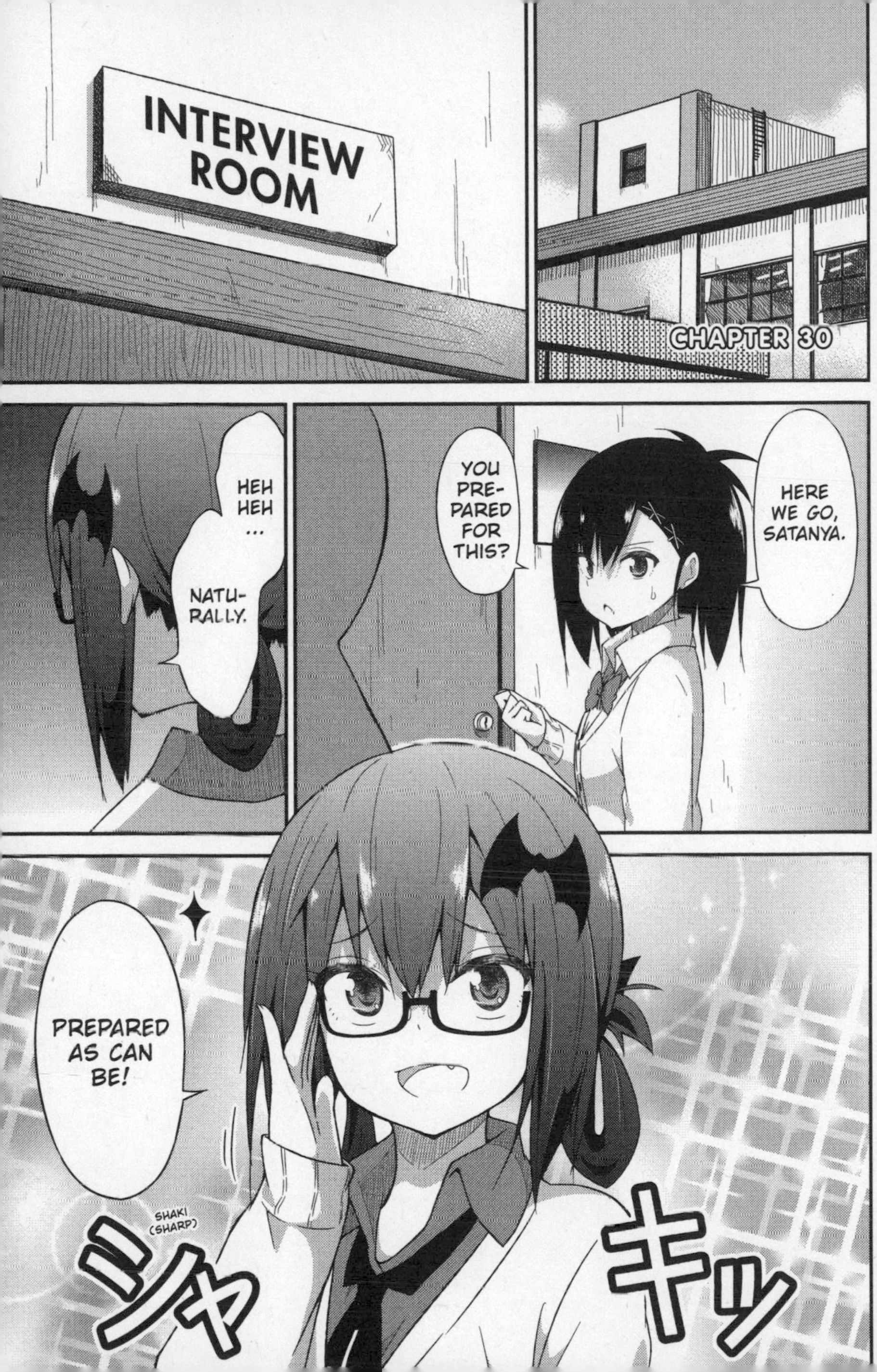
CHAPTER 30
INTERVIEW ROOM
HERE WE GO, SATANYA.
YOU PRE-PARED FOR THIS?
HEH HEH ...
NATU-RALLY.
PREPARED AS CAN BE!
シャキッ
SHAKI (SHARP)

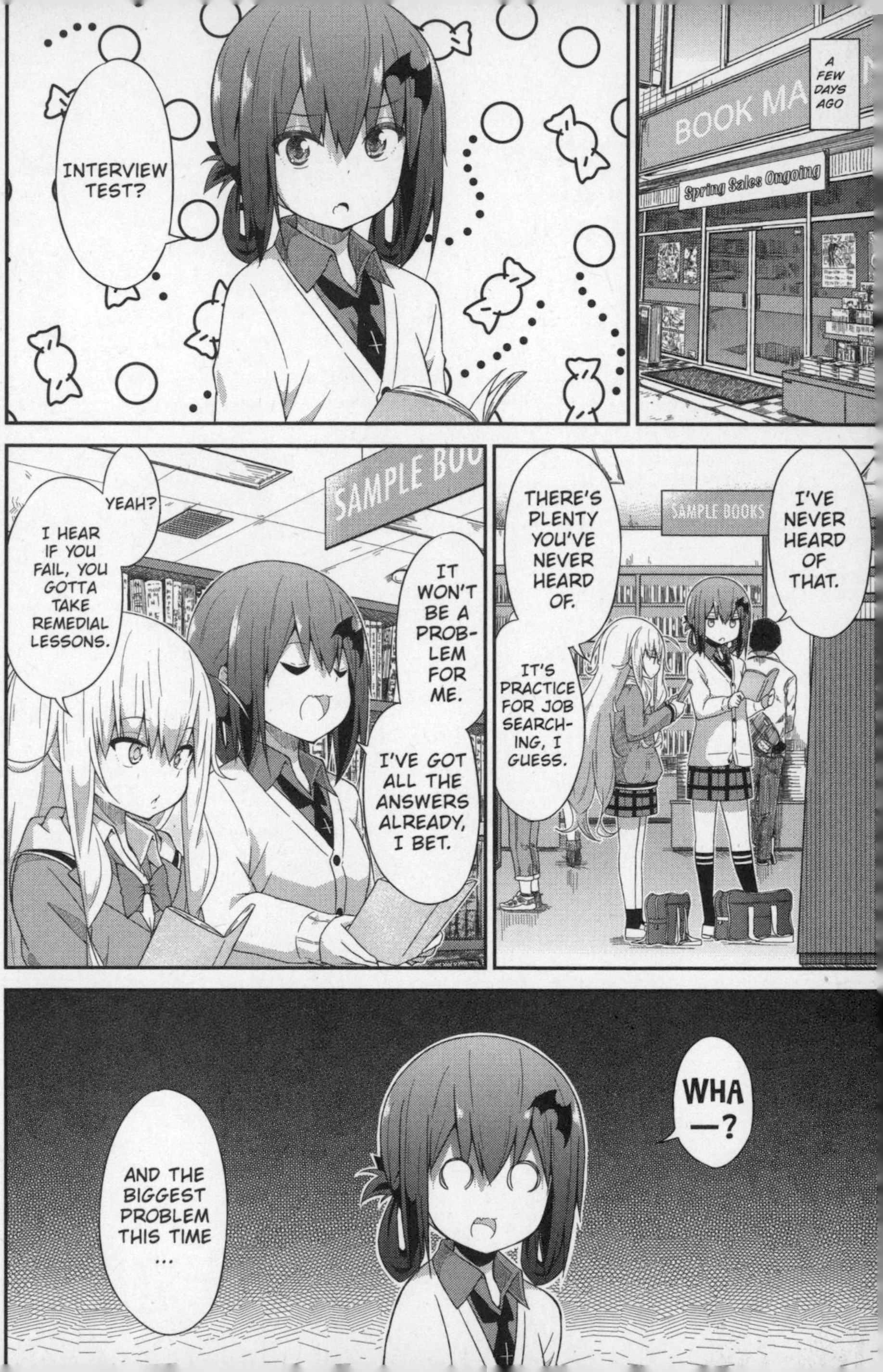
A FEW DAYS AGO
BOOK MA
Spring Sales Ongoing
INTERVIEW TEST?
I'VE NEVER HEARD OF THAT.
THERE'S PLENTY YOU'VE NEVER HEARD OF.
SAMPLE BOOKS
IT'S PRACTICE FOR JOB SEARCHING, I GUESS.
SAMPLE BO
YEAH?
I HEAR IF YOU FAIL, YOU GOTTA TAKE REMEDIAL LESSONS.
IT WON'T BE A PROBLEM FOR ME.
I'VE GOT ALL THE ANSWERS ALREADY, I BET.
WHA—?
AND THE BIGGEST PROBLEM THIS TIME...

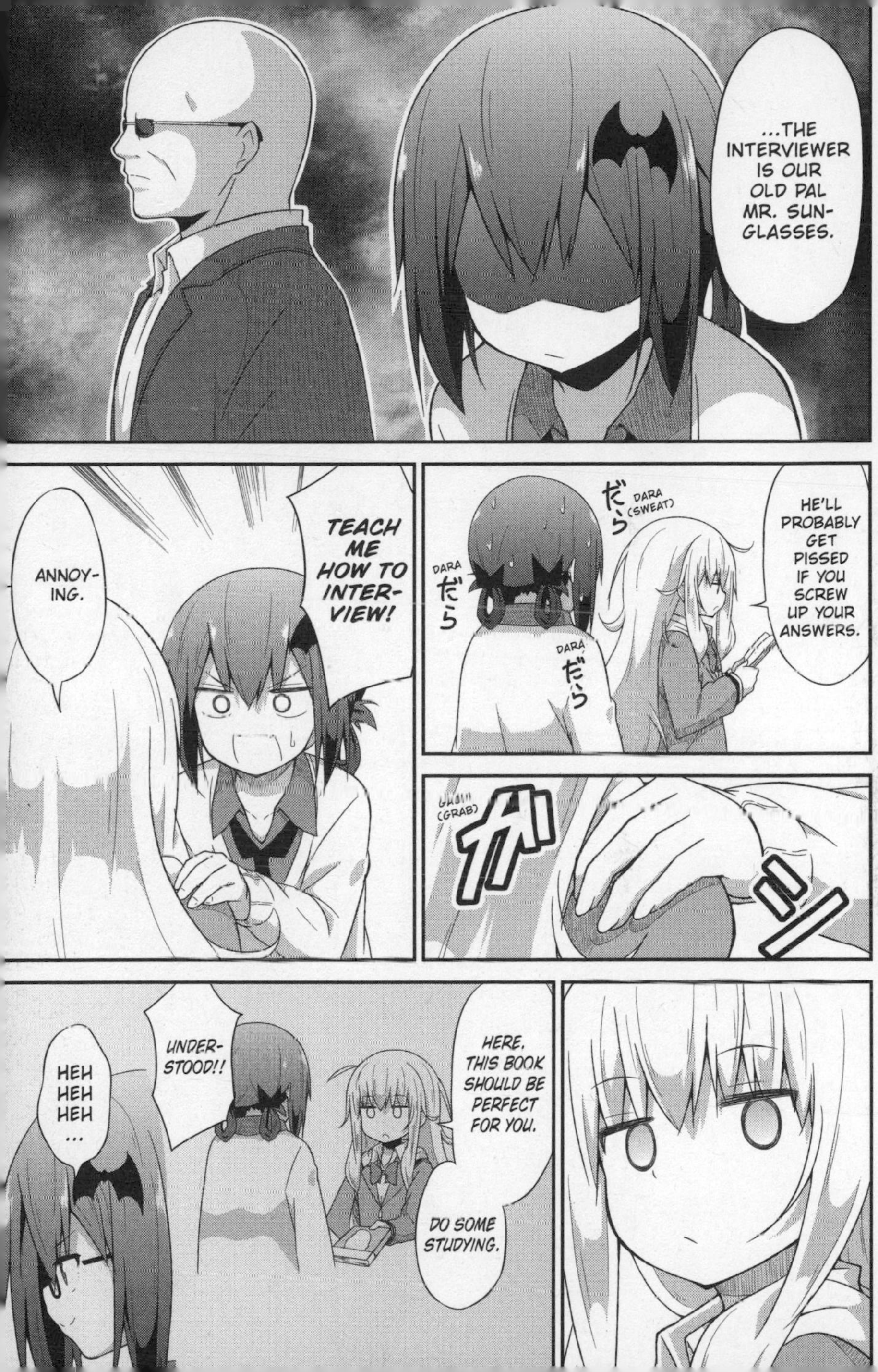
...THE INTERVIEWER IS OUR OLD PAL MR. SUN-GLASSES.
HE'LL PROBABLY GET PISSED IF YOU SCREW UP YOUR ANSWERS.
だら DARA (SWEAT)
だら DARA
だら DARA
(GRAB)
が
TEACH ME HOW TO INTER-VIEW!
ANNOY-ING.
HERE. THIS BOOK SHOULD BE PERFECT FOR YOU.
DO SOME STUDYING.
UNDER-STOOD!!
HEH HEH HEH ...

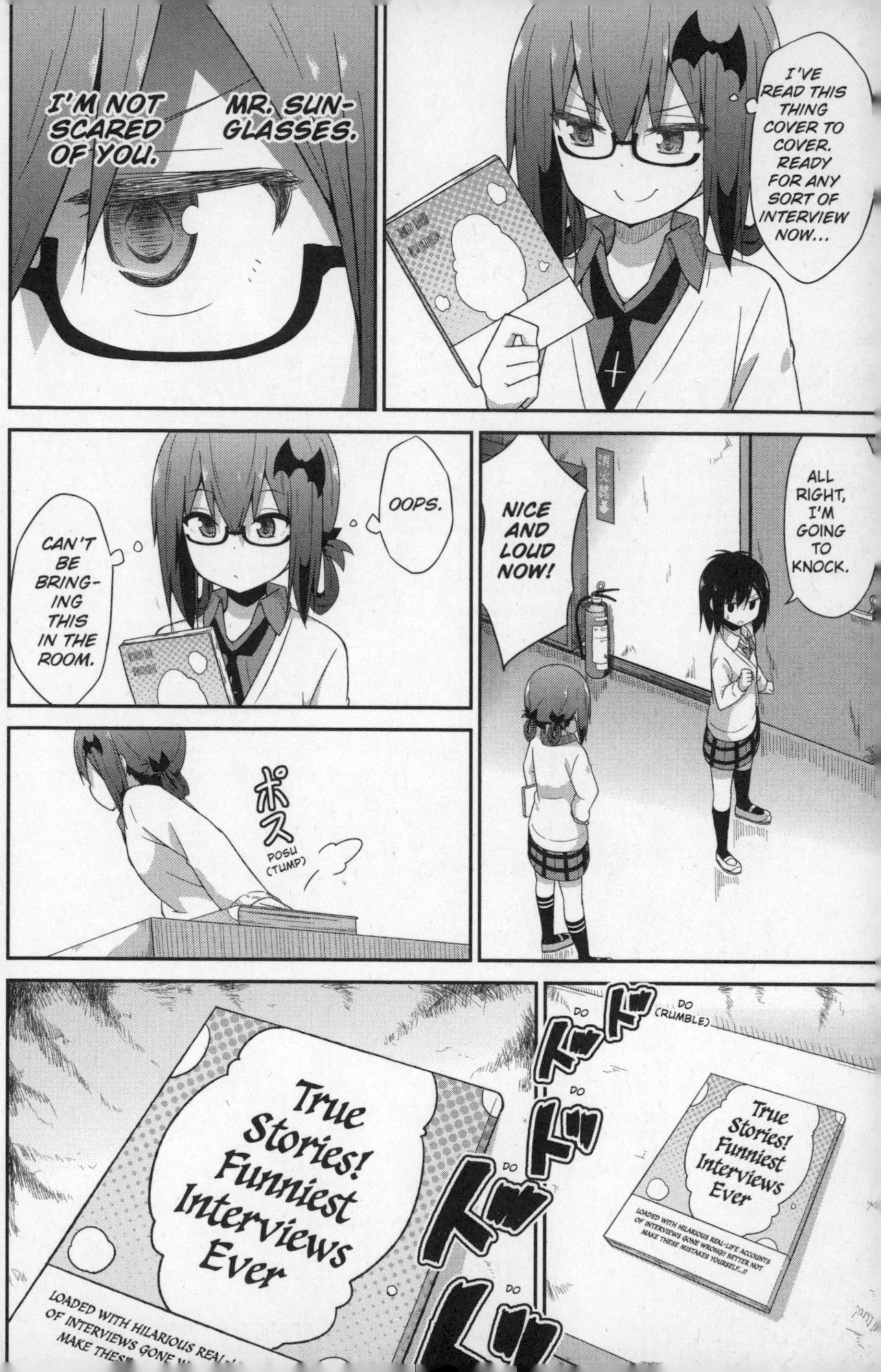
I'VE READ THIS THING COVER TO COVER. READY FOR ANY SORT OF INTERVIEW NOW...
MR. SUN-GLASSES.
I'M NOT SCARED OF YOU.
ALL RIGHT, I'M GOING TO KNOCK.
NICE AND LOUD NOW!
OOPS.
CAN'T BE BRINGING THIS IN THE ROOM.
ポス
POSU (TUMP)
DO DO (RUMBLE)
DO
DO
DO
True Stories! Funniest Interviews Ever
LOADED WITH HILARIOUS REAL-LIFE ACCOUNTS OF INTERVIEWS GONE WRONG!! BETTER NOT MAKE THESE MISTAKES YOURSELF...!!
True Stories! Funniest Interviews Ever
LOADED WITH HILARIOUS
OF INTERVIEWS GONE
MAKE THESE

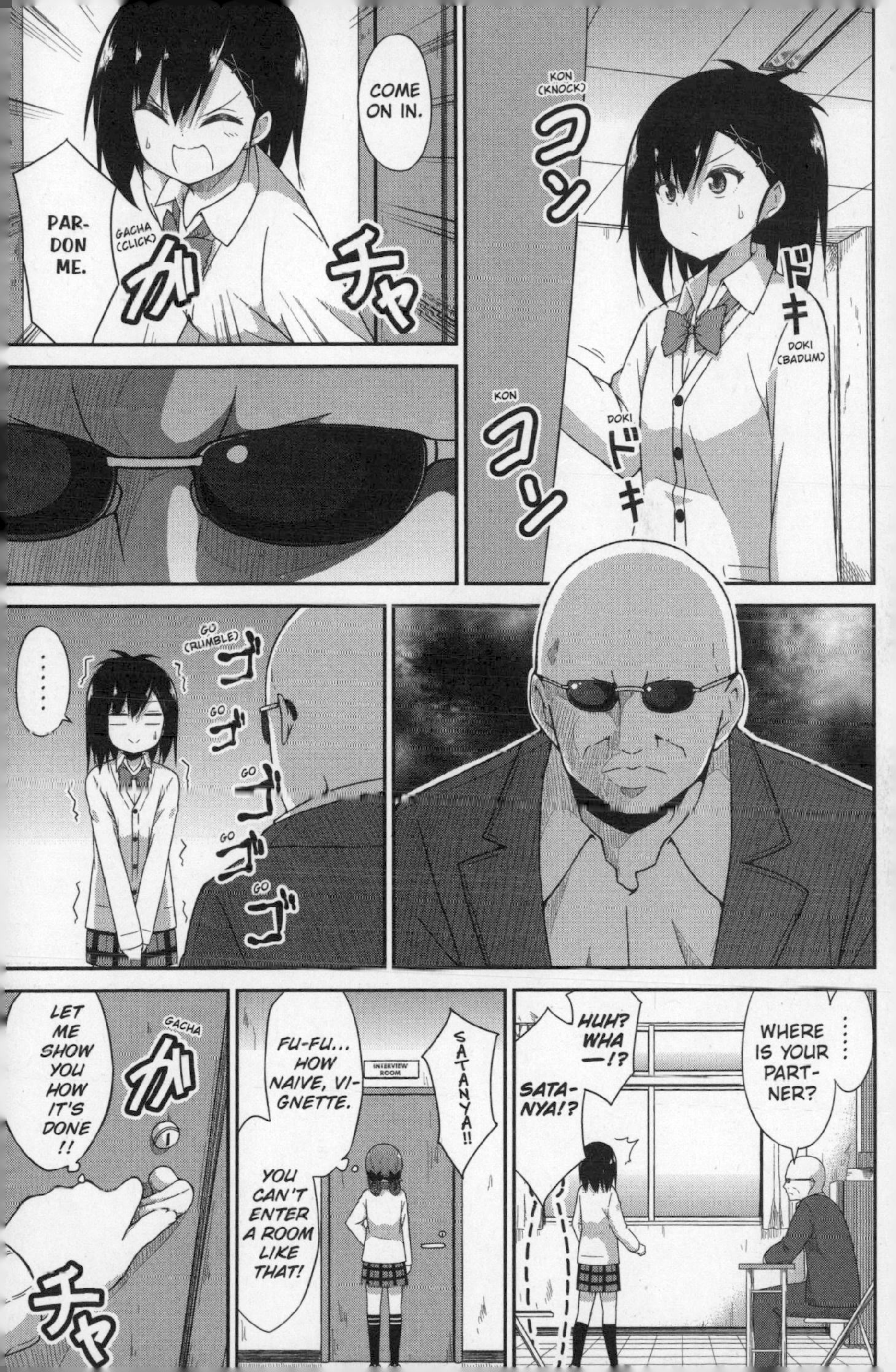
KON (KNOCK)
コン
DOKI (BADUM)
ドキ
KON
コン
DOKI
ドキ
COME ON IN.
PARDON ME.
GACHA (CLICK)
ガチャ
......
GO (RUMBLE)
ゴ
GO
ゴ
GO
ゴ
GO
ゴ
GO
ゴ
......
WHERE IS YOUR PARTNER?
HUH? WHA—!?
SATANYA!?
SATANYA!!
INTERVIEW ROOM
FU-FU... HOW NAIVE, VIGNETTE.
YOU CAN'T ENTER A ROOM LIKE THAT!
GACHA
ガチャ
LET ME SHOW YOU HOW IT'S DONE!!

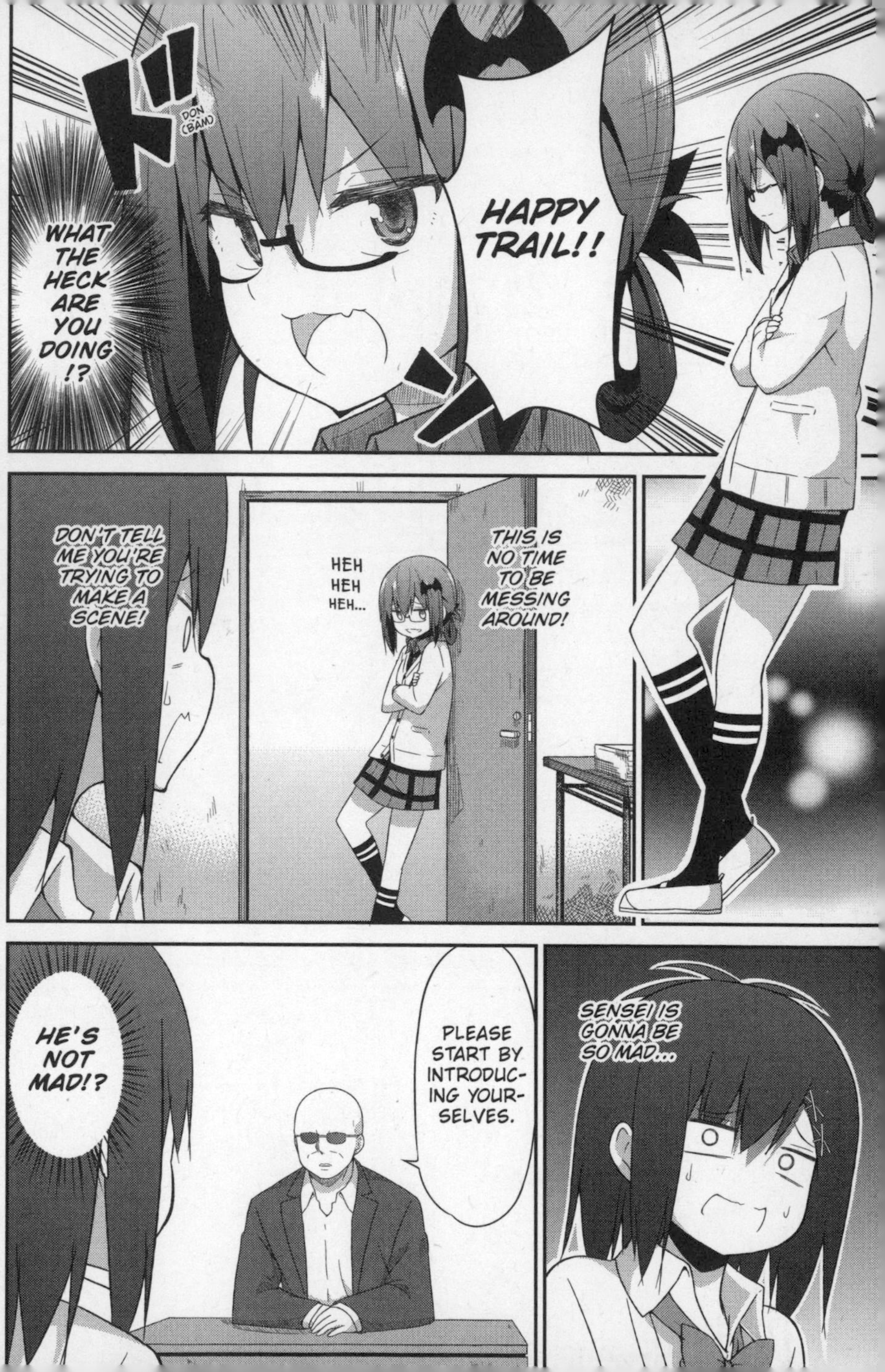
HAPPY TRAIL!!
DON (BAM)
WHAT THE HECK ARE YOU DOING!?
THIS IS NO TIME TO BE MESSING AROUND!
HEH HEH HEH...
DON'T TELL ME YOU'RE TRYING TO MAKE A SCENE!
SENSEI IS GONNA BE SO MAD...
PLEASE START BY INTRODUC-ING YOUR-SELVES.
HE'S NOT MAD!?

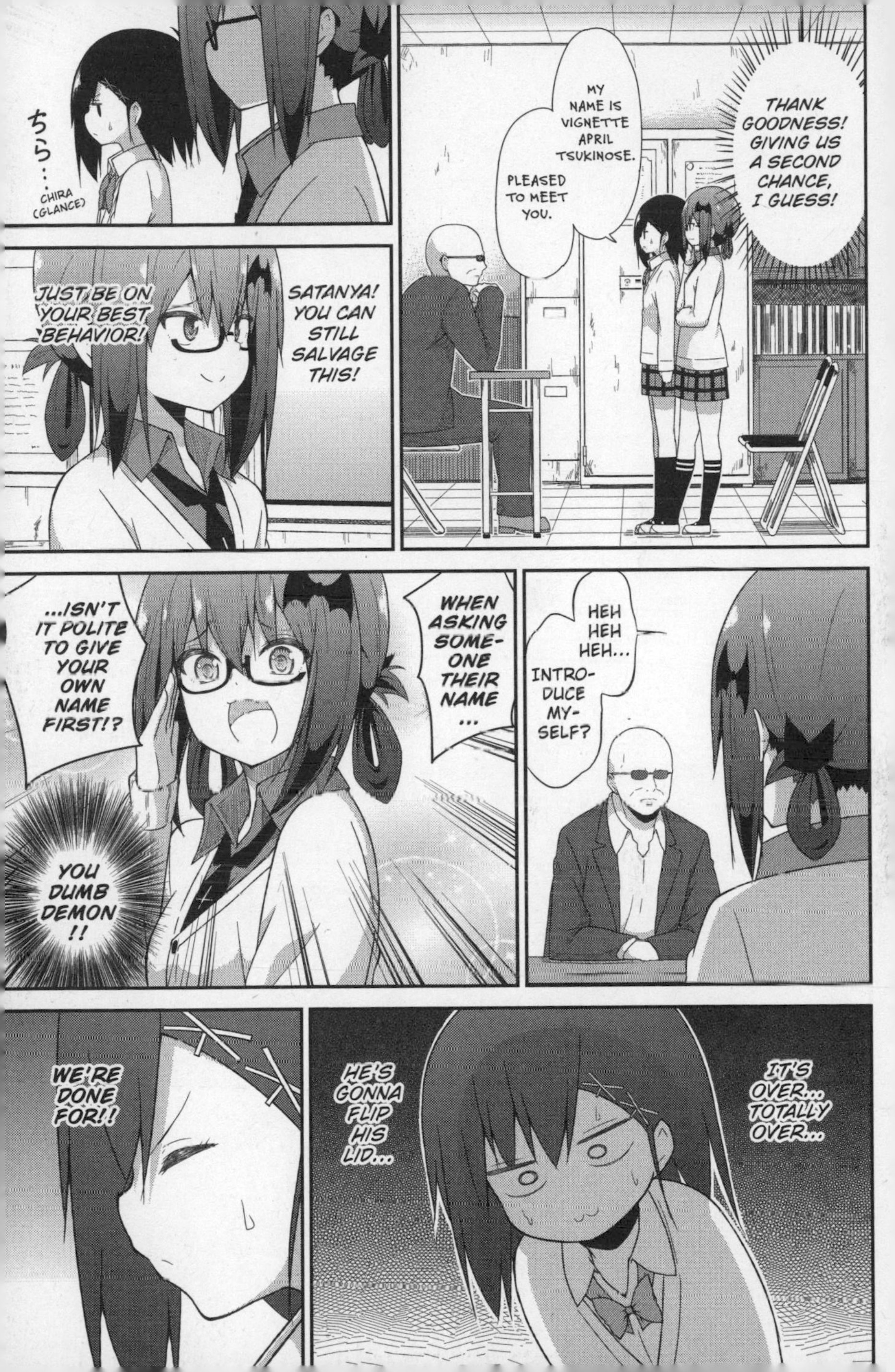
THANK GOODNESS! GIVING US A SECOND CHANCE, I GUESS!
MY NAME IS VIGNETTE APRIL TSUKINOSE.
PLEASED TO MEET YOU.
ちら…
CHIRA (GLANCE)
SATANYA! YOU CAN STILL SALVAGE THIS!
JUST BE ON YOUR BEST BEHAVIOR!
HEH HEH HEH...
INTRO-DUCE MY-SELF?
WHEN ASKING SOME-ONE THEIR NAME...
...ISN'T IT POLITE TO GIVE YOUR OWN NAME FIRST!?
YOU DUMB DEMON!!
IT'S OVER... TOTALLY OVER...
HE'S GONNA FLIP HIS LID...
WE'RE DONE FOR!!

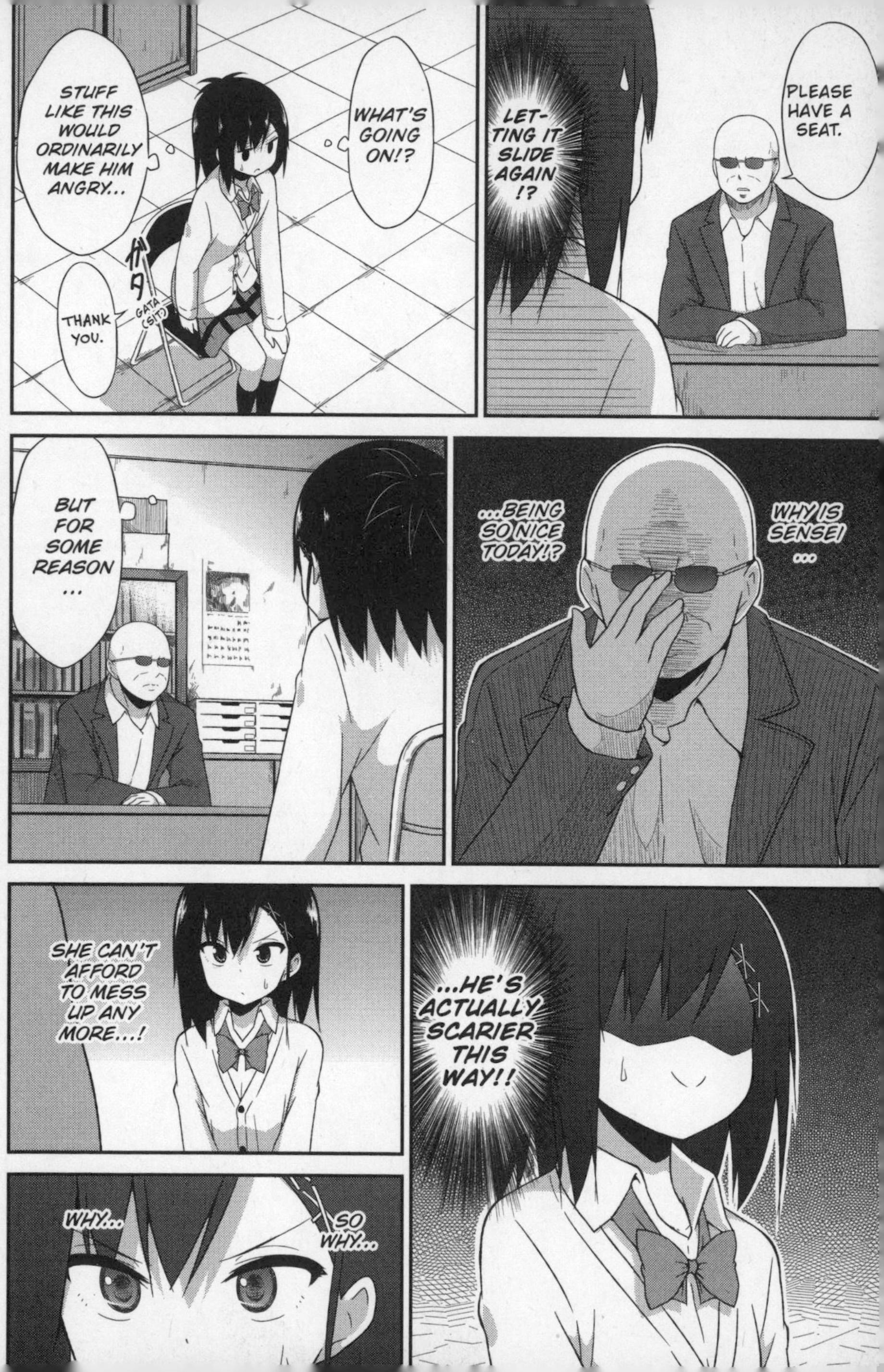
PLEASE HAVE A SEAT.
LET-TING IT SLIDE AGAIN!?
WHAT'S GOING ON!?
STUFF LIKE THIS WOULD ORDINARILY MAKE HIM ANGRY...
GATA (SIT)
THANK YOU.
WHY IS SENSEI ...
...BEING SO NICE TODAY!?
BUT FOR SOME REASON ...
...HE'S ACTUALLY SCARIER THIS WAY!!
SHE CAN'T AFFORD TO MESS UP ANY MORE...!
WHY...
SO WHY...

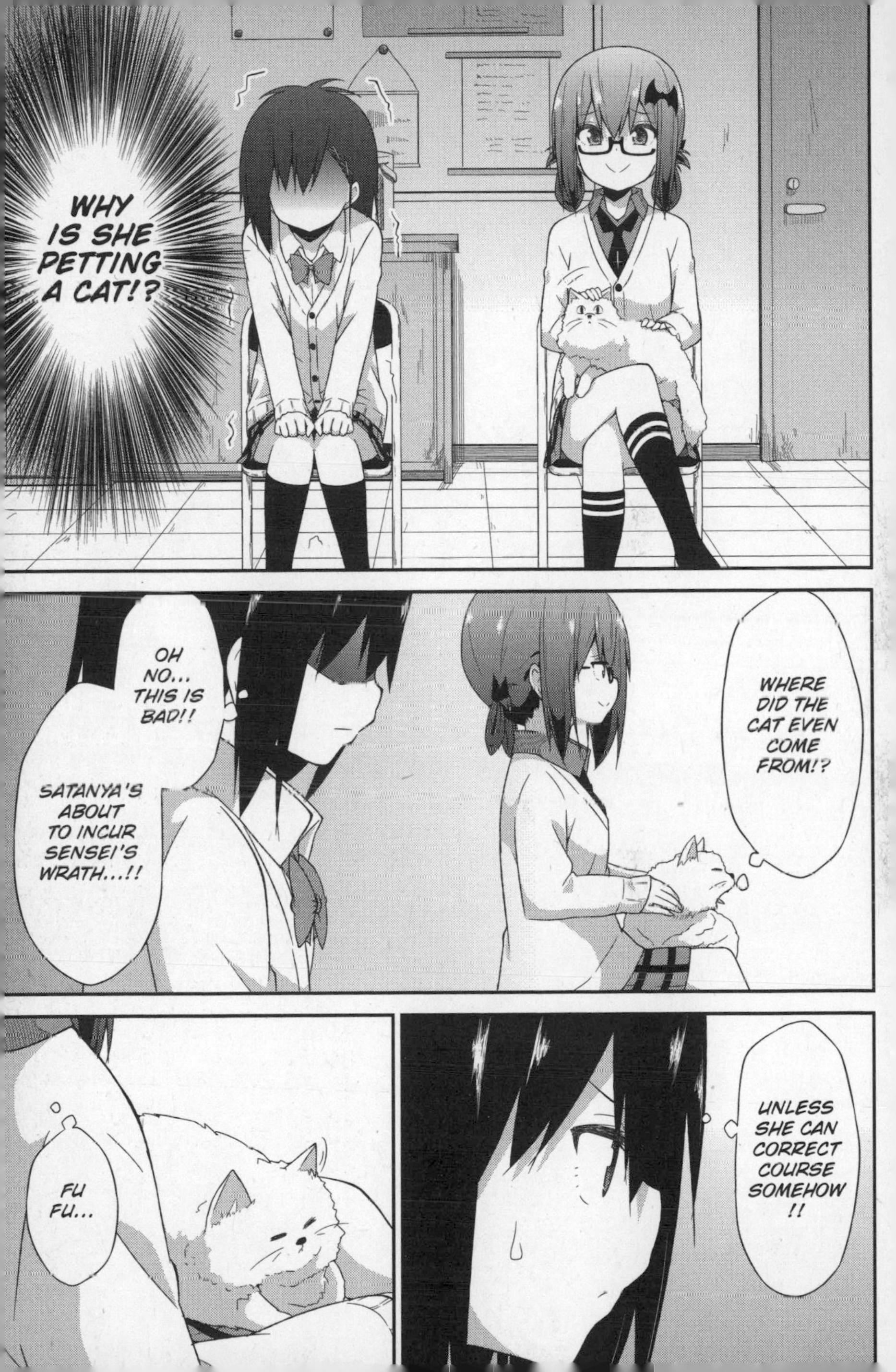
WHY IS SHE PETTING A CAT!?
WHERE DID THE CAT EVEN COME FROM!?
OH NO... THIS IS BAD!!
SATANYA'S ABOUT TO INCUR SENSEI'S WRATH...!!
UNLESS SHE CAN CORRECT COURSE SOMEHOW!!
FU FU...

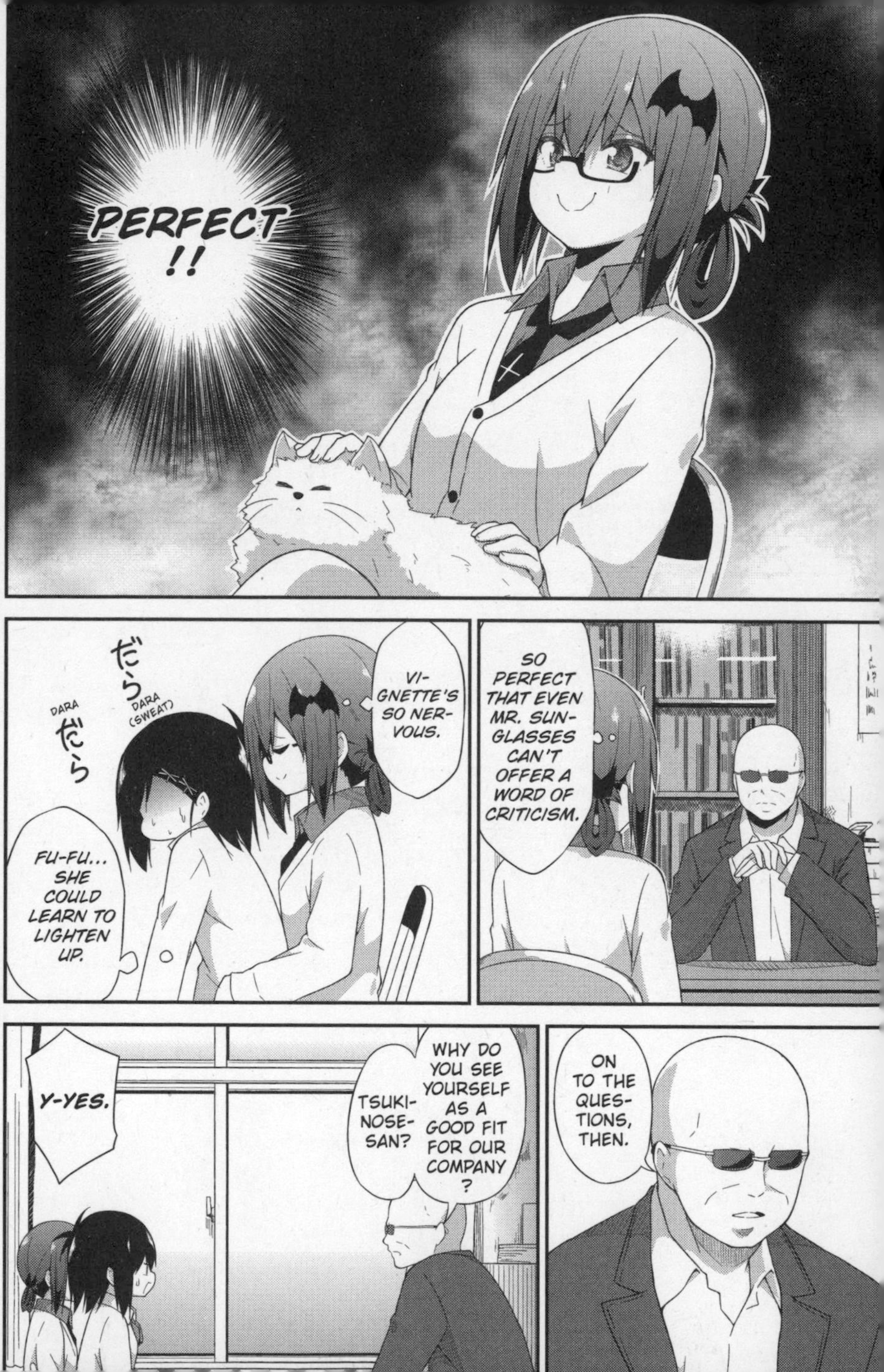
PERFECT !!
SO PERFECT THAT EVEN MR. SUNGLASSES CAN'T OFFER A WORD OF CRITICISM.
だら DARA (SWEAT)
だら DARA
VIGNETTE'S SO NERVOUS.
FU-FU... SHE COULD LEARN TO LIGHTEN UP.
ON TO THE QUESTIONS, THEN.
WHY DO YOU SEE YOURSELF AS A GOOD FIT FOR OUR COMPANY?
TSUKINOSE-SAN?
Y-YES.

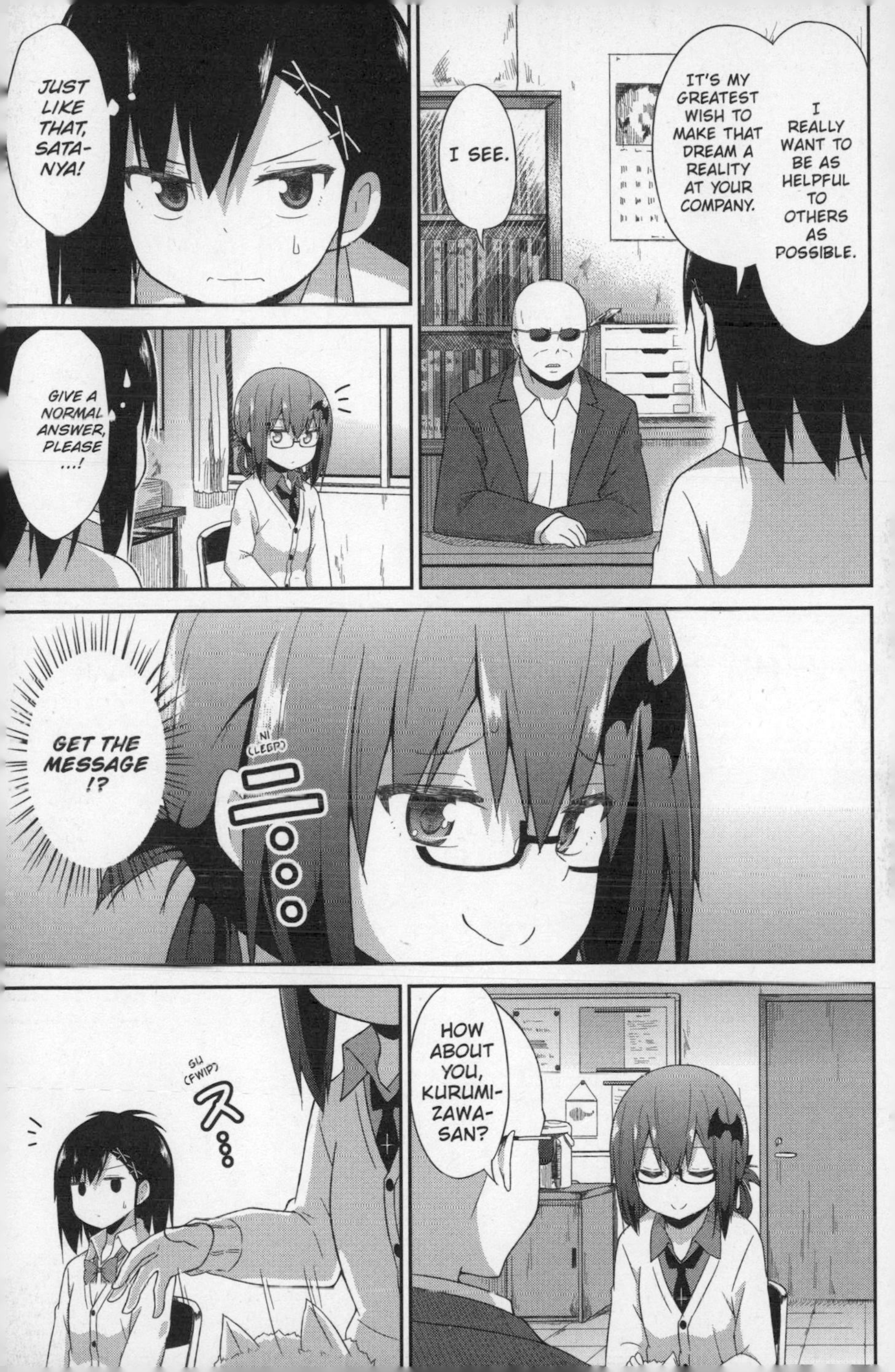
I REALLY WANT TO BE AS HELPFUL TO OTHERS AS POSSIBLE.
IT'S MY GREATEST WISH TO MAKE THAT DREAM A REALITY AT YOUR COMPANY.
I SEE.
JUST LIKE THAT, SATA-NYA!
GIVE A NORMAL ANSWER, PLEASE ...!
GET THE MESSAGE !?
NI (LEER)
HOW ABOUT YOU, KURUMI-ZAWA-SAN?
SU (FWIP)

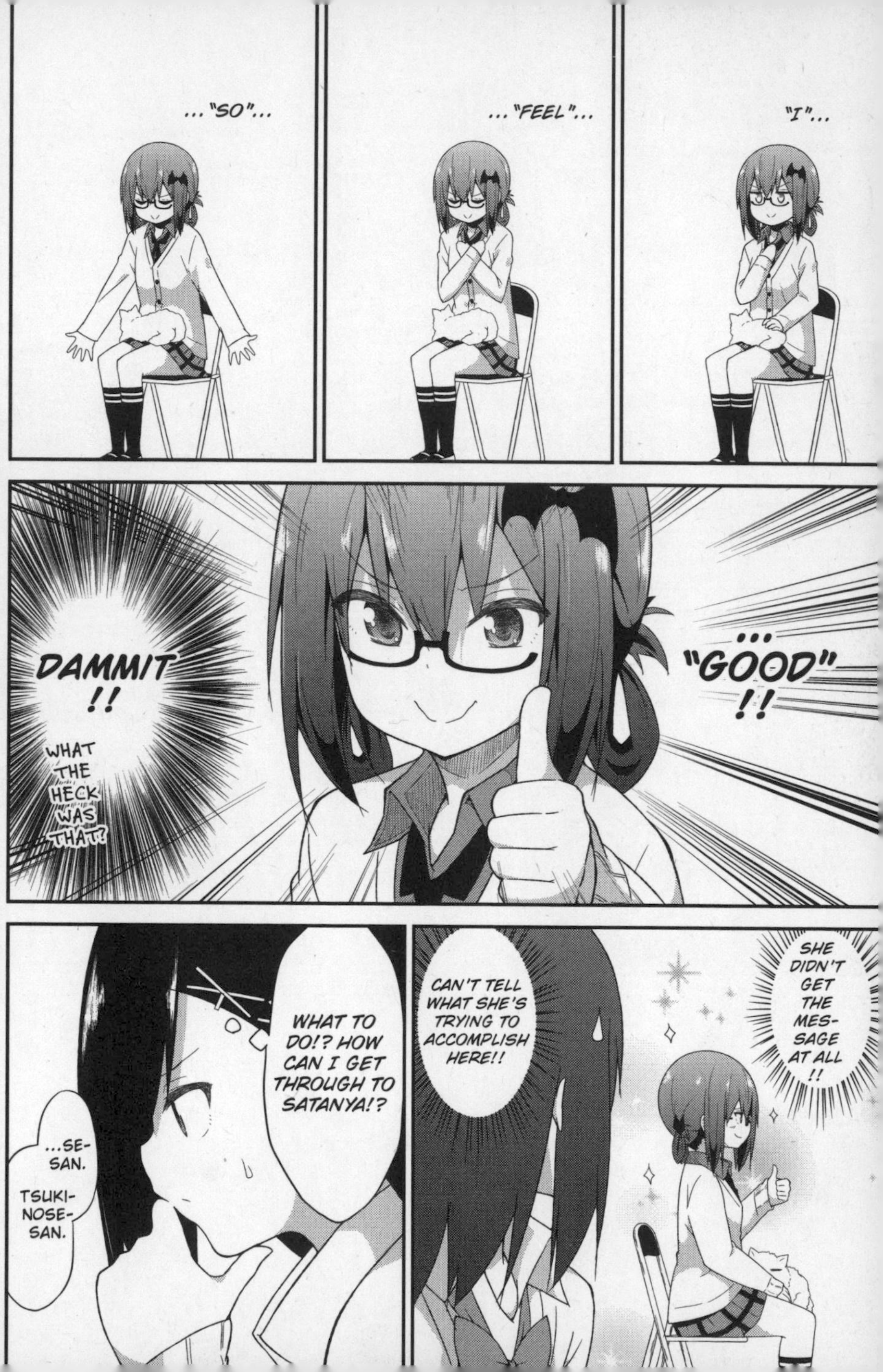
"I"...
..."FEEL"...
..."SO"...
..."GOOD"!!
DAMMIT!!
WHAT THE HECK WAS THAT?
SHE DIDN'T GET THE MESSAGE AT ALL!!
CAN'T TELL WHAT SHE'S TRYING TO ACCOMPLISH HERE!!
WHAT TO DO!? HOW CAN I GET THROUGH TO SATANYA!?
...SE-SAN.
TSUKINOSE-SAN.

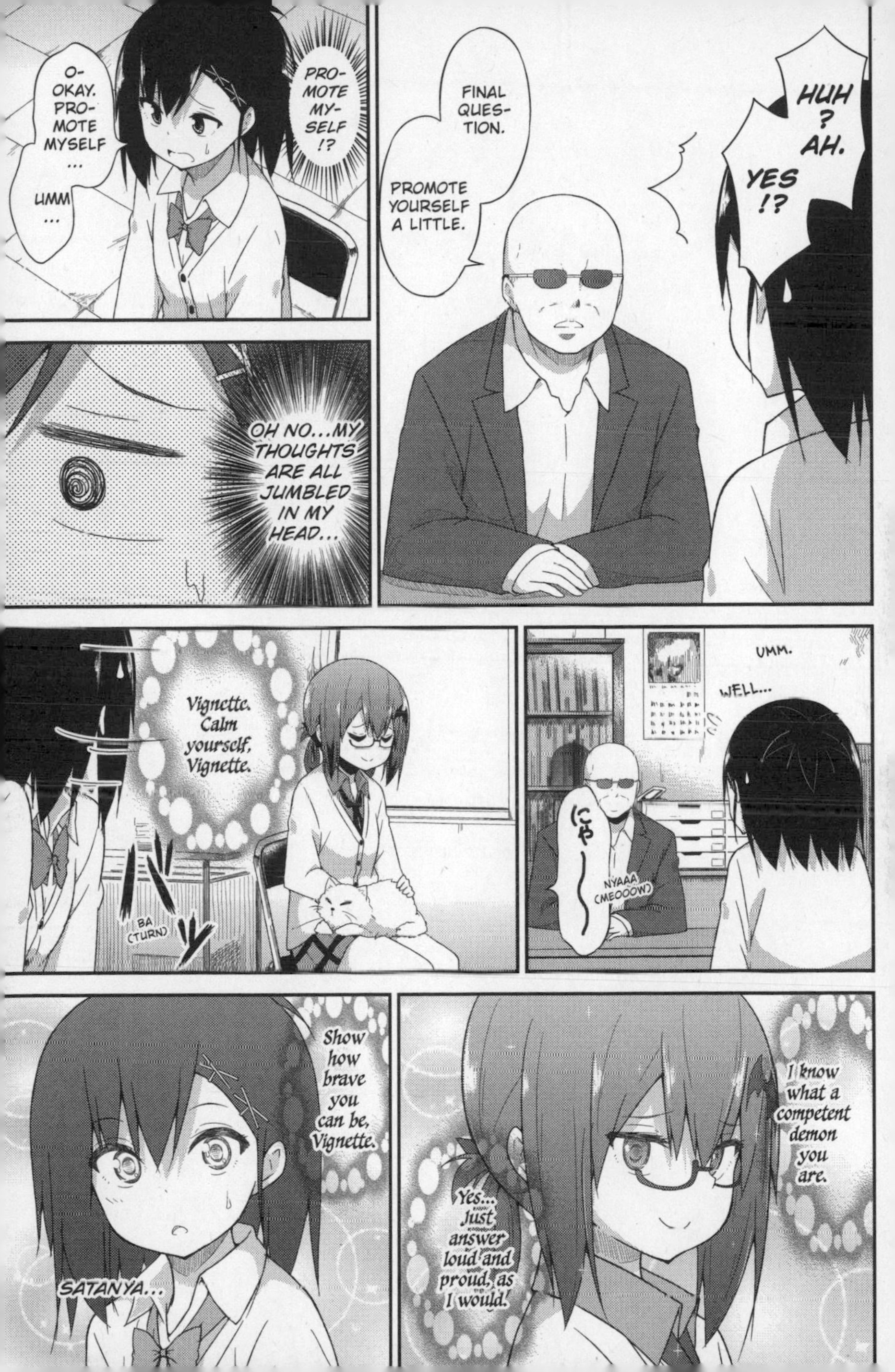
HUH? AH. YES!?
FINAL QUESTION.
PROMOTE YOURSELF A LITTLE.
PROMOTE MYSELF!?
O-OKAY. PROMOTE MYSELF...
UMM...
OH NO...MY THOUGHTS ARE ALL JUMBLED IN MY HEAD...
UMM.
WELL...
にゃ〜
NYAAA (MEOOOW)
Vignette. Calm yourself, Vignette.
BA (TURN)
I know what a competent demon you are.
Yes... Just answer loud and proud, as I would!
Show how brave you can be, Vignette.
SATANYA...

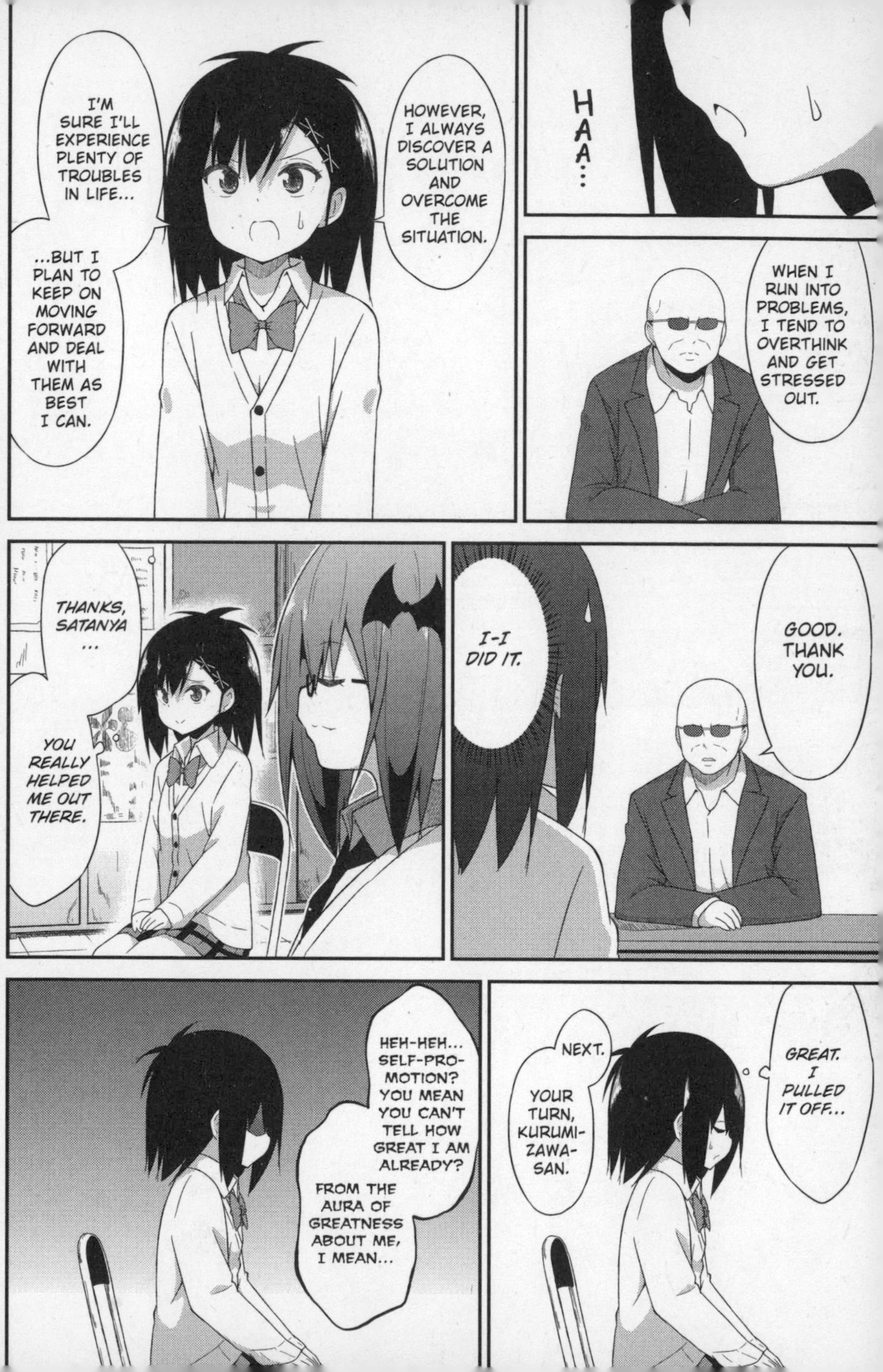
HAA...
WHEN I RUN INTO PROBLEMS, I TEND TO OVERTHINK AND GET STRESSED OUT.
HOWEVER, I ALWAYS DISCOVER A SOLUTION AND OVERCOME THE SITUATION.
I'M SURE I'LL EXPERIENCE PLENTY OF TROUBLES IN LIFE...
...BUT I PLAN TO KEEP ON MOVING FORWARD AND DEAL WITH THEM AS BEST I CAN.
GOOD. THANK YOU.
I-I DID IT.
THANKS, SATANYA...
YOU REALLY HELPED ME OUT THERE.
GREAT. I PULLED IT OFF...
NEXT.
YOUR TURN, KURUMIZAWA-SAN.
HEH-HEH... SELF-PROMOTION? YOU MEAN YOU CAN'T TELL HOW GREAT I AM ALREADY?
FROM THE AURA OF GREATNESS ABOUT ME, I MEAN...

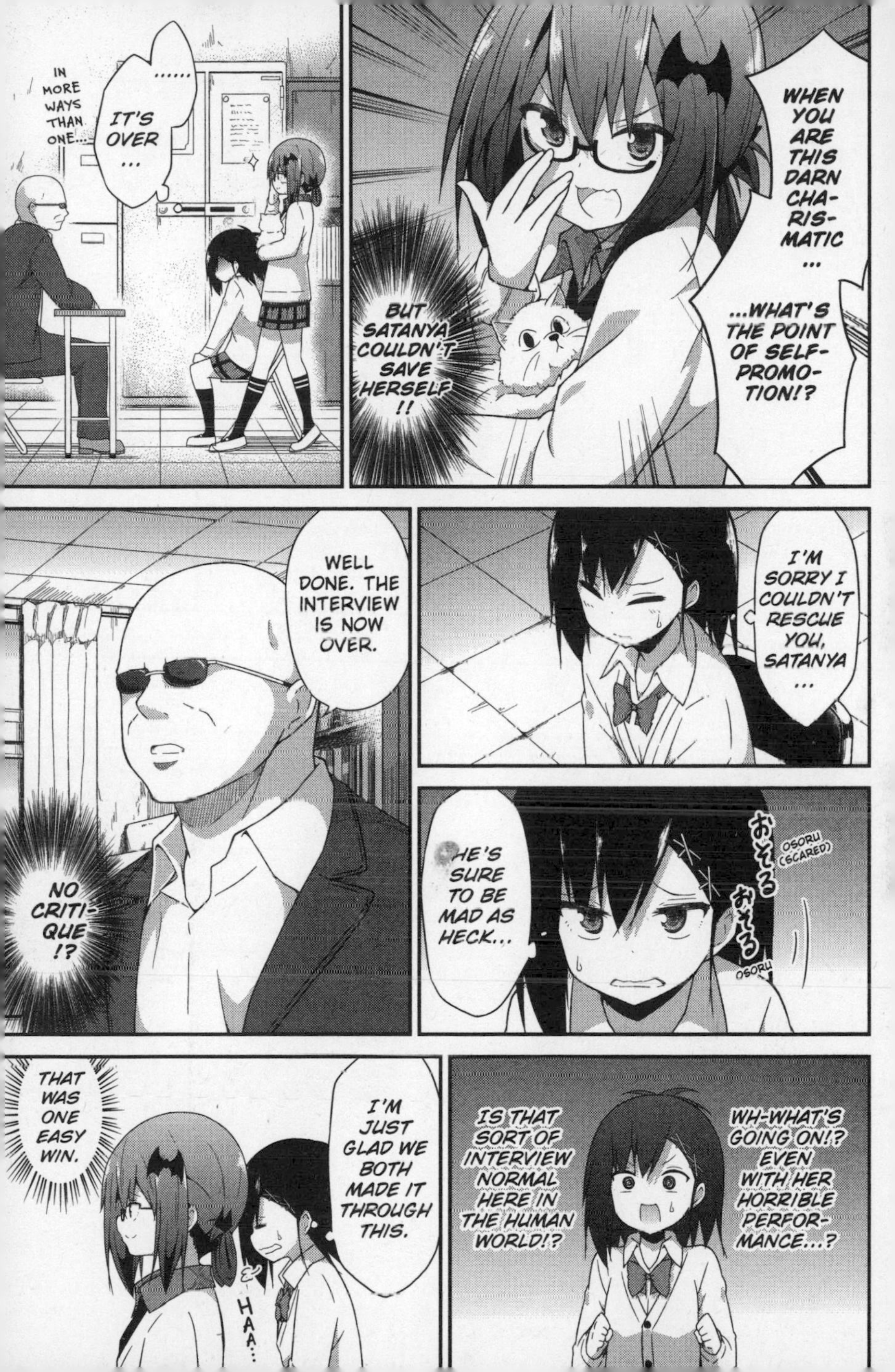
WHEN YOU ARE THIS DARN CHARISMATIC...
...WHAT'S THE POINT OF SELF-PROMOTION!?
BUT SATANYA COULDN'T SAVE HERSELF!!
...... IT'S OVER...
IN MORE WAYS THAN ONE...
I'M SORRY I COULDN'T RESCUE YOU, SATANYA...
おそる おそる
OSORU (SCARED)
OSORU
HE'S SURE TO BE MAD AS HECK...
WELL DONE. THE INTERVIEW IS NOW OVER.
NO CRITIQUE!?
WH-WHAT'S GOING ON!? EVEN WITH HER HORRIBLE PERFORMANCE...?
IS THAT SORT OF INTERVIEW NORMAL HERE IN THE HUMAN WORLD!?
THAT WAS ONE EASY WIN.
I'M JUST GLAD WE BOTH MADE IT THROUGH THIS.
HAA...

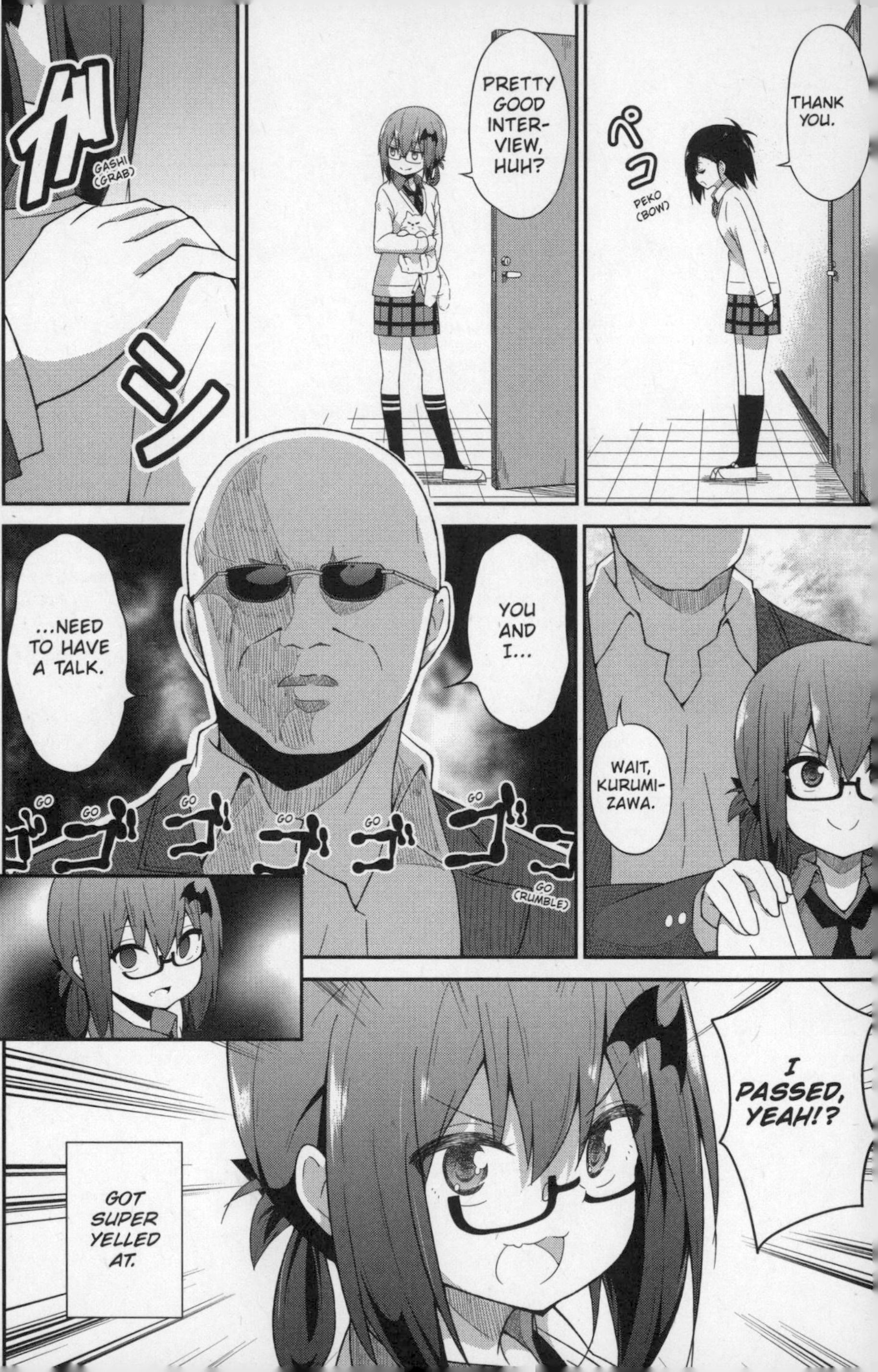
THANK YOU.
ペコ
PEKO (BOW)
PRETTY GOOD INTER-VIEW, HUH?
ガシッ
GASHI (GRAB)
WAIT, KURUMI-ZAWA.
YOU AND I...
...NEED TO HAVE A TALK.
ゴゴゴゴゴゴ
GO GO GO GO GO GO GO (RUMBLE)
I PASSED, YEAH!?
GOT SUPER YELLED AT.

HER SOUL...

TEN
MIN-
UTES
LATER

Gabriel Dropout

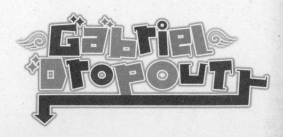

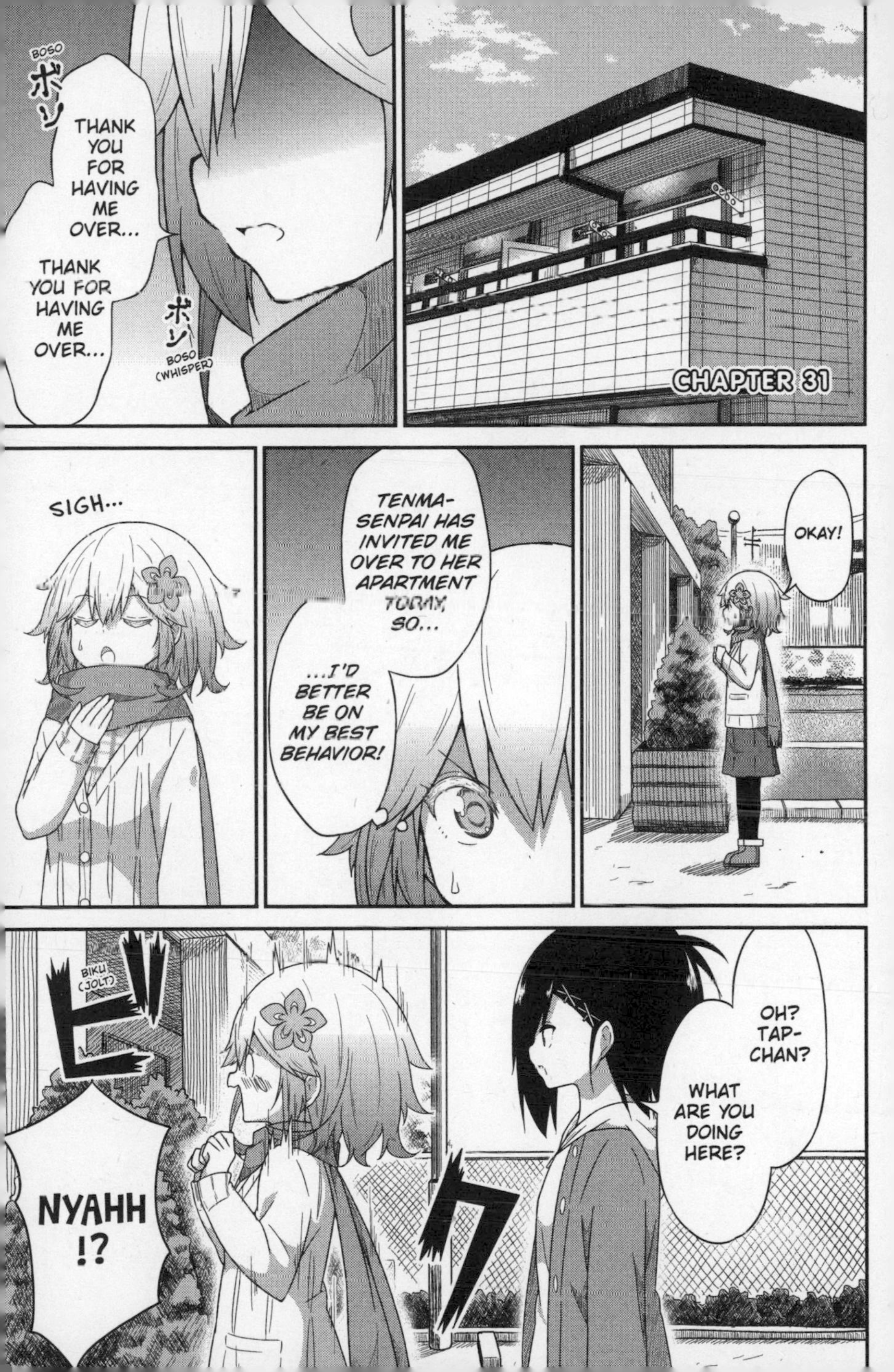
CHAPTER 31
BOSO
ボソ
THANK YOU FOR HAVING ME OVER...
ボソ
BOSO (WHISPER)
THANK YOU FOR HAVING ME OVER...
OKAY!
TENMA-SENPAI HAS INVITED ME OVER TO HER APARTMENT TODAY, SO...
...I'D BETTER BE ON MY BEST BEHAVIOR!
SIGH...
OH? TAP-CHAN?
WHAT ARE YOU DOING HERE?
ビク
BIKU (JOLT)
NYAHH!?

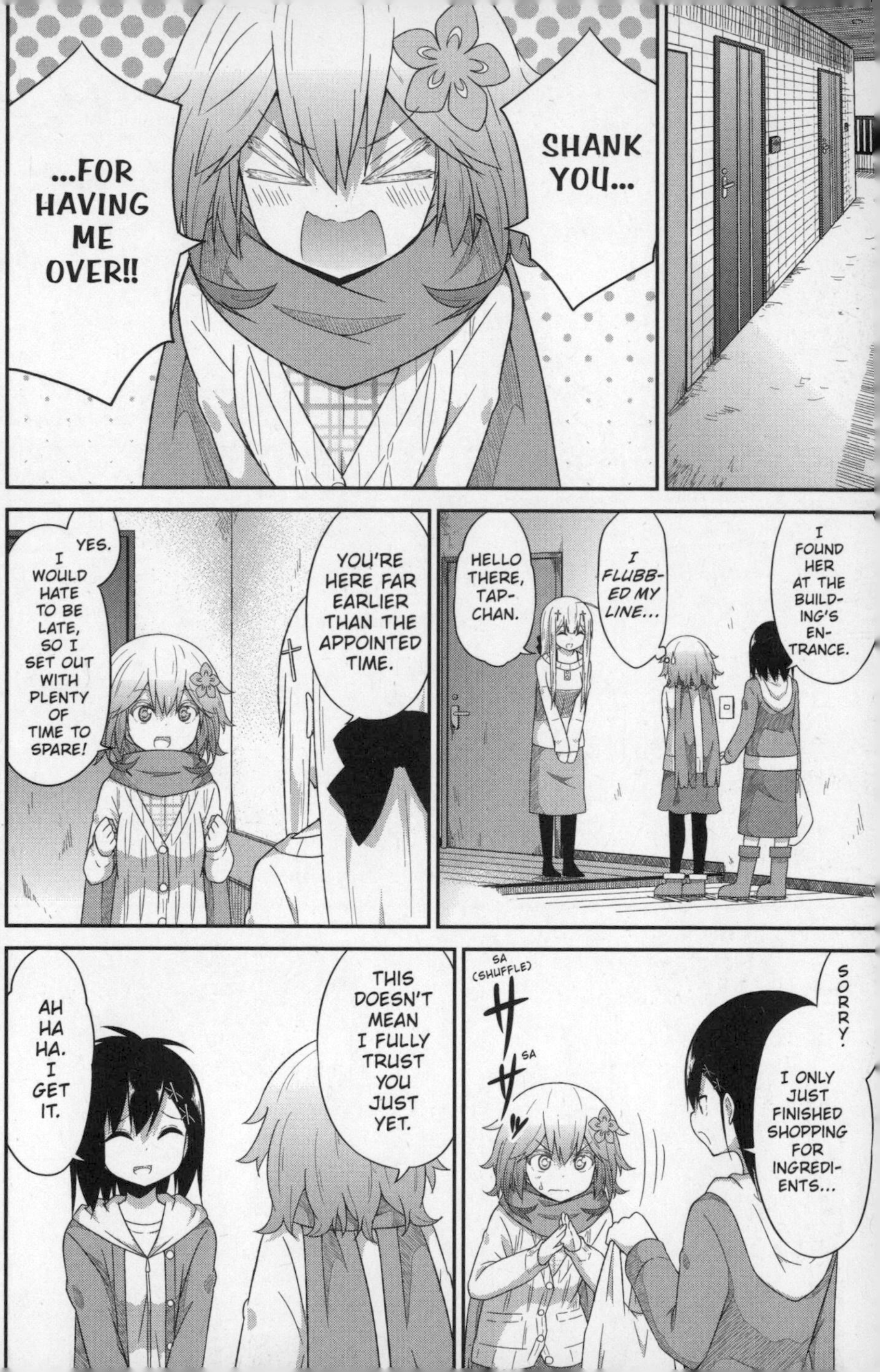
SHANK YOU...
...FOR HAVING ME OVER!!
I FOUND HER AT THE BUILDING'S ENTRANCE.
I FLUBBED MY LINE...
HELLO THERE, TAP-CHAN.
YOU'RE HERE FAR EARLIER THAN THE APPOINTED TIME.
YES. I WOULD HATE TO BE LATE, SO I SET OUT WITH PLENTY OF TIME TO SPARE!
SORRY.
I ONLY JUST FINISHED SHOPPING FOR INGREDIENTS...
SA (SHUFFLE)
SA
THIS DOESN'T MEAN I FULLY TRUST YOU JUST YET.
AH HA HA. I GET IT.

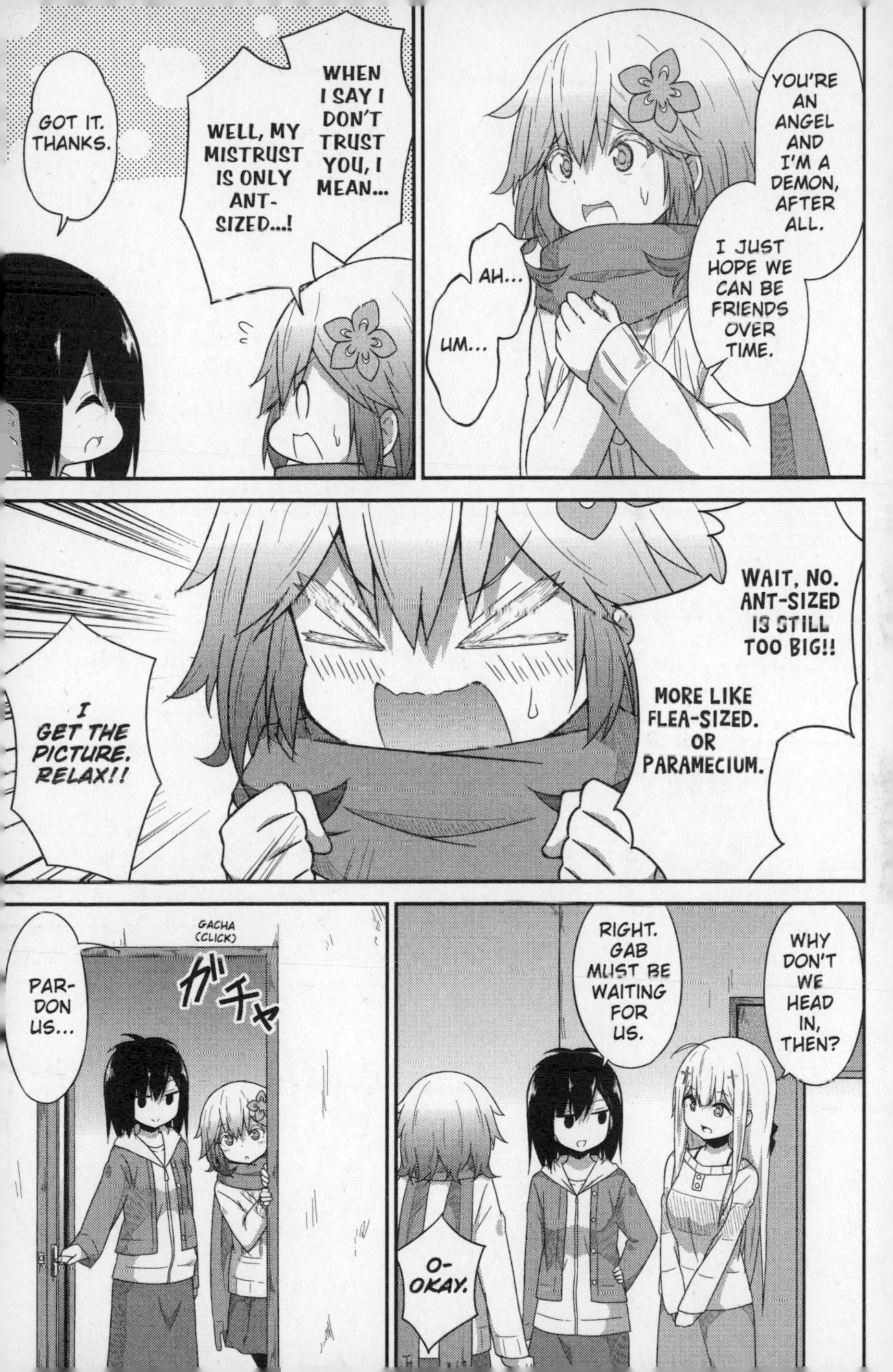
YOU'RE AN ANGEL AND I'M A DEMON, AFTER ALL.
I JUST HOPE WE CAN BE FRIENDS OVER TIME.
AH...
UM...
WHEN I SAY I DON'T TRUST YOU, I MEAN...
WELL, MY MISTRUST IS ONLY ANT-SIZED...!
GOT IT. THANKS.
WAIT, NO. ANT-SIZED IS STILL TOO BIG!!
MORE LIKE FLEA-SIZED. OR PARAMECIUM.
I GET THE PICTURE. RELAX!!
WHY DON'T WE HEAD IN, THEN?
RIGHT. GAB MUST BE WAITING FOR US.
O-OKAY.
GACHA (CLICK)
ガチャ
PAR-DON US...

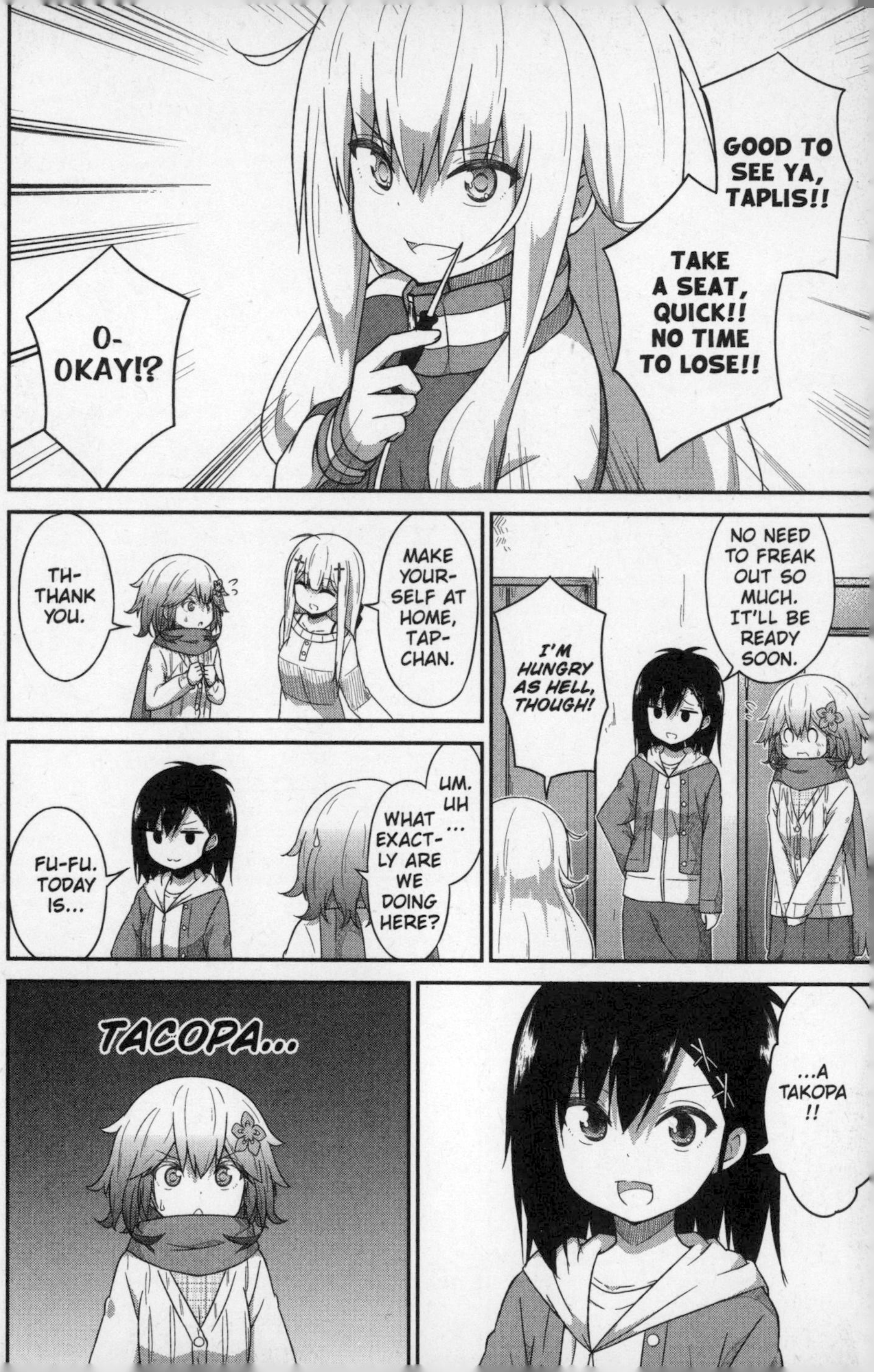
GOOD TO SEE YA, TAPLIS!!
TAKE A SEAT, QUICK!! NO TIME TO LOSE!!
O-OKAY!?
NO NEED TO FREAK OUT SO MUCH. IT'LL BE READY SOON.
I'M HUNGRY AS HELL, THOUGH!
MAKE YOUR-SELF AT HOME, TAP-CHAN.
TH-THANK YOU.
UM. UH... WHAT EXACT-LY ARE WE DOING HERE?
FU-FU. TODAY IS...
...A TAKOPA!!
TACOPA...

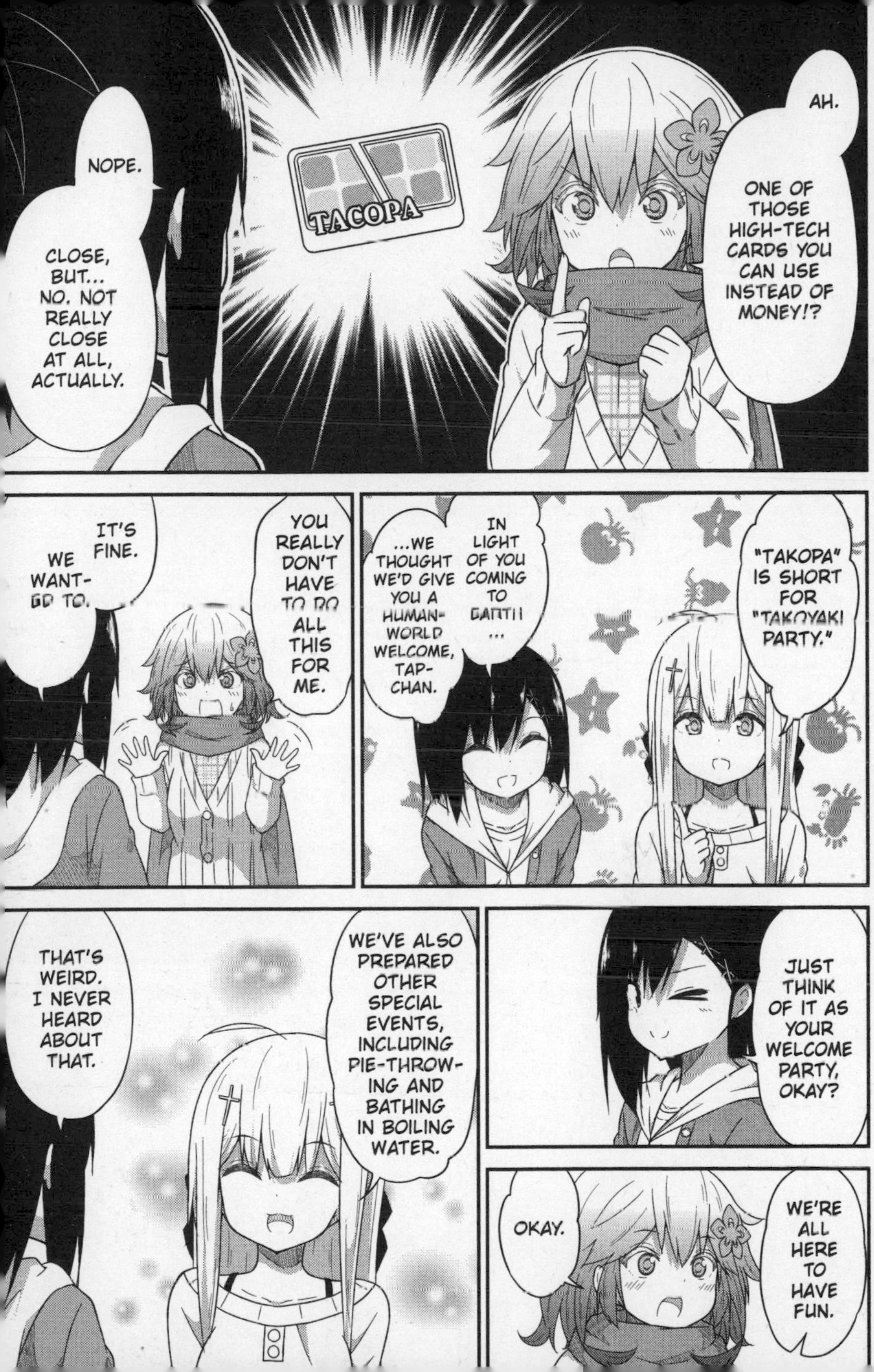
AH.
ONE OF THOSE HIGH-TECH CARDS YOU CAN USE INSTEAD OF MONEY!?
TACOPA
NOPE.
CLOSE, BUT... NO. NOT REALLY CLOSE AT ALL, ACTUALLY.
"TAKOPA" IS SHORT FOR "TAKOYAKI PARTY."
IN LIGHT OF YOU COMING TO EARTH ...
...WE THOUGHT WE'D GIVE YOU A HUMAN-WORLD WELCOME, TAP-CHAN.
YOU REALLY DON'T HAVE TO DO ALL THIS FOR ME.
IT'S FINE.
WE WANT-ED TO.
JUST THINK OF IT AS YOUR WELCOME PARTY, OKAY?
WE'RE ALL HERE TO HAVE FUN.
OKAY.
WE'VE ALSO PREPARED OTHER SPECIAL EVENTS, INCLUDING PIE-THROW-ING AND BATHING IN BOILING WATER.
THAT'S WEIRD. I NEVER HEARD ABOUT THAT.

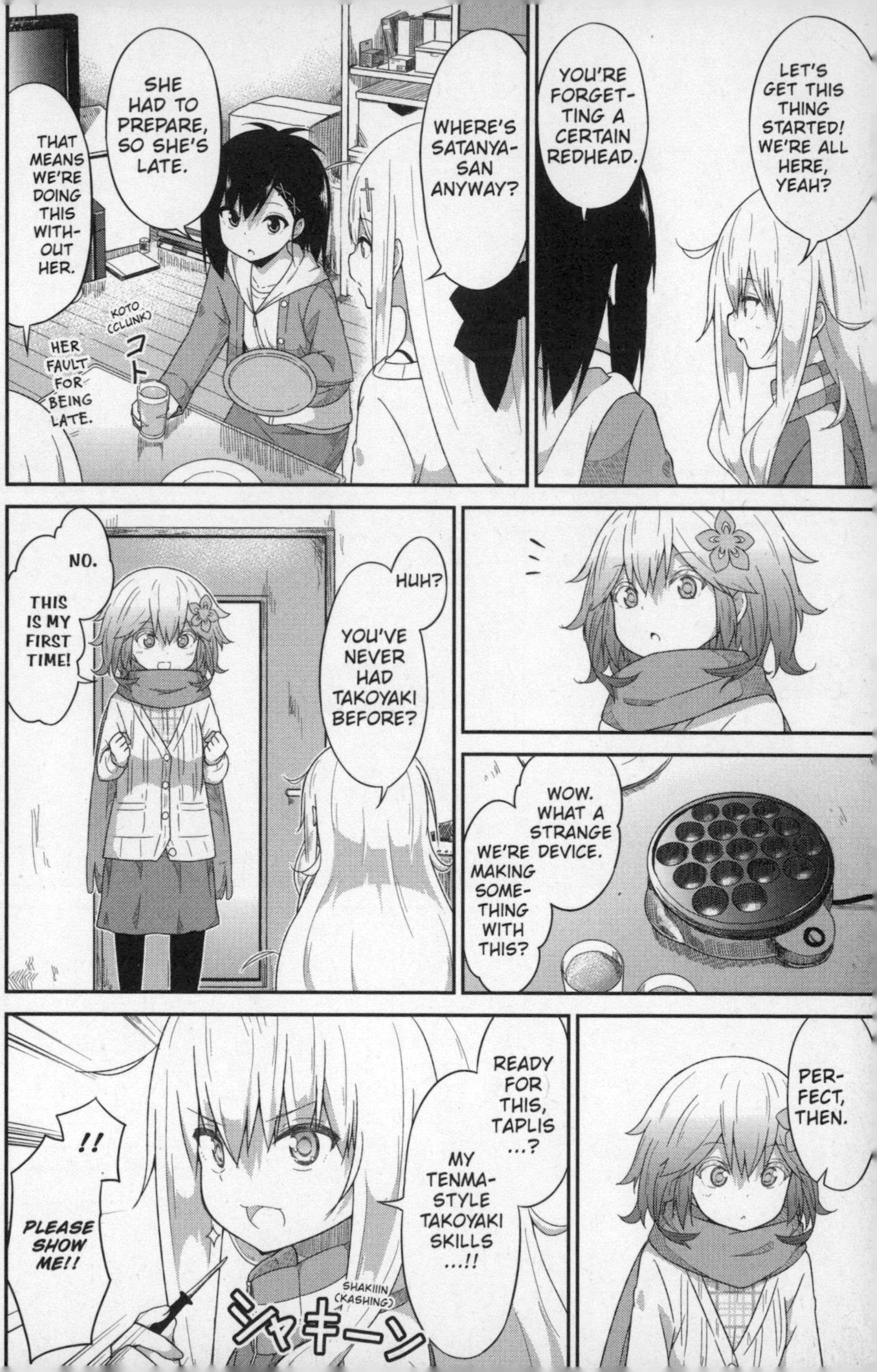

LET'S GET THIS THING STARTED! WE'RE ALL HERE, YEAH?
YOU'RE FORGET-TING A CERTAIN REDHEAD.
WHERE'S SATANYA-SAN ANYWAY?
SHE HAD TO PREPARE, SO SHE'S LATE.
THAT MEANS WE'RE DOING THIS WITH-OUT HER.
KOTO (CLUNK)
コト
HER FAULT FOR BEING LATE.
WOW. WHAT A STRANGE DEVICE.
WE'RE MAKING SOME-THING WITH THIS?
HUH?
YOU'VE NEVER HAD TAKOYAKI BEFORE?
NO.
THIS IS MY FIRST TIME!
PER-FECT, THEN.
READY FOR THIS, TAPLIS ...?
MY TENMA-STYLE TAKOYAKI SKILLS ...!!
SHAKIIIN (KASHING)
シャキーン
!!
PLEASE SHOW ME!!

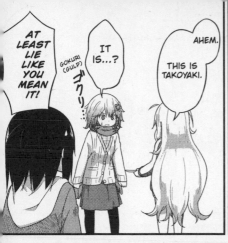

ぐちゃ
GUCHA (WOMP)
AHEM.
THIS IS TAKOYAKI.
IT IS...?
GOKURI (GULP)
ゴクリ…
AT LEAST LIE LIKE YOU MEAN IT!
WOULD YOU LIKE TO GIVE IT A TRY, TAP-CHAN?
NO.
THIS SEEMS BEYOND ME!
GIVE IT A SHOT!
......
VERY WELL.
JUDGING FROM THE STRUCTURE OF THIS MACHINE, TAKOYAKI MUST BE...
...BALL-SHAPED FOOD!!

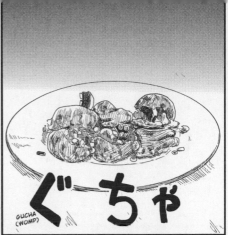

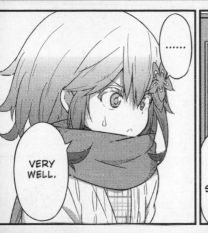

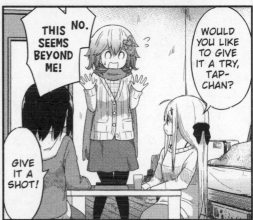

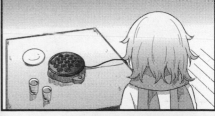

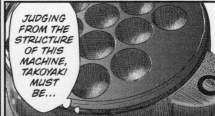

KOGE

KOGE

PUSU
(SMOKE)

PUSU
(SMOKE)

KOGE
(BURNT)

I'LL DO IT. JUST GIVE ME A MINUTE.

KYU
(TUG)

THIS WAS YOUR FIRST TIME, SO IT MAKES SENSE.

I'M SORRY... I REALLY DID TRY MY BEST.

OHH.

KURU
(FLIK)

PARA
(TOSS)

PARA

BA
(POUR)

THERE, ALL DONE!
OHHHHH!!
SO THESE ARE TAKO-YAKI!
THEY ARE ALSO PRETTY TASTY WITH MAYO.
BETTER EAT THEM WHILE THEY'RE HOT.
OKAY.
AHHH...
MMMMM.
THAT WAS DELICIOUS!!
HAFU (PUFF) はふ
HAFU はふ
GLAD TO HEAR IT.
HMM. PASSABLE.
SHALL I...TEACH YOU THE TENMA STYLE?
MUGU (MUNCH) むぐ
MUGU むぐ
NOT SURE WHAT THAT MEANS, BUT NO THANK YOU.

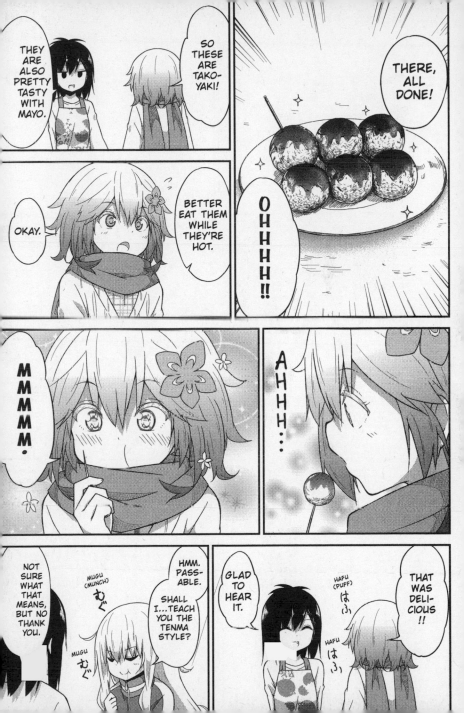

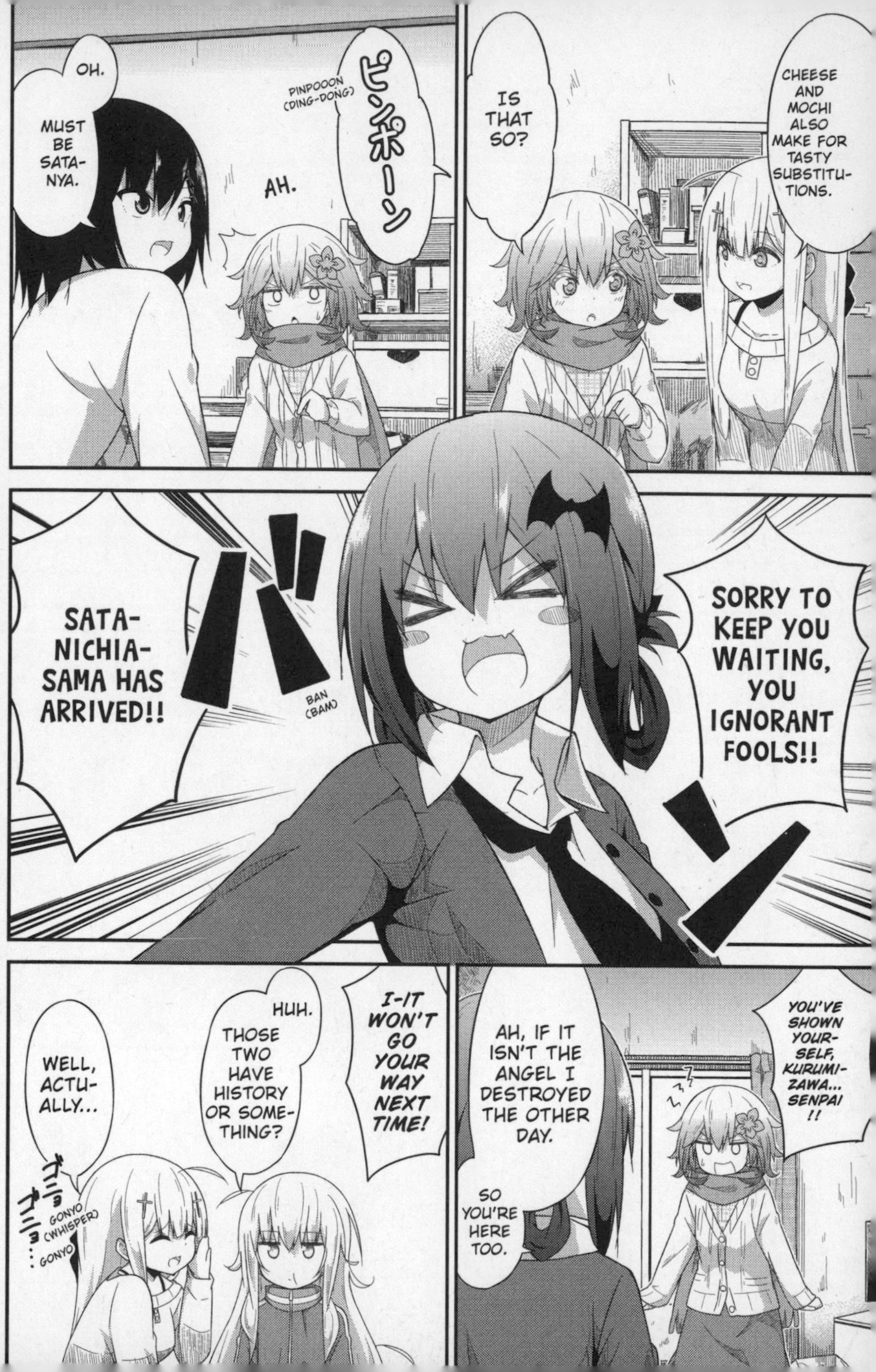

CHEESE AND MOCHI ALSO MAKE FOR TASTY SUBSTITUTIONS.
IS THAT SO?
ピンポーン
PINPOOON (DING-DONG)
AH.
OH.
MUST BE SATANYA.
SORRY TO KEEP YOU WAITING, YOU IGNORANT FOOLS!!
バン
BAN (BAM)
SATANICHIA-SAMA HAS ARRIVED!!
YOU'VE SHOWN YOURSELF, KURUMIZAWA... SENPAI!!
AH, IF IT ISN'T THE ANGEL I DESTROYED THE OTHER DAY.
SO YOU'RE HERE TOO.
I-IT WON'T GO YOUR WAY NEXT TIME!
HUH. THOSE TWO HAVE HISTORY OR SOMETHING?
WELL, ACTUALLY...
ゴニョゴニョ…
GONYO GONYO (WHISPER)

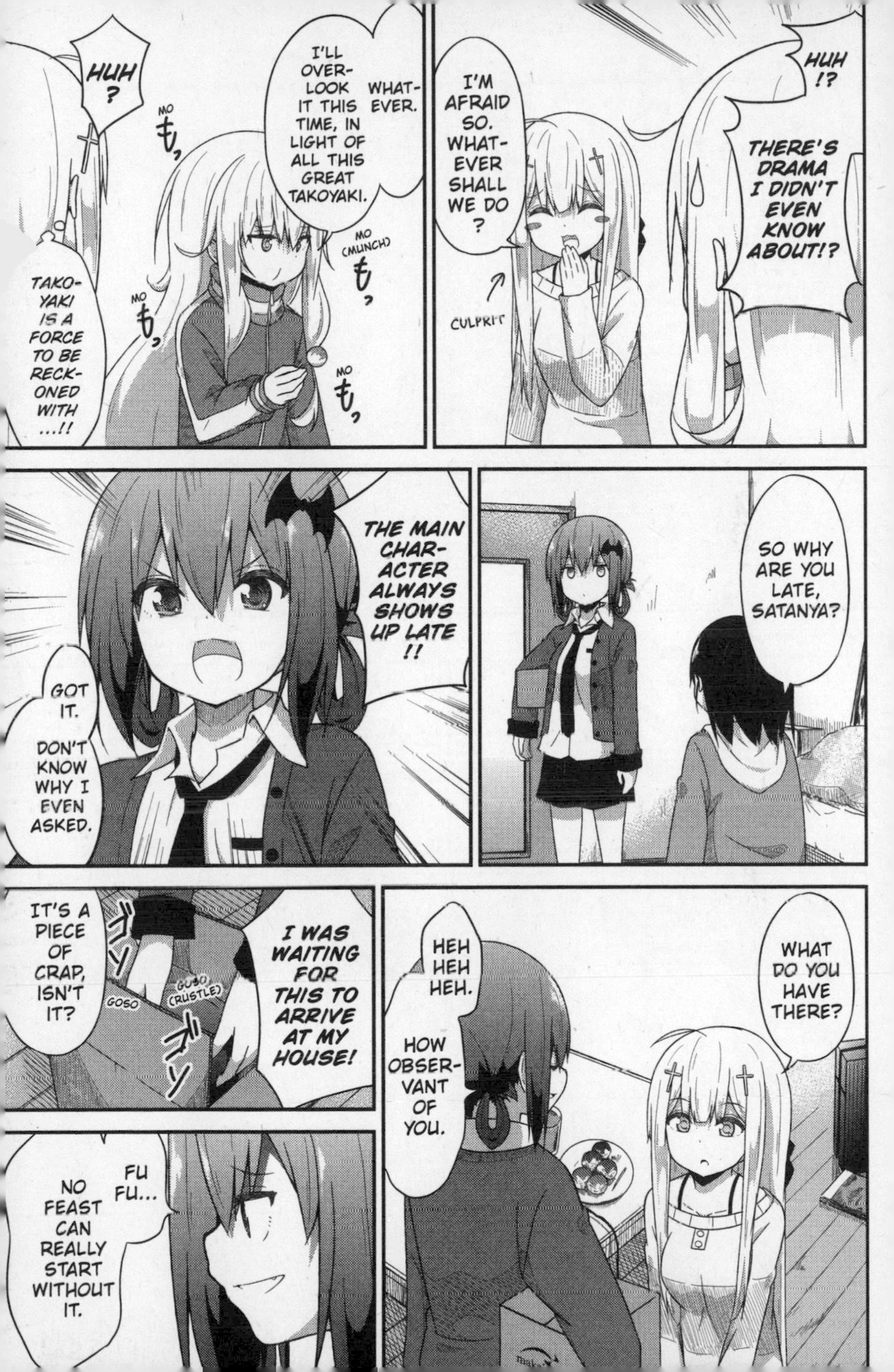
HUH !?
THERE'S DRAMA I DIDN'T EVEN KNOW ABOUT!?
I'M AFRAID SO. WHATEVER SHALL WE DO?
CULPRIT
WHATEVER.
I'LL OVERLOOK IT THIS TIME, IN LIGHT OF ALL THIS GREAT TAKOYAKI.
MO (MUNCH)
HUH?
MO
MO
MO
TAKOYAKI IS A FORCE TO BE RECKONED WITH ...!!
SO WHY ARE YOU LATE, SATANYA?
THE MAIN CHARACTER ALWAYS SHOWS UP LATE!!
GOT IT.
DON'T KNOW WHY I EVEN ASKED.
WHAT DO YOU HAVE THERE?
HEH HEH HEH.
HOW OBSERVANT OF YOU.
I WAS WAITING FOR THIS TO ARRIVE AT MY HOUSE!
GOSO (RUSTLE)
GOSO
IT'S A PIECE OF CRAP, ISN'T IT?
FU FU...
NO FEAST CAN REALLY START WITHOUT IT.

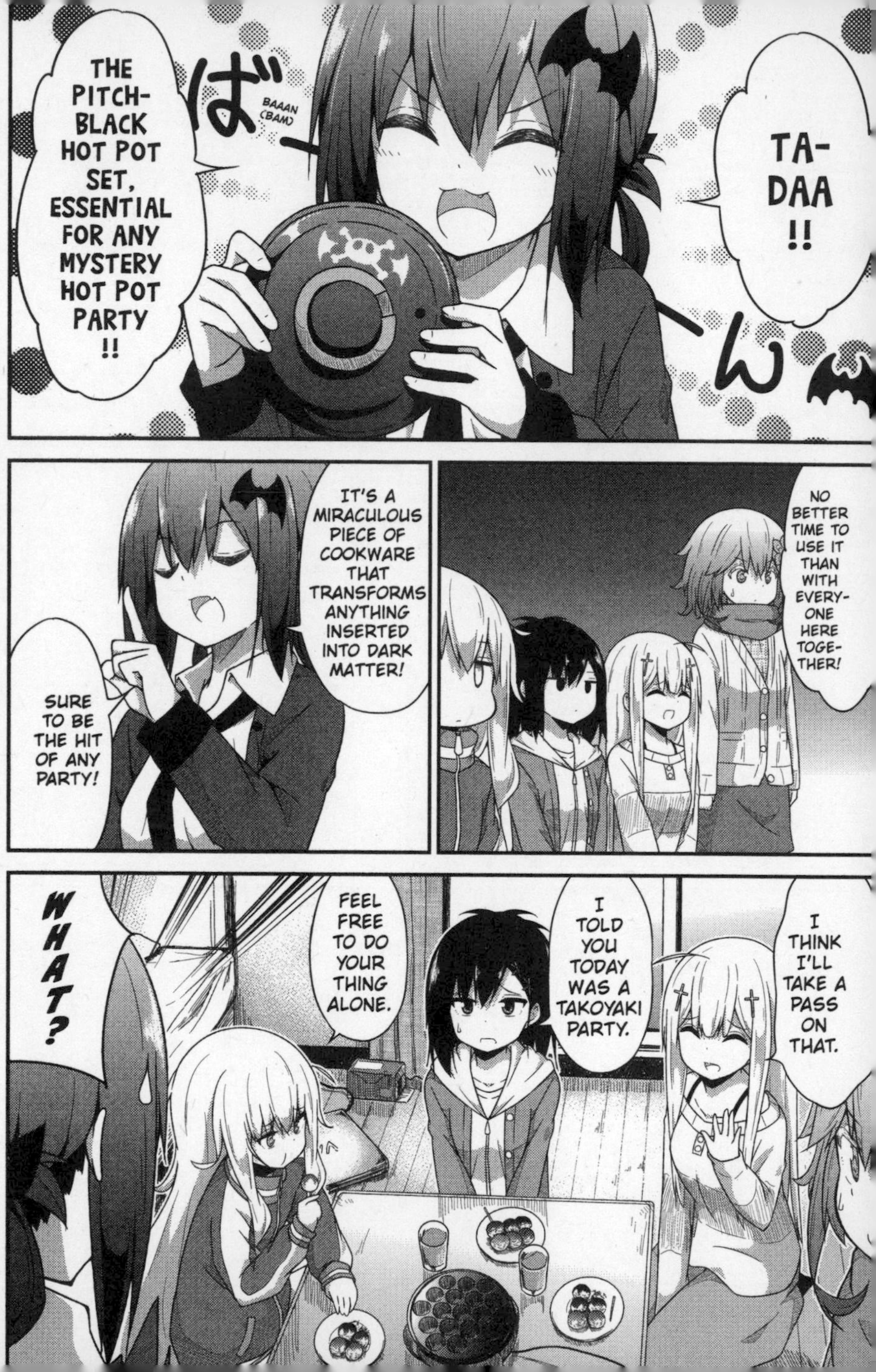
TA-DAA!!
ばーん
BAAAN (BAM)
THE PITCH-BLACK HOT POT SET, ESSENTIAL FOR ANY MYSTERY HOT POT PARTY!!
NO BETTER TIME TO USE IT THAN WITH EVERY-ONE HERE TOGE-THER!
IT'S A MIRACULOUS PIECE OF COOKWARE THAT TRANSFORMS ANYTHING INSERTED INTO DARK MATTER!
SURE TO BE THE HIT OF ANY PARTY!
I THINK I'LL TAKE A PASS ON THAT.
I TOLD YOU TODAY WAS A TAKOYAKI PARTY.
FEEL FREE TO DO YOUR THING ALONE.
WHAT?

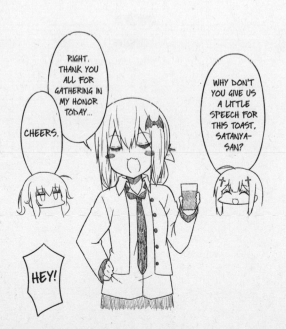

WHY DON'T YOU GIVE US A LITTLE SPEECH FOR THIS TOAST, SATANYA-SAN?
RIGHT. THANK YOU ALL FOR GATHERING IN MY HONOR TODAY...
CHEERS.
HEY!

Gabriel Dropout

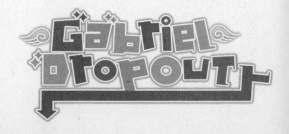

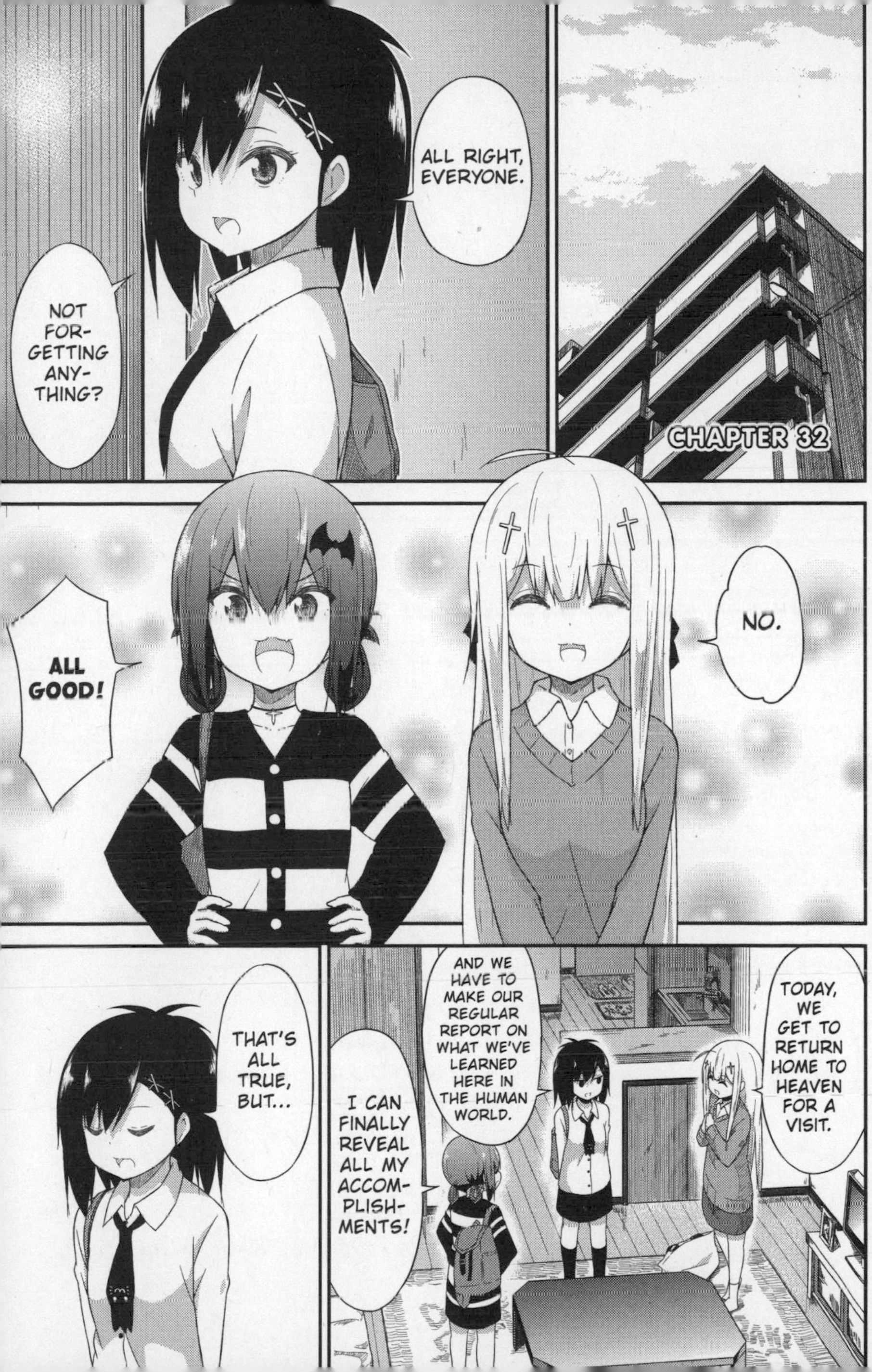
CHAPTER 32
ALL RIGHT, EVERYONE.
NOT FOR-GETTING ANY-THING?
NO.
ALL GOOD!
TODAY, WE GET TO RETURN HOME TO HEAVEN FOR A VISIT.
AND WE HAVE TO MAKE OUR REGULAR REPORT ON WHAT WE'VE LEARNED HERE IN THE HUMAN WORLD.
I CAN FINALLY REVEAL ALL MY ACCOMP-LISH-MENTS!
THAT'S ALL TRUE, BUT...

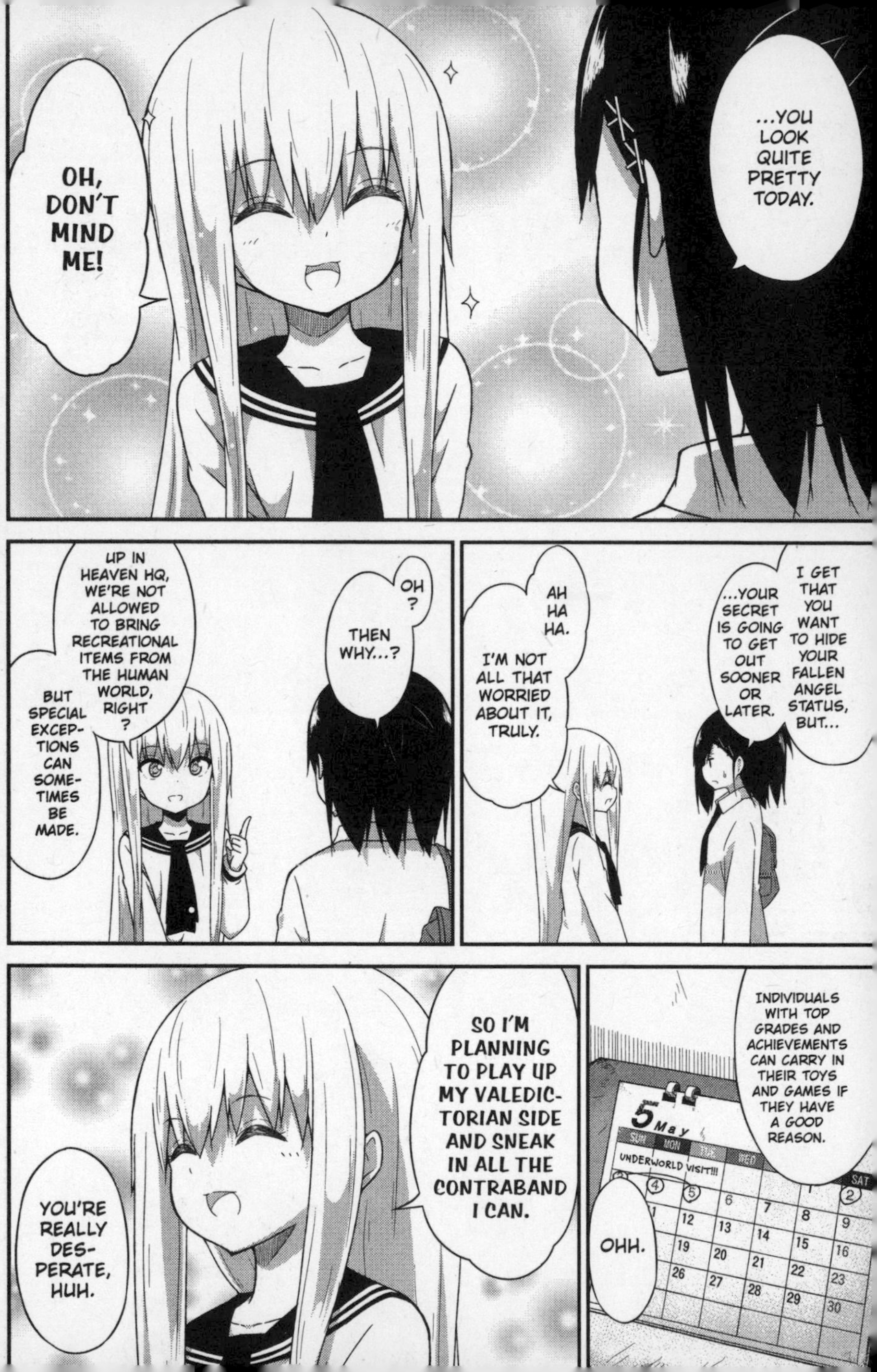
...YOU LOOK QUITE PRETTY TODAY.
OH, DON'T MIND ME!
I GET THAT YOU WANT TO HIDE YOUR FALLEN ANGEL STATUS, BUT...
...YOUR SECRET IS GOING TO GET OUT SOONER OR LATER.
AH HA HA.
I'M NOT ALL THAT WORRIED ABOUT IT, TRULY.
OH?
THEN WHY...?
UP IN HEAVEN HQ, WE'RE NOT ALLOWED TO BRING RECREATIONAL ITEMS FROM THE HUMAN WORLD, RIGHT?
BUT SPECIAL EXCEPTIONS CAN SOMETIMES BE MADE.
INDIVIDUALS WITH TOP GRADES AND ACHIEVEMENTS CAN CARRY IN THEIR TOYS AND GAMES IF THEY HAVE A GOOD REASON.
5 May
UNDERWORLD VISIT!!!
OHH.
SO I'M PLANNING TO PLAY UP MY VALEDICTORIAN SIDE AND SNEAK IN ALL THE CONTRABAND I CAN.
YOU'RE REALLY DESPERATE, HUH.

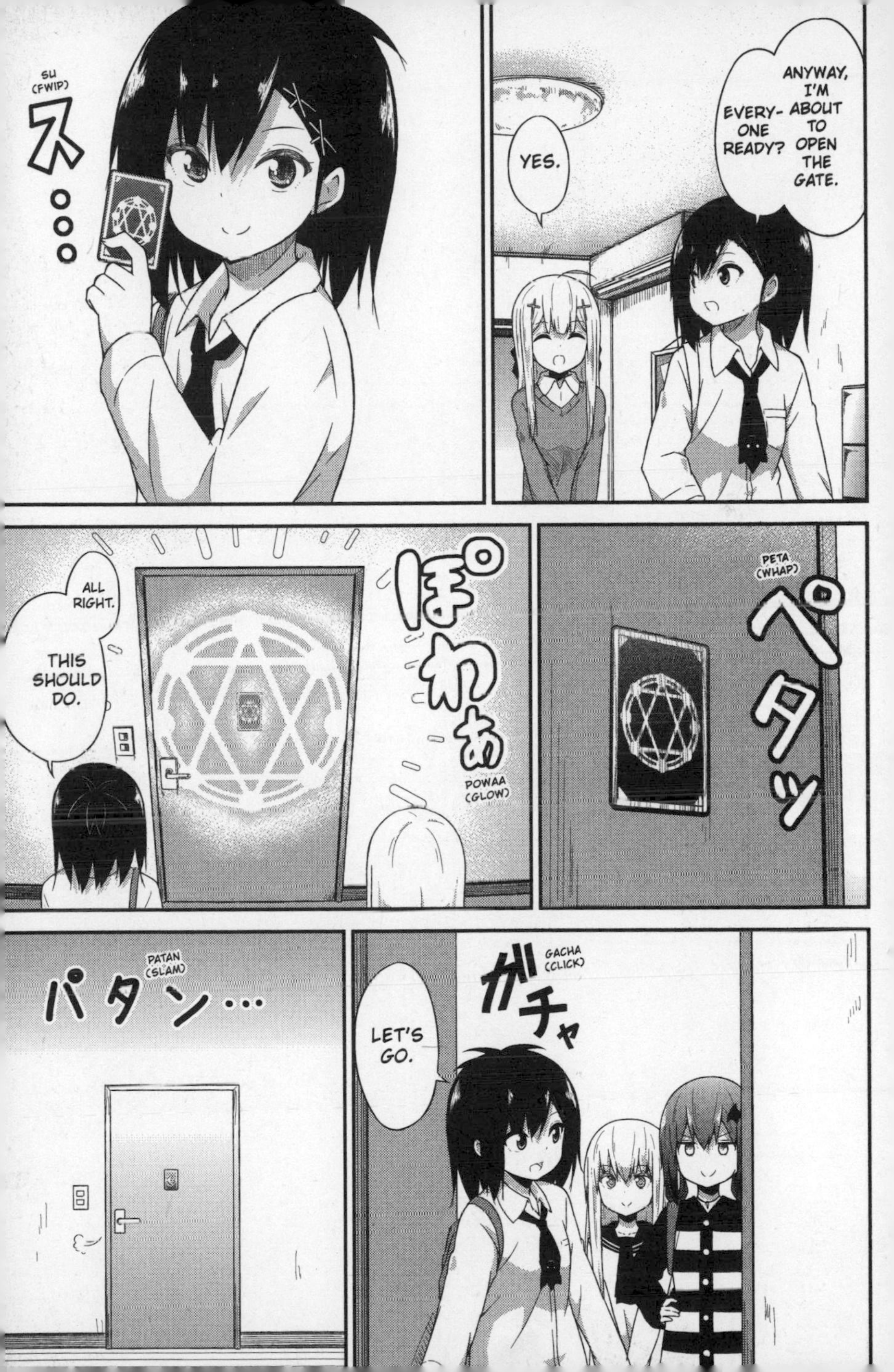
ANYWAY, I'M ABOUT TO OPEN THE GATE.
EVERY-ONE READY?
YES.
ス…
SU (FWIP)
ペタッ
PETA (WHAP)
ぽわあ
POWAA (GLOW)
ALL RIGHT.
THIS SHOULD DO.
ガチャ
GACHA (CLICK)
LET'S GO.
パタン…
PATAN (SLAM)

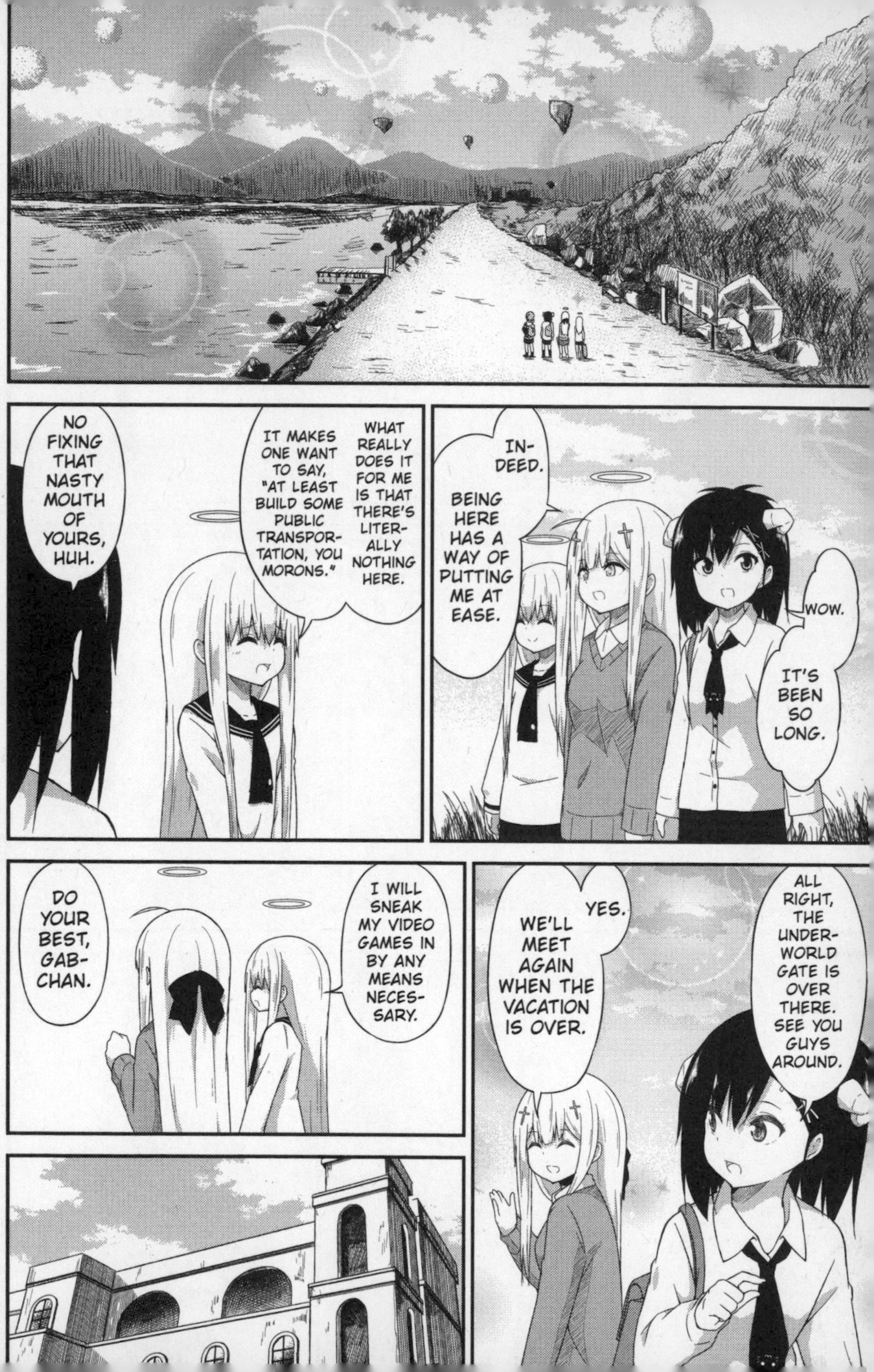
WOW.
IT'S BEEN SO LONG.
IN-DEED.
BEING HERE HAS A WAY OF PUTTING ME AT EASE.
WHAT REALLY DOES IT FOR ME IS THAT THERE'S LITER-ALLY NOTHING HERE.
IT MAKES ONE WANT TO SAY, "AT LEAST BUILD SOME PUBLIC TRANSPOR-TATION, YOU MORONS."
NO FIXING THAT NASTY MOUTH OF YOURS, HUH.
ALL RIGHT, THE UNDER-WORLD GATE IS OVER THERE. SEE YOU GUYS AROUND.
YES.
WE'LL MEET AGAIN WHEN THE VACATION IS OVER.
I WILL SNEAK MY VIDEO GAMES IN BY ANY MEANS NECES-SARY.
DO YOUR BEST, GAB-CHAN.

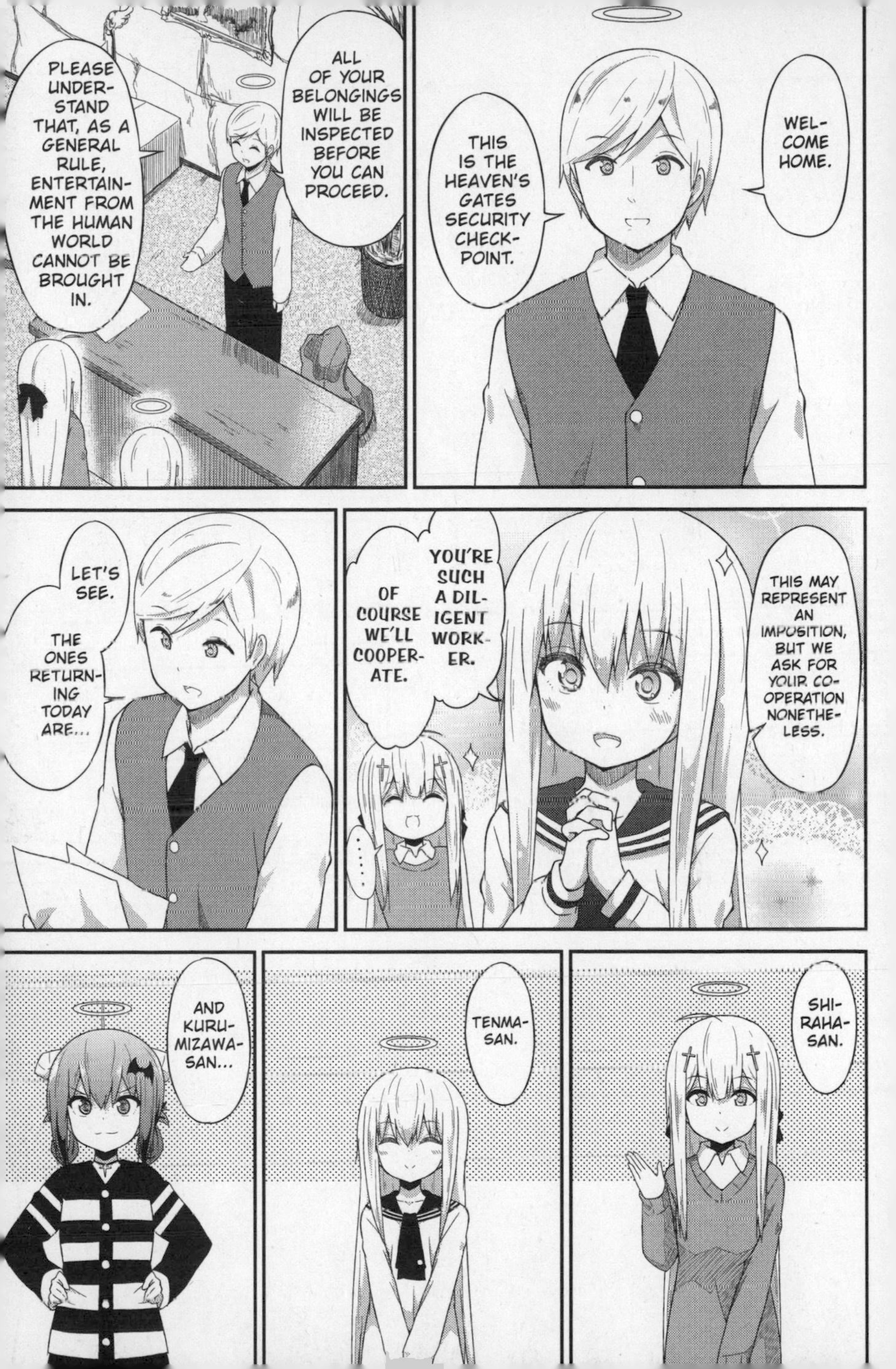

WELCOME HOME.
THIS IS THE HEAVEN'S GATES SECURITY CHECKPOINT.
ALL OF YOUR BELONGINGS WILL BE INSPECTED BEFORE YOU CAN PROCEED.
PLEASE UNDERSTAND THAT, AS A GENERAL RULE, ENTERTAINMENT FROM THE HUMAN WORLD CANNOT BE BROUGHT IN.
THIS MAY REPRESENT AN IMPOSITION, BUT WE ASK FOR YOUR COOPERATION NONETHELESS.
YOU'RE SUCH A DILIGENT WORKER.
OF COURSE WE'LL COOPERATE.
......
LET'S SEE.
THE ONES RETURNING TODAY ARE...
SHIRAHA-SAN.
TENMA-SAN.
AND KURUMIZAWA-SAN...

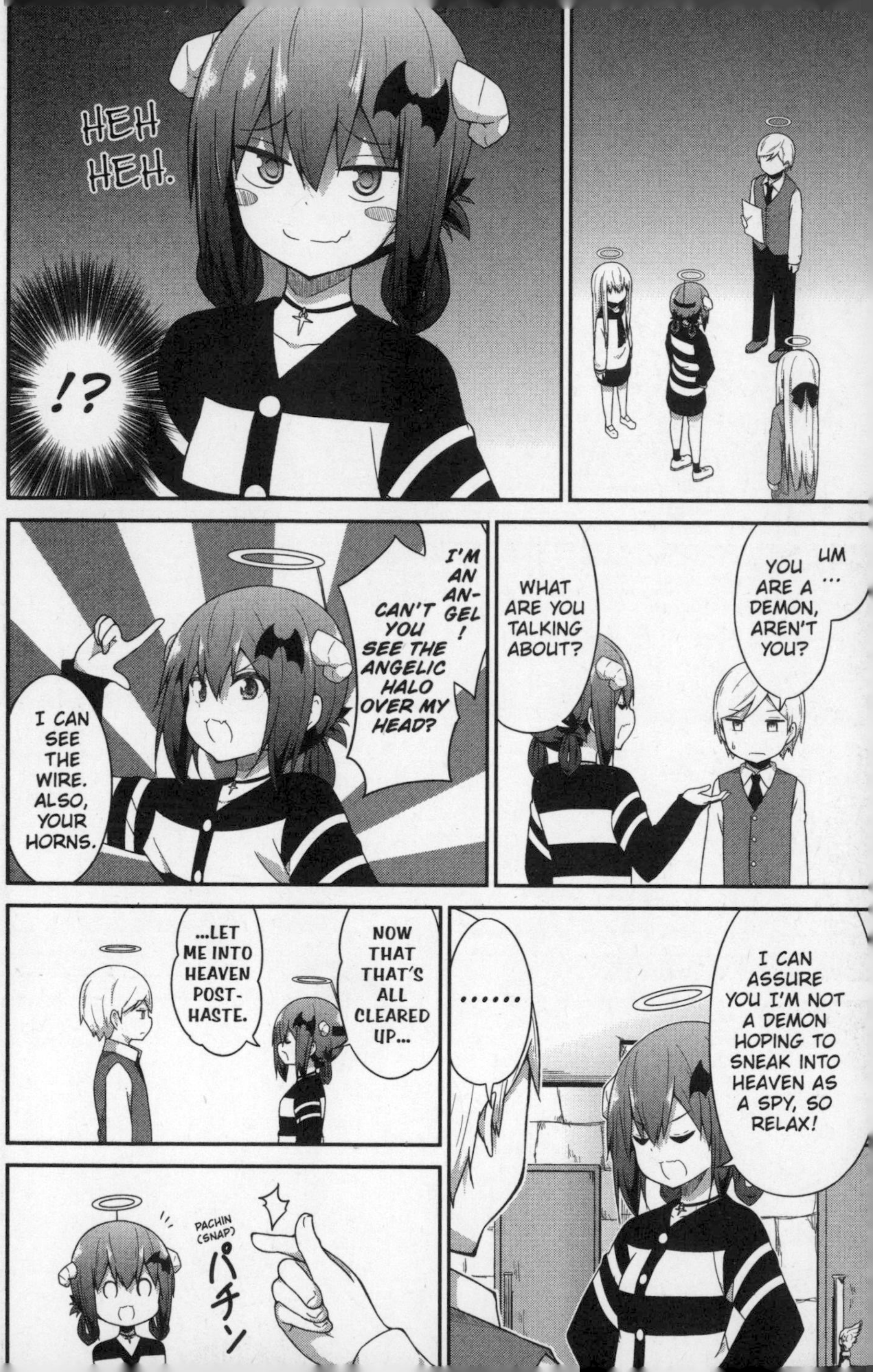
HEH HEH.
!?
UM... YOU ARE A DEMON, AREN'T YOU?
WHAT ARE YOU TALKING ABOUT?
I'M AN ANGEL! CAN'T YOU SEE THE ANGELIC HALO OVER MY HEAD?
I CAN SEE THE WIRE. ALSO, YOUR HORNS.
I CAN ASSURE YOU I'M NOT A DEMON HOPING TO SNEAK INTO HEAVEN AS A SPY, SO RELAX!
......
NOW THAT THAT'S ALL CLEARED UP...
...LET ME INTO HEAVEN POST-HASTE.
PACHIN (SNAP)
パチン

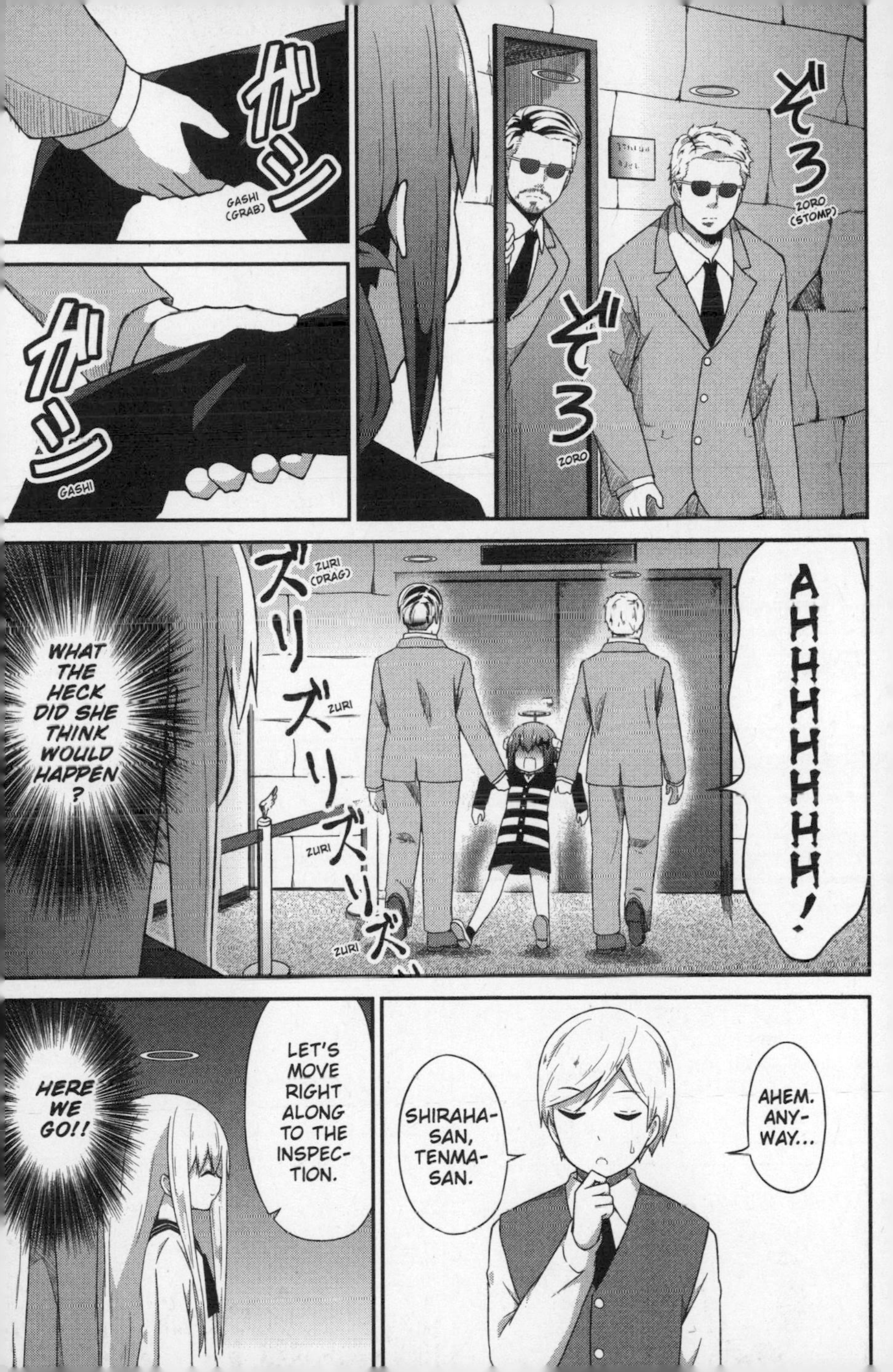
ぞろ
ZORO (STOMP)
ぞろ
ZORO
ガシッ
GASHI (GRAB)
ガシッ
GASHI
AHHHHHHHHH!
ズリ
ZURI (DRAG)
ズリ
ZURI
ズリ
ZURI
ズリ
ZURI
WHAT THE HECK DID SHE THINK WOULD HAPPEN?
AHEM. ANYWAY...
SHIRAHA-SAN, TENMA-SAN.
LET'S MOVE RIGHT ALONG TO THE INSPECTION.
HERE WE GO!!

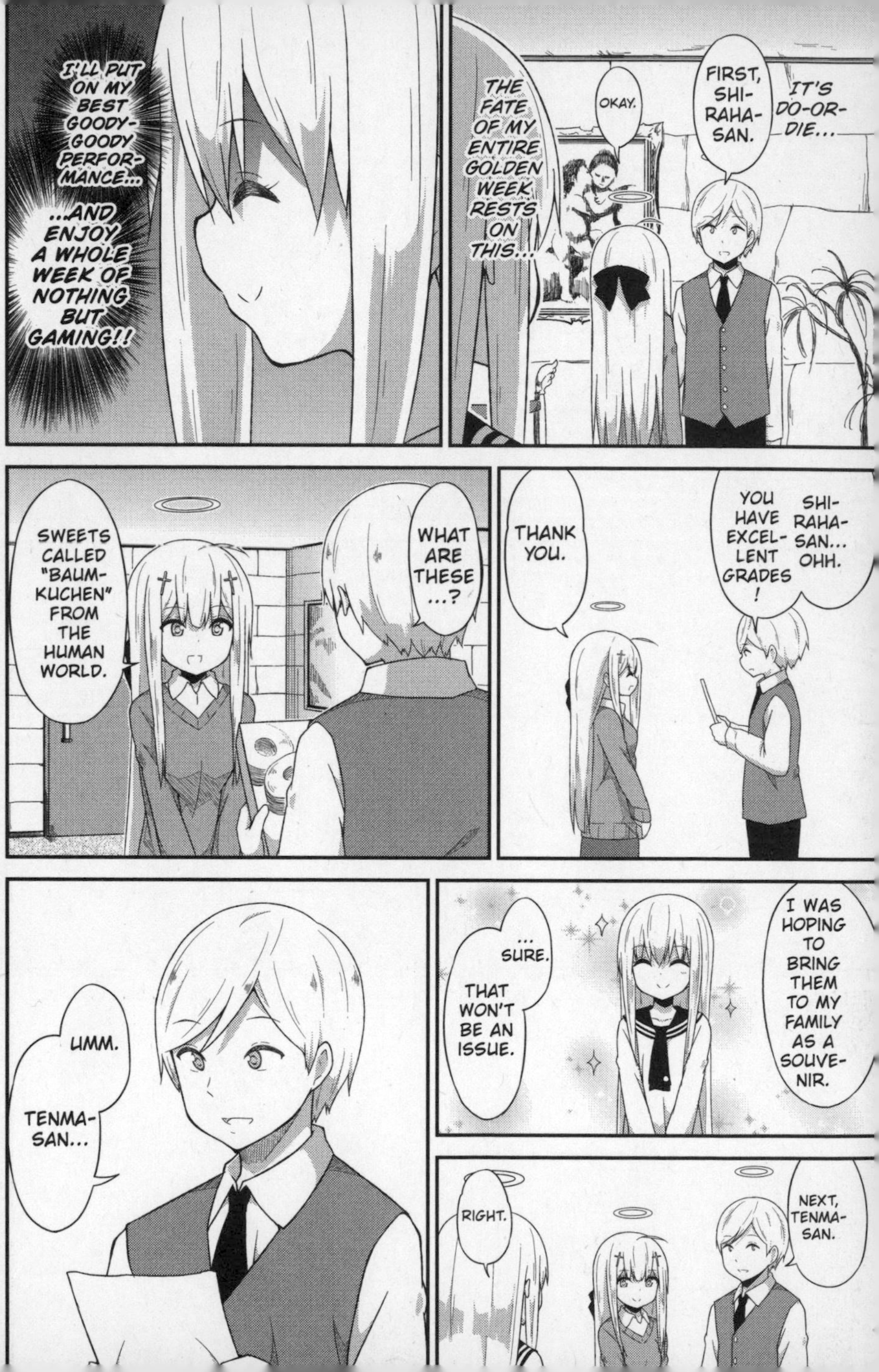
IT'S DO-OR-DIE...
FIRST, SHIRAHA-SAN.
OKAY.
THE FATE OF MY ENTIRE GOLDEN WEEK RESTS ON THIS...
I'LL PUT ON MY BEST GOODY-GOODY PERFORMANCE...
...AND ENJOY A WHOLE WEEK OF NOTHING BUT GAMING!!
SHIRAHA-SAN... OHH.
YOU HAVE EXCELLENT GRADES!
THANK YOU.
WHAT ARE THESE...?
SWEETS CALLED "BAUMKUCHEN" FROM THE HUMAN WORLD.
I WAS HOPING TO BRING THEM TO MY FAMILY AS A SOUVENIR.
...SURE.
THAT WON'T BE AN ISSUE.
NEXT, TENMA-SAN.
RIGHT.
UMM.
TENMA-SAN...

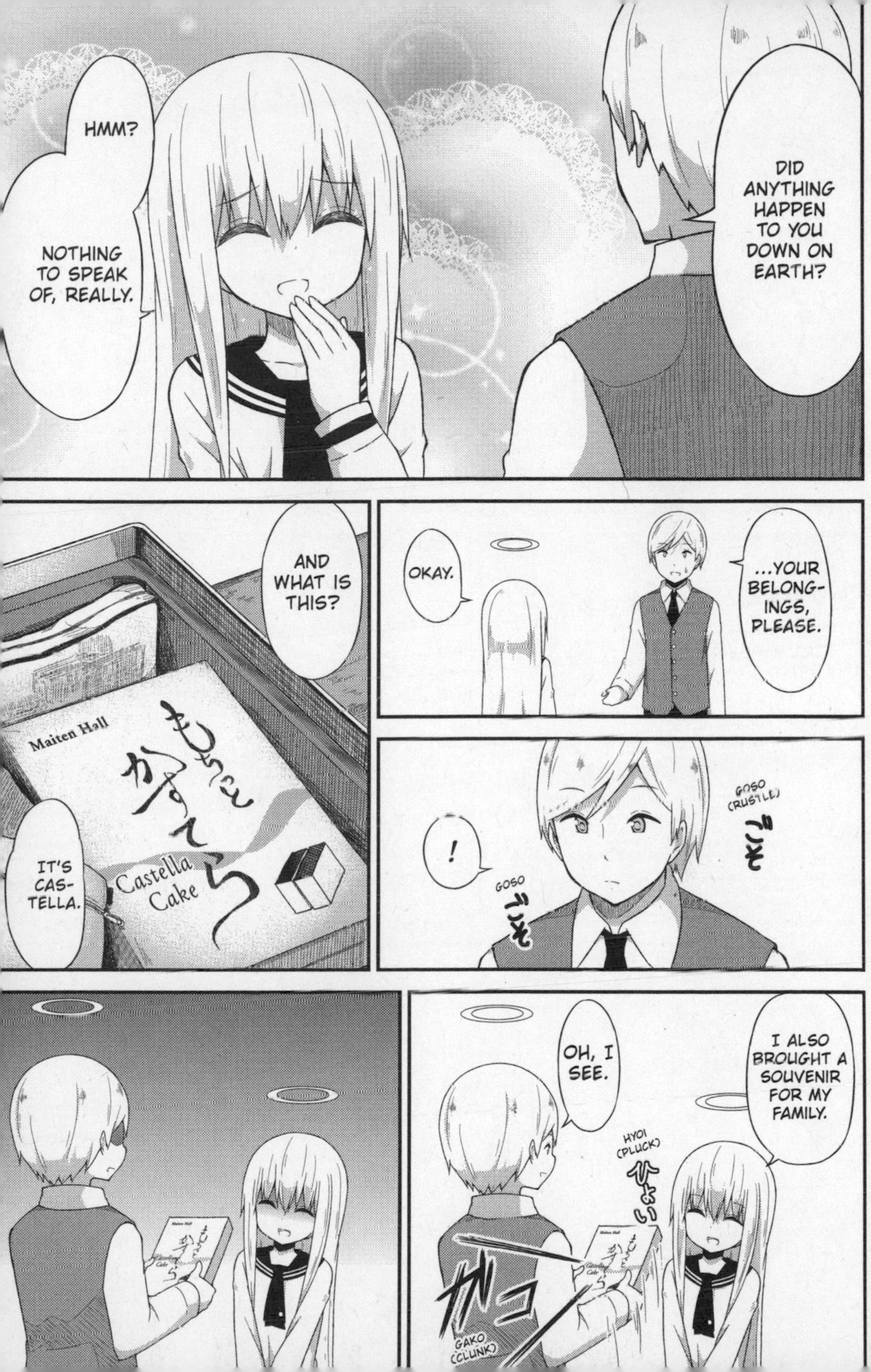
DID ANYTHING HAPPEN TO YOU DOWN ON EARTH?
HMM?
NOTHING TO SPEAK OF, REALLY.
...YOUR BELONGINGS, PLEASE.
OKAY.
GOSO (RUSTLE)
ごそ
!
GOSO
ごそ
AND WHAT IS THIS?
Maiten Hall
Castella Cake
IT'S CASTELLA.
I ALSO BROUGHT A SOUVENIR FOR MY FAMILY.
OH, I SEE.
HYOI (PLUCK)
ひょい
GAKO (CLUNK)

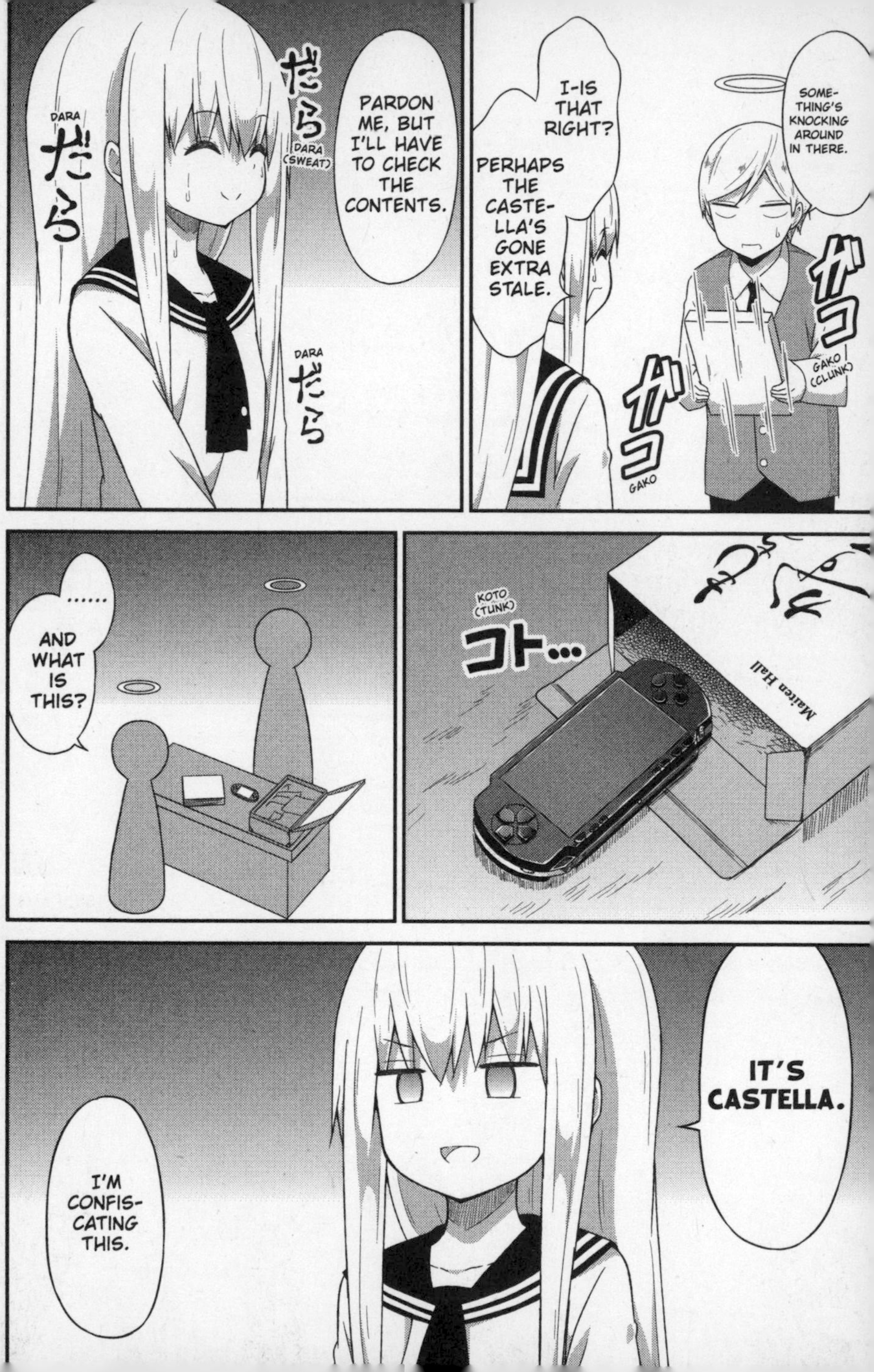
SOME-THING'S KNOCKING AROUND IN THERE.
がっ
GAKO (CLUNK)
がっ
GAKO
I-IS THAT RIGHT?
PERHAPS THE CASTE-LLA'S GONE EXTRA STALE.
PARDON ME, BUT I'LL HAVE TO CHECK THE CONTENTS.
だら
DARA (SWEAT)
だら
DARA
だら
DARA
KOTO (TUNK)
コト…
Maiten Hall
......
AND WHAT IS THIS?
IT'S CASTELLA.
I'M CONFIS-CATING THIS.

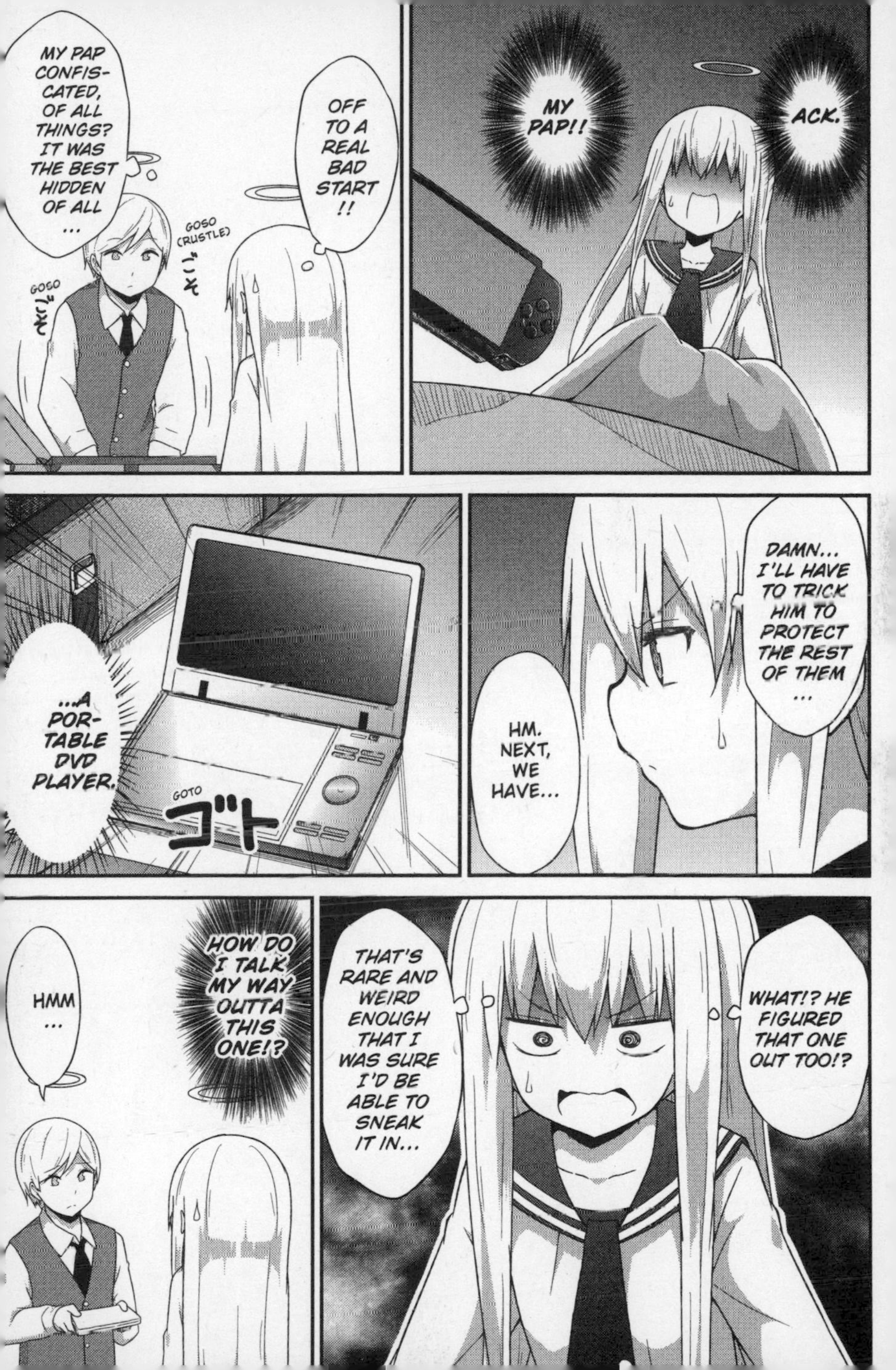
ACK.
MY PAP!!
OFF TO A REAL BAD START!!
GOSO (RUSTLE)
MY PAP CONFISCATED, OF ALL THINGS? IT WAS THE BEST HIDDEN OF ALL...
GOSO
DAMN... I'LL HAVE TO TRICK HIM TO PROTECT THE REST OF THEM...
HM. NEXT, WE HAVE...
...A PORTABLE DVD PLAYER.
GOTO
ゴト
WHAT!? HE FIGURED THAT ONE OUT TOO!?
THAT'S RARE AND WEIRD ENOUGH THAT I WAS SURE I'D BE ABLE TO SNEAK IT IN...
HOW DO I TALK MY WAY OUTTA THIS ONE!?
HMM...

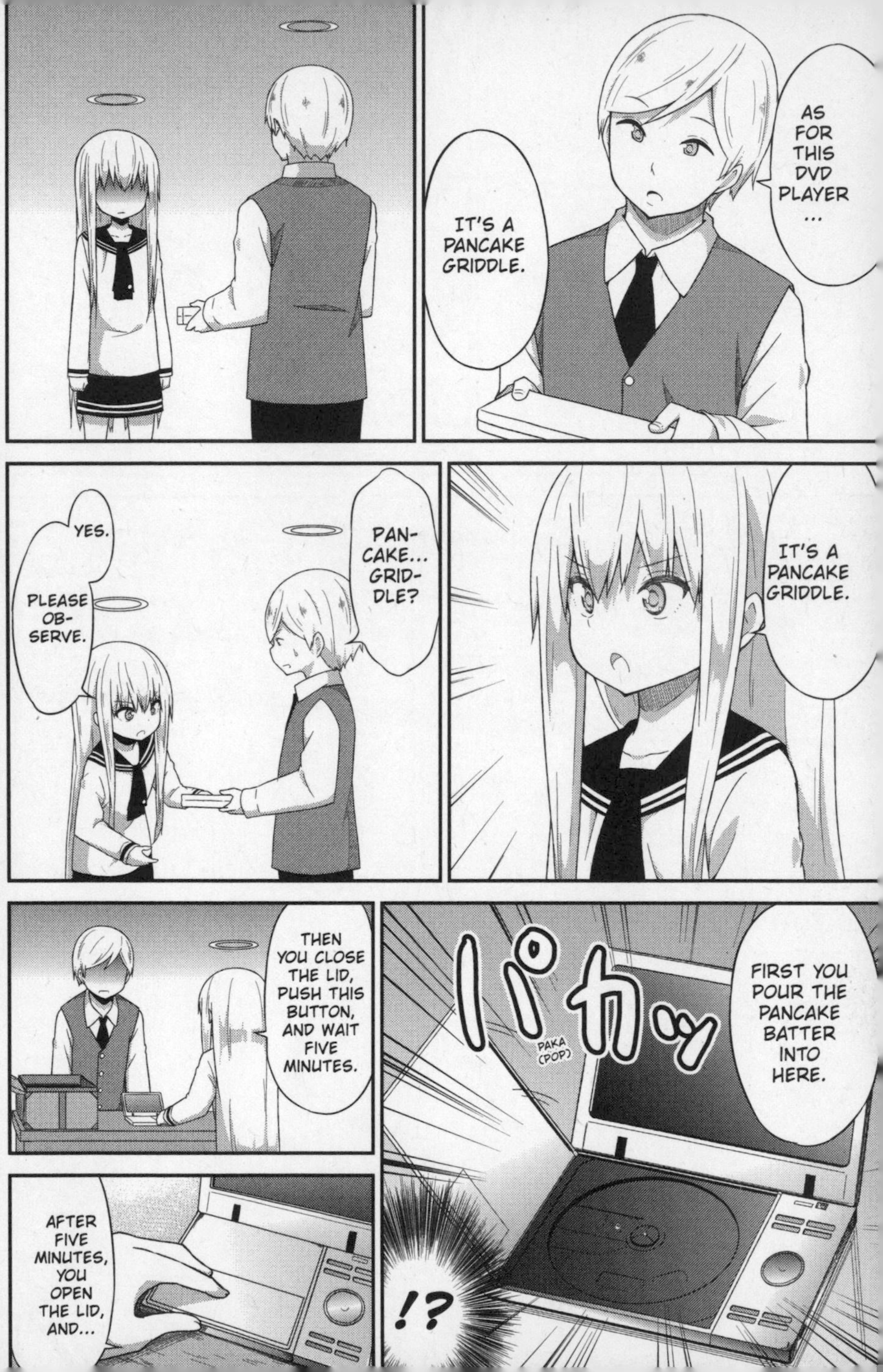
AS FOR THIS DVD PLAYER...
IT'S A PANCAKE GRIDDLE.
IT'S A PANCAKE GRIDDLE.
PAN-CAKE... GRID-DLE?
YES.
PLEASE OB-SERVE.
FIRST YOU POUR THE PANCAKE BATTER INTO HERE.
パカッ
PAKA (POP)
!?
THEN YOU CLOSE THE LID, PUSH THIS BUTTON, AND WAIT FIVE MINUTES.
AFTER FIVE MINUTES, YOU OPEN THE LID, AND...

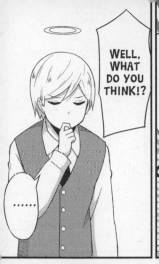

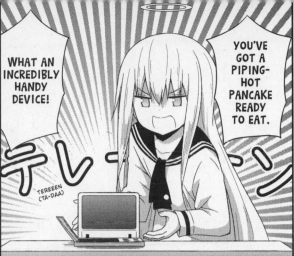

YOU'VE GOT A PIPING-HOT PANCAKE READY TO EAT.
WHAT AN INCREDIBLY HANDY DEVICE!
テレーーン
TEREEEN (TA-DAA)
WELL, WHAT DO YOU THINK!?
......
SORRY, I'M CONFISCATING THIS TOO.
SAW THAT COMING!!
PANCAKES? REALLY? I'M AN IDIOT!!
I'LL LOSE EVERYTHING AT THIS RATE!!
ゴソ
GOSO (RUSTLE)
ゴソ
GOSO
CRAP. MY GOLDEN WEEK VACATION IS DOOMED...
WHAT... WHAT CAN I DO...?
FINALLY, WE HAVE THIS...
MY LAPTOP!!

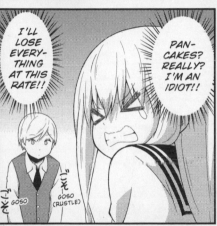

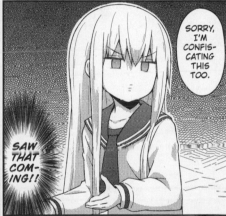

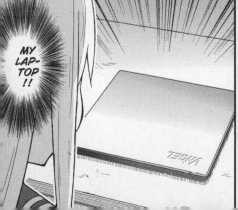

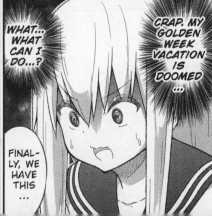

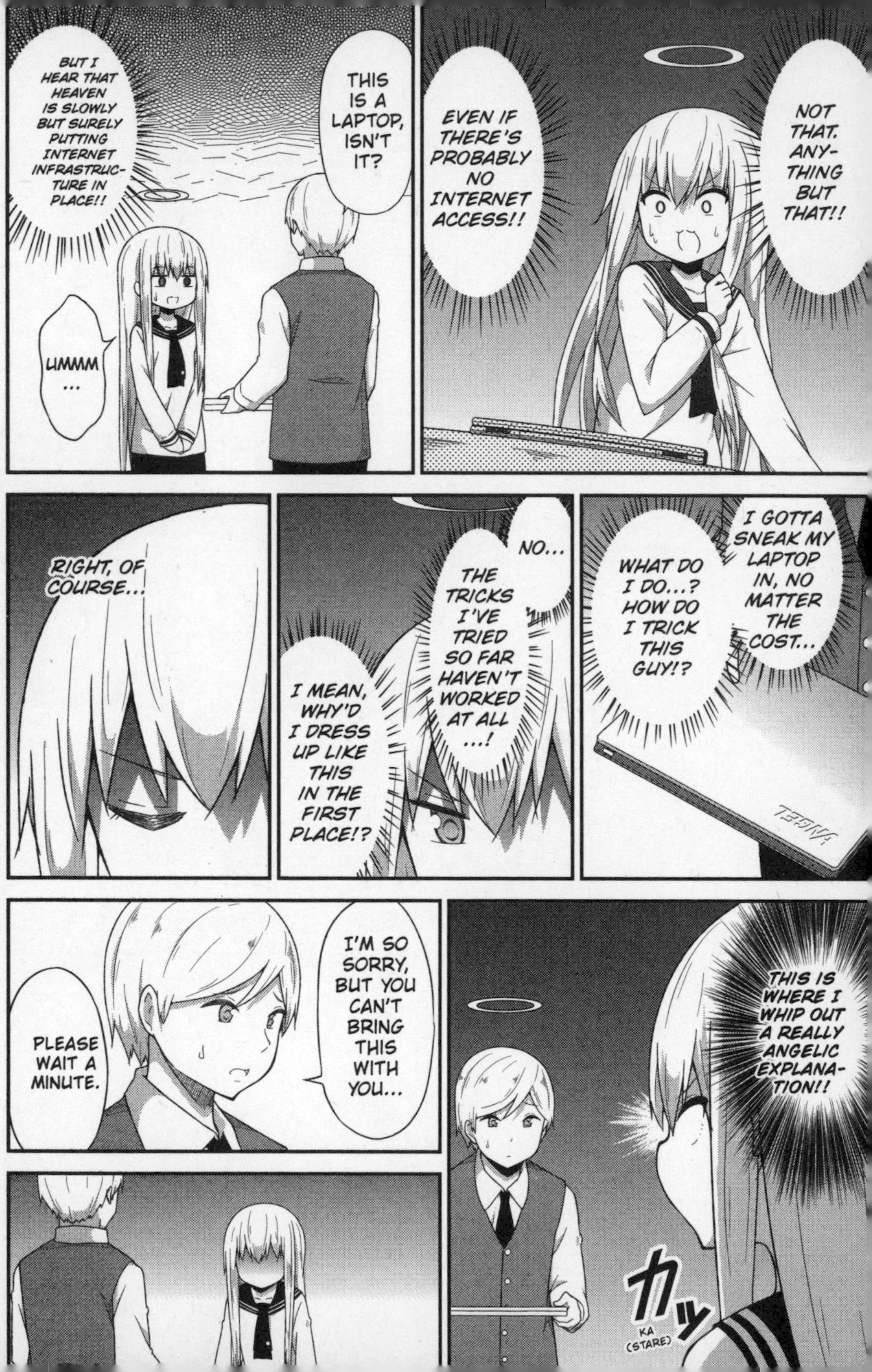
NOT THAT. ANY-THING BUT THAT!!
EVEN IF THERE'S PROBABLY NO INTERNET ACCESS!!
THIS IS A LAPTOP, ISN'T IT?
BUT I HEAR THAT HEAVEN IS SLOWLY BUT SURELY PUTTING INTERNET INFRASTRUC-TURE IN PLACE!!
UMMM ...
I GOTTA SNEAK MY LAPTOP IN, NO MATTER THE COST...
WHAT DO I DO...? HOW DO I TRICK THIS GUY!?
NO...
THE TRICKS I'VE TRIED SO FAR HAVEN'T WORKED AT ALL ...!
I MEAN, WHY'D I DRESS UP LIKE THIS IN THE FIRST PLACE!?
RIGHT, OF COURSE...
THIS IS WHERE I WHIP OUT A REALLY ANGELIC EXPLANA-TION!!
カッ
KA (STARE)
I'M SO SORRY, BUT YOU CAN'T BRING THIS WITH YOU...
PLEASE WAIT A MINUTE.

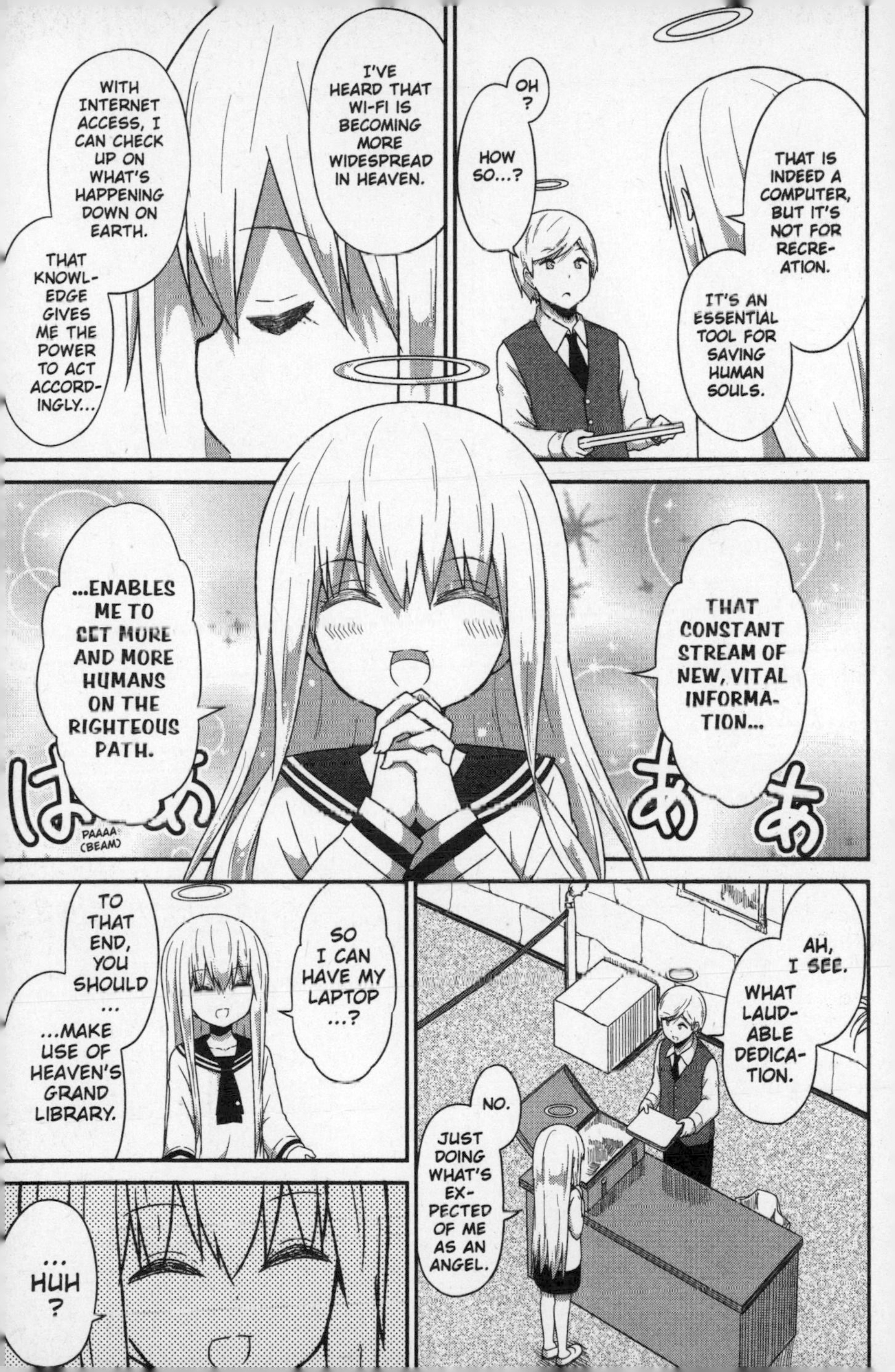
THAT IS INDEED A COMPUTER, BUT IT'S NOT FOR RECRE-ATION.
IT'S AN ESSENTIAL TOOL FOR SAVING HUMAN SOULS.
OH?
HOW SO...?
I'VE HEARD THAT WI-FI IS BECOMING MORE WIDESPREAD IN HEAVEN.
WITH INTERNET ACCESS, I CAN CHECK UP ON WHAT'S HAPPENING DOWN ON EARTH.
THAT KNOWL-EDGE GIVES ME THE POWER TO ACT ACCORD-INGLY...
THAT CONSTANT STREAM OF NEW, VITAL INFORMA-TION...
...ENABLES ME TO GET MORE AND MORE HUMANS ON THE RIGHTEOUS PATH.
PAAAA (BEAM)
AH, I SEE.
WHAT LAUD-ABLE DEDICA-TION.
NO.
JUST DOING WHAT'S EX-PECTED OF ME AS AN ANGEL.
SO I CAN HAVE MY LAPTOP ...?
TO THAT END, YOU SHOULD ...
...MAKE USE OF HEAVEN'S GRAND LIBRARY.
... HUH ?

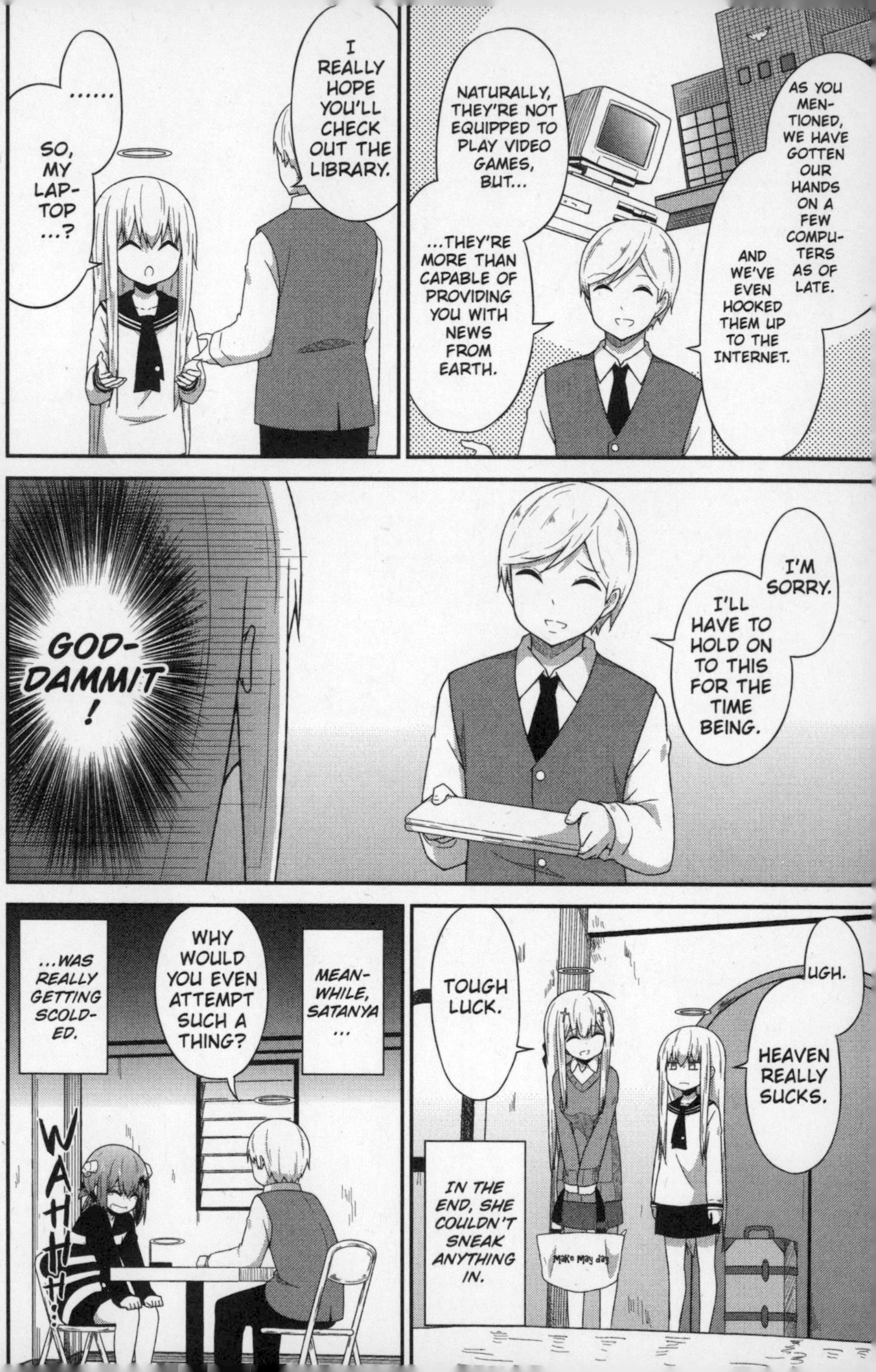
AS YOU MENTIONED, WE HAVE GOTTEN OUR HANDS ON A FEW COMPUTERS AS OF LATE.
AND WE'VE EVEN HOOKED THEM UP TO THE INTERNET.
NATURALLY, THEY'RE NOT EQUIPPED TO PLAY VIDEO GAMES, BUT...
...THEY'RE MORE THAN CAPABLE OF PROVIDING YOU WITH NEWS FROM EARTH.
I REALLY HOPE YOU'LL CHECK OUT THE LIBRARY.
......
SO, MY LAPTOP...?
I'M SORRY.
I'LL HAVE TO HOLD ON TO THIS FOR THE TIME BEING.
GOD-DAMMIT!
UGH.
HEAVEN REALLY SUCKS.
TOUGH LUCK.
IN THE END, SHE COULDN'T SNEAK ANYTHING IN.
Make May day
MEAN-WHILE, SATANYA...
WHY WOULD YOU EVEN ATTEMPT SUCH A THING?
...WAS REALLY GETTING SCOLD-ED.
WAHHH...

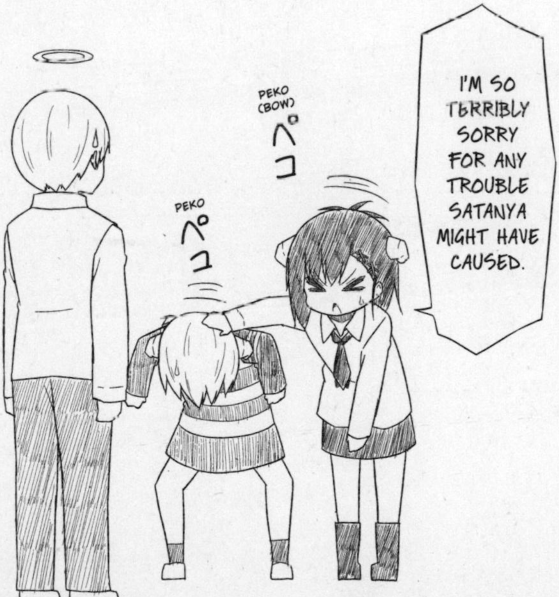
I'M SO TERRIBLY SORRY FOR ANY TROUBLE SATANYA MIGHT HAVE CAUSED.
PEKO (BOW)
ペコ
PEKO
ペコ

Gabriel Dropout

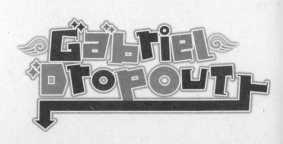

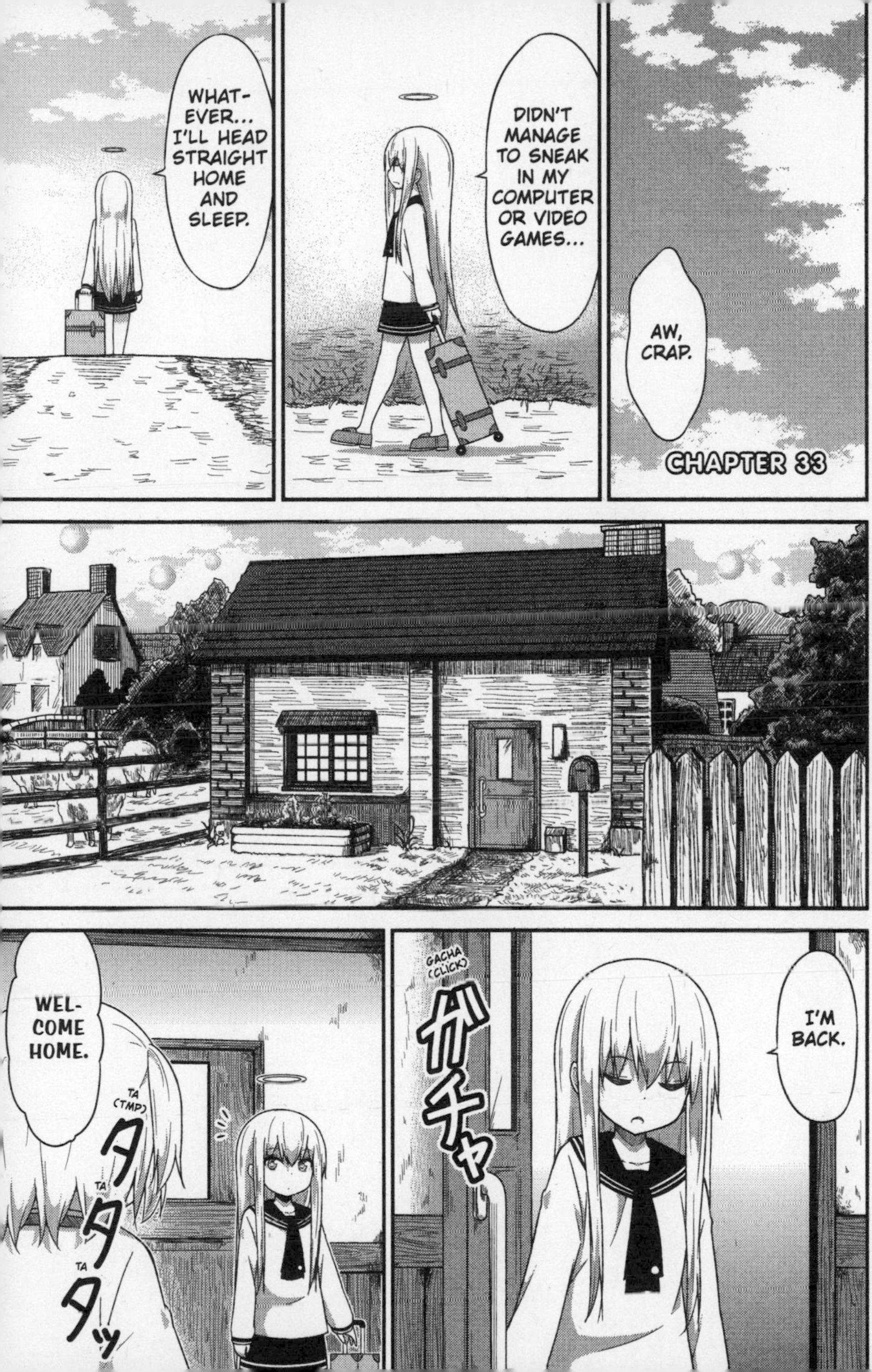
AW, CRAP.
CHAPTER 33
DIDN'T MANAGE TO SNEAK IN MY COMPUTER OR VIDEO GAMES...
WHAT-EVER... I'LL HEAD STRAIGHT HOME AND SLEEP.
I'M BACK.
GACHA (CLICK)
ガチャ
WEL-COME HOME.
TA (TMP)
タ
TA
タ
TA
タッ

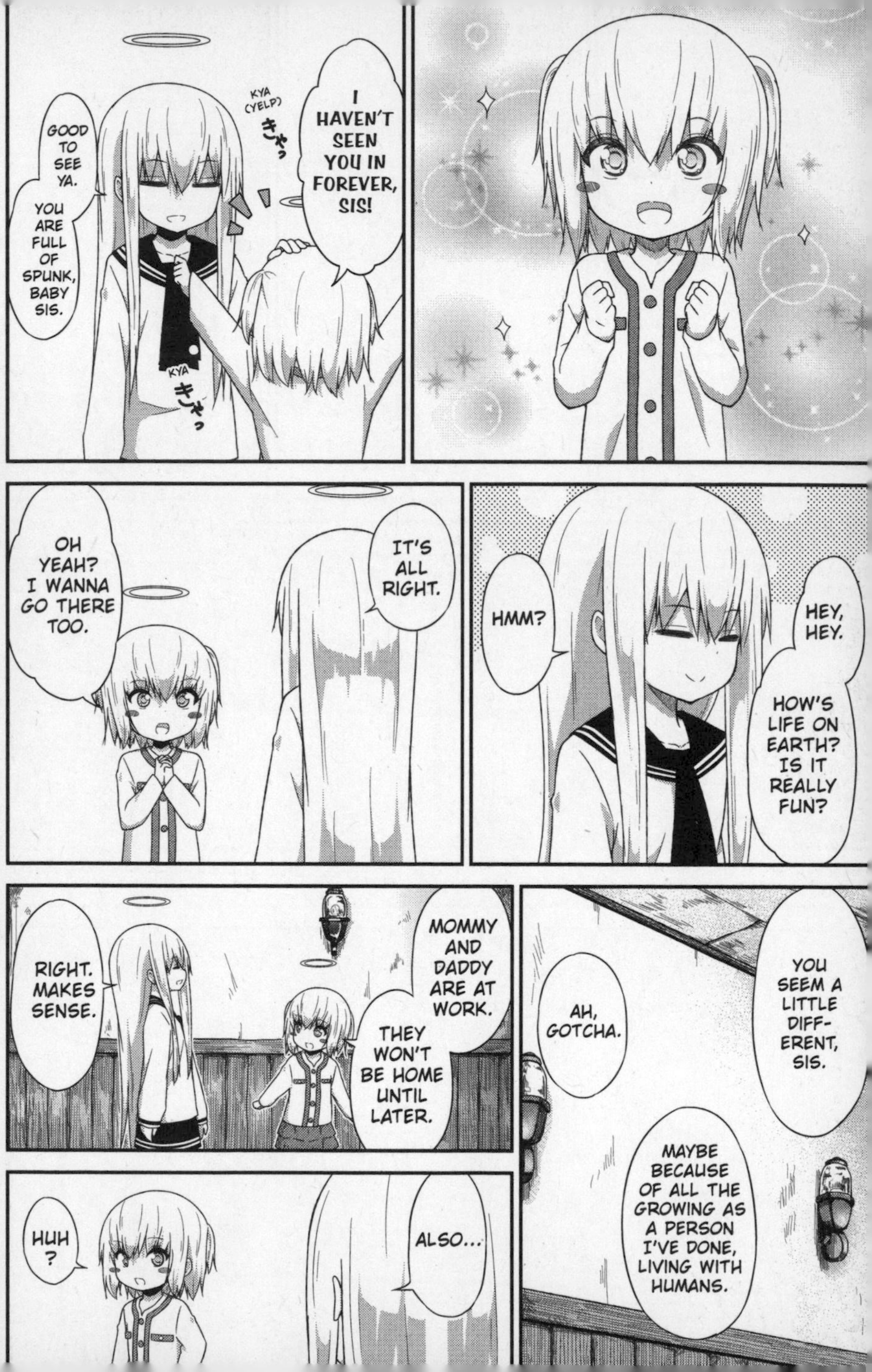
I HAVEN'T SEEN YOU IN FOREVER, SIS!
KYA (YELP) きゃっ
GOOD TO SEE YA.
YOU ARE FULL OF SPUNK, BABY SIS.
KYA きゃっ
HEY, HEY.
HOW'S LIFE ON EARTH? IS IT REALLY FUN?
HMM?
IT'S ALL RIGHT.
OH YEAH? I WANNA GO THERE TOO.
YOU SEEM A LITTLE DIFF-ERENT, SIS.
AH, GOTCHA.
MAYBE BECAUSE OF ALL THE GROWING AS A PERSON I'VE DONE, LIVING WITH HUMANS.
MOMMY AND DADDY ARE AT WORK.
THEY WON'T BE HOME UNTIL LATER.
RIGHT. MAKES SENSE.
ALSO...
HUH?

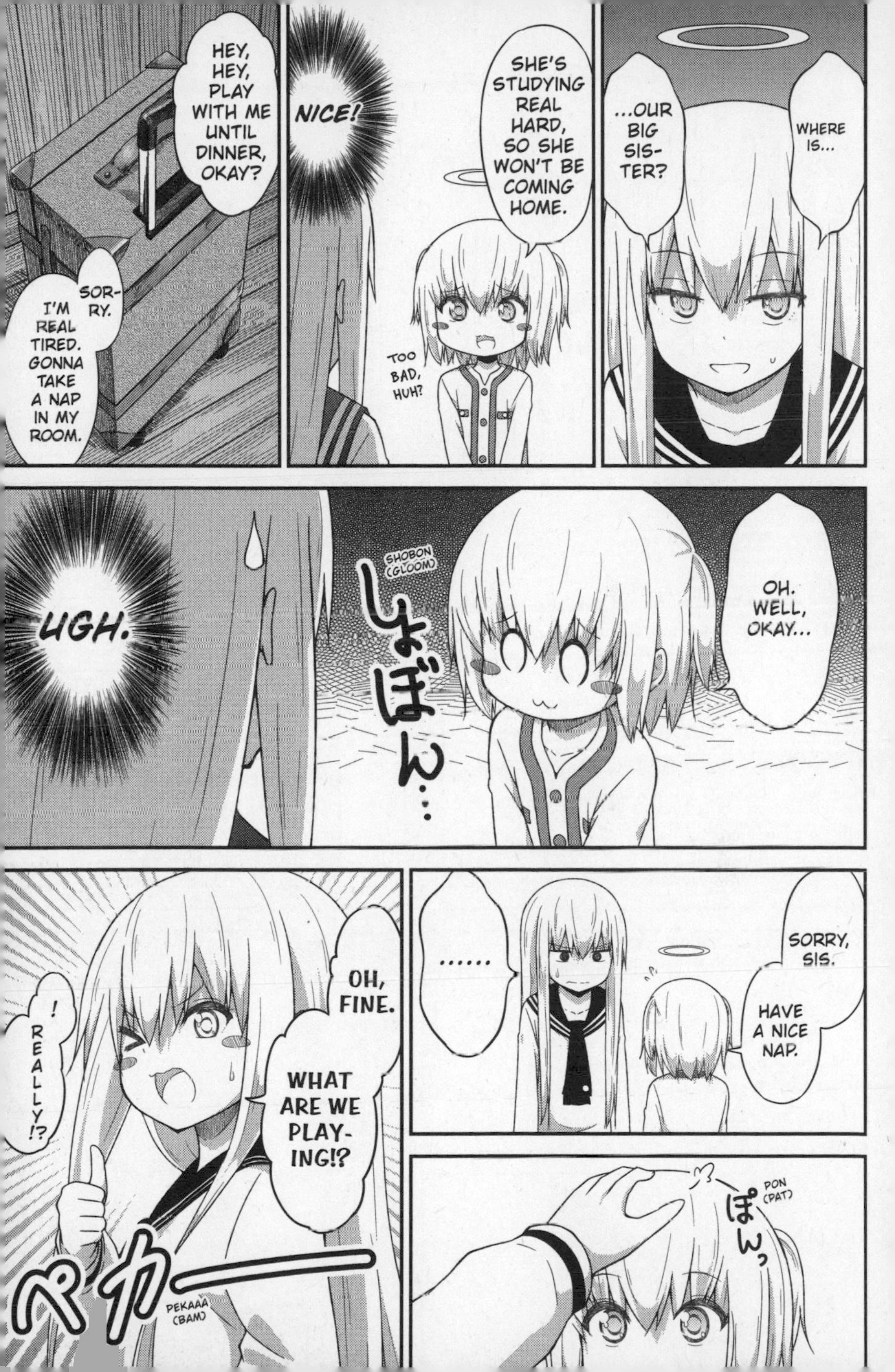
WHERE IS...
...OUR BIG SIS-TER?
SHE'S STUDYING REAL HARD, SO SHE WON'T BE COMING HOME.
TOO BAD, HUH?
NICE!
HEY, HEY, PLAY WITH ME UNTIL DINNER, OKAY?
SORRY. I'M REAL TIRED. GONNA TAKE A NAP IN MY ROOM.
OH. WELL, OKAY...
しょぼん…
SHOBON (GLOOM)
UGH.
SORRY, SIS. HAVE A NICE NAP.
......
ぽんっ
PON (PAT)
OH, FINE.
WHAT ARE WE PLAYING!?
! REALLY!?
ペカー
PEKAAA (BAM)

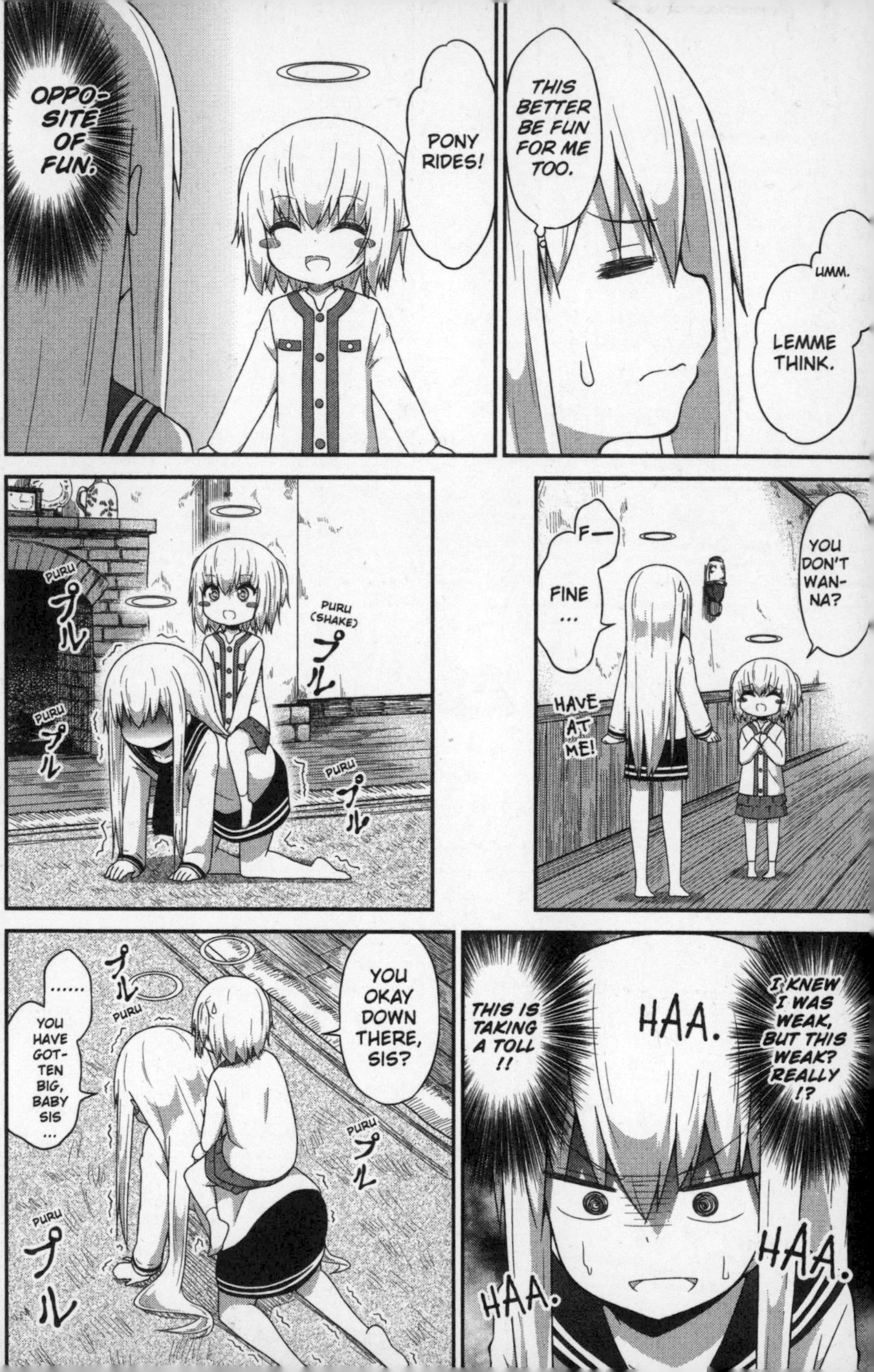
THIS BETTER BE FUN FOR ME TOO.
UMM.
LEMME THINK.
PONY RIDES!
OPPO-SITE OF FUN.
YOU DON'T WAN-NA?
F—
FINE ...
HAVE AT ME!
PURU (SHAKE) プル
PURU プル
PURU プル
PURU プル
I KNEW I WAS WEAK, BUT THIS WEAK? REALLY !?
HAA.
THIS IS TAKING A TOLL !!
HAA.
HAA.
YOU OKAY DOWN THERE, SIS?
.... YOU HAVE GOT-TEN BIG, BABY SIS ...
プル PURU
PURU プル
PURU プル

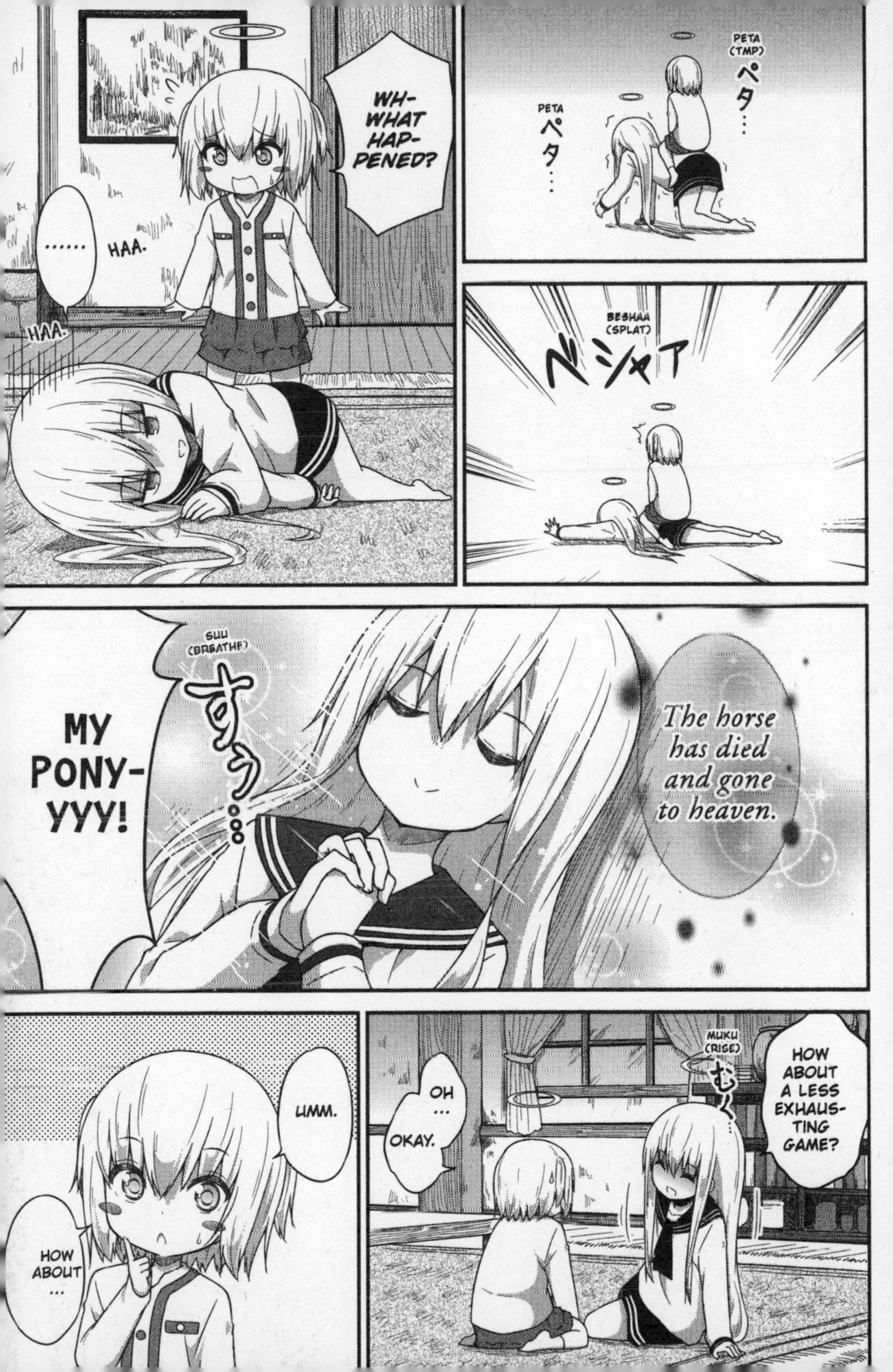
PETA (TMP)
ペタ…
PETA
ペタ…
BESHAA (SPLAT)
ベシャア
WH-WHAT HAP-PENED?
…… HAA.
HAA.
The horse has died and gone to heaven.
SUU (BREATHE)
すぅ…
MY PONY-YYY!
HOW ABOUT A LESS EXHAUS-TING GAME?
MUKU (RISE)
むく…
OH … OKAY.
UMM.
HOW ABOUT …

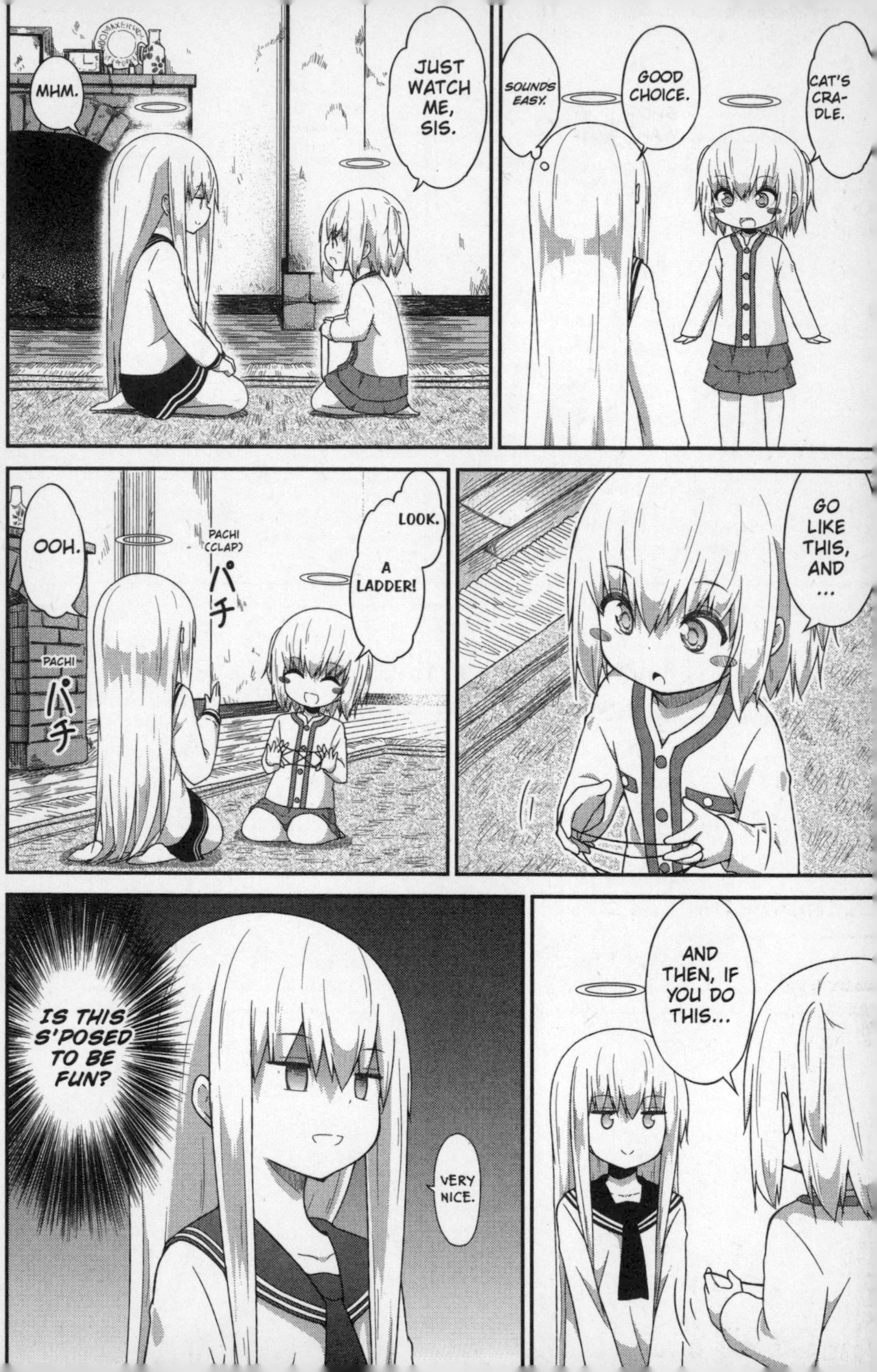
CAT'S CRA-DLE.
GOOD CHOICE.
SOUNDS EASY.
JUST WATCH ME, SIS.
MHM.
GO LIKE THIS, AND ...
LOOK.
A LADDER!
PACHI (CLAP)
パチ
PACHI
パチ
OOH.
AND THEN, IF YOU DO THIS...
VERY NICE.
IS THIS S'POSED TO BE FUN?

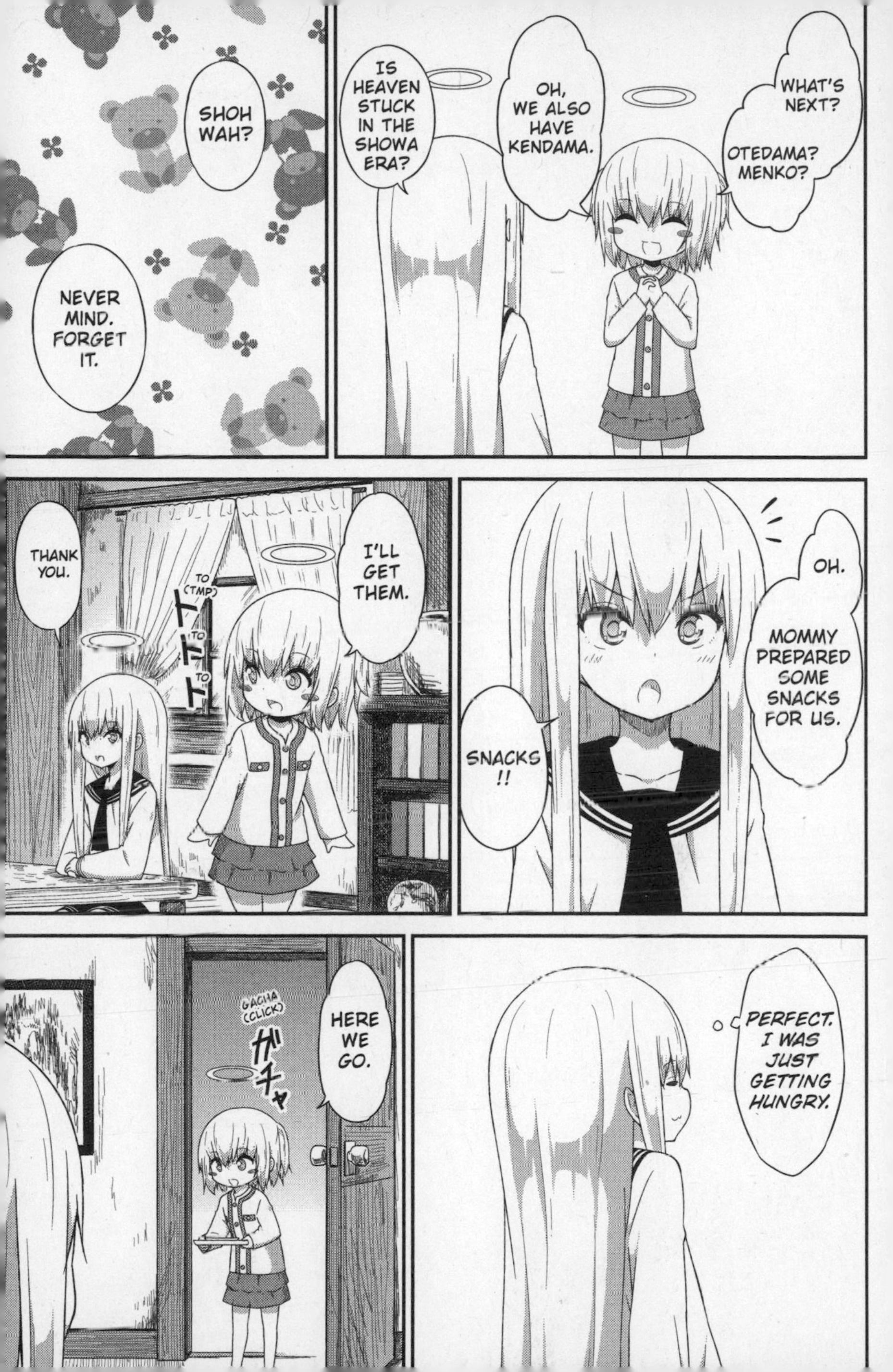
WHAT'S NEXT?
OTEDAMA? MENKO?
OH, WE ALSO HAVE KENDAMA.
IS HEAVEN STUCK IN THE SHOWA ERA?
SHOH WAH?
NEVER MIND. FORGET IT.
OH.
MOMMY PREPARED SOME SNACKS FOR US.
SNACKS!!
I'LL GET THEM.
TO (TMP) TO TO TO
トトトト
THANK YOU.
PERFECT. I WAS JUST GETTING HUNGRY.
HERE WE GO.
GACHA (CLICK)
ガチャ

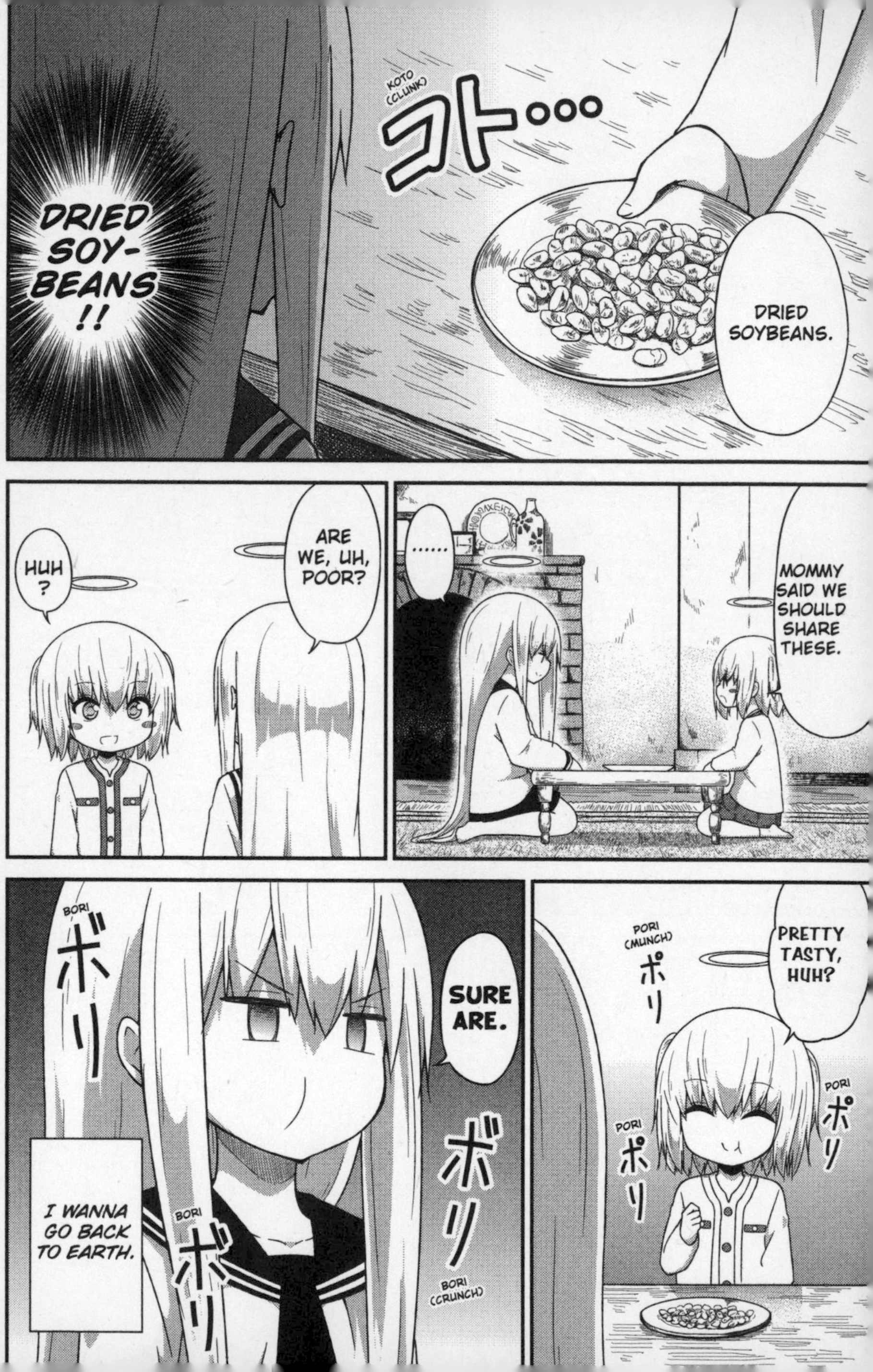
KOTO (CLUNK)
コト…
DRIED SOYBEANS.
DRIED SOY-BEANS!!
MOMMY SAID WE SHOULD SHARE THESE.
……
ARE WE, UH, POOR?
HUH?
PRETTY TASTY, HUH?
PORI (MUNCH)
ポリ
PORI
ポリ
PORI
ポリ
SURE ARE.
BORI
ボリ
BORI (CRUNCH)
ボリ
BORI
ボリ
I WANNA GO BACK TO EARTH.

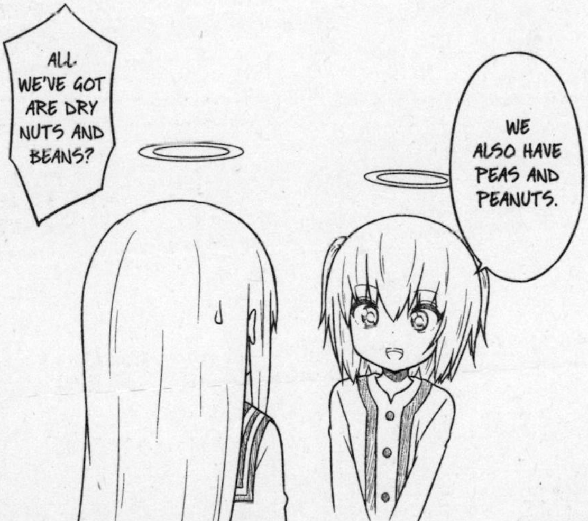
ALL. WE'VE GOT ARE DRY NUTS AND BEANS?
WE ALSO HAVE PEAS AND PEANUTS.

Gabriel Dropout

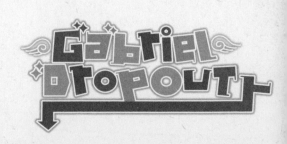

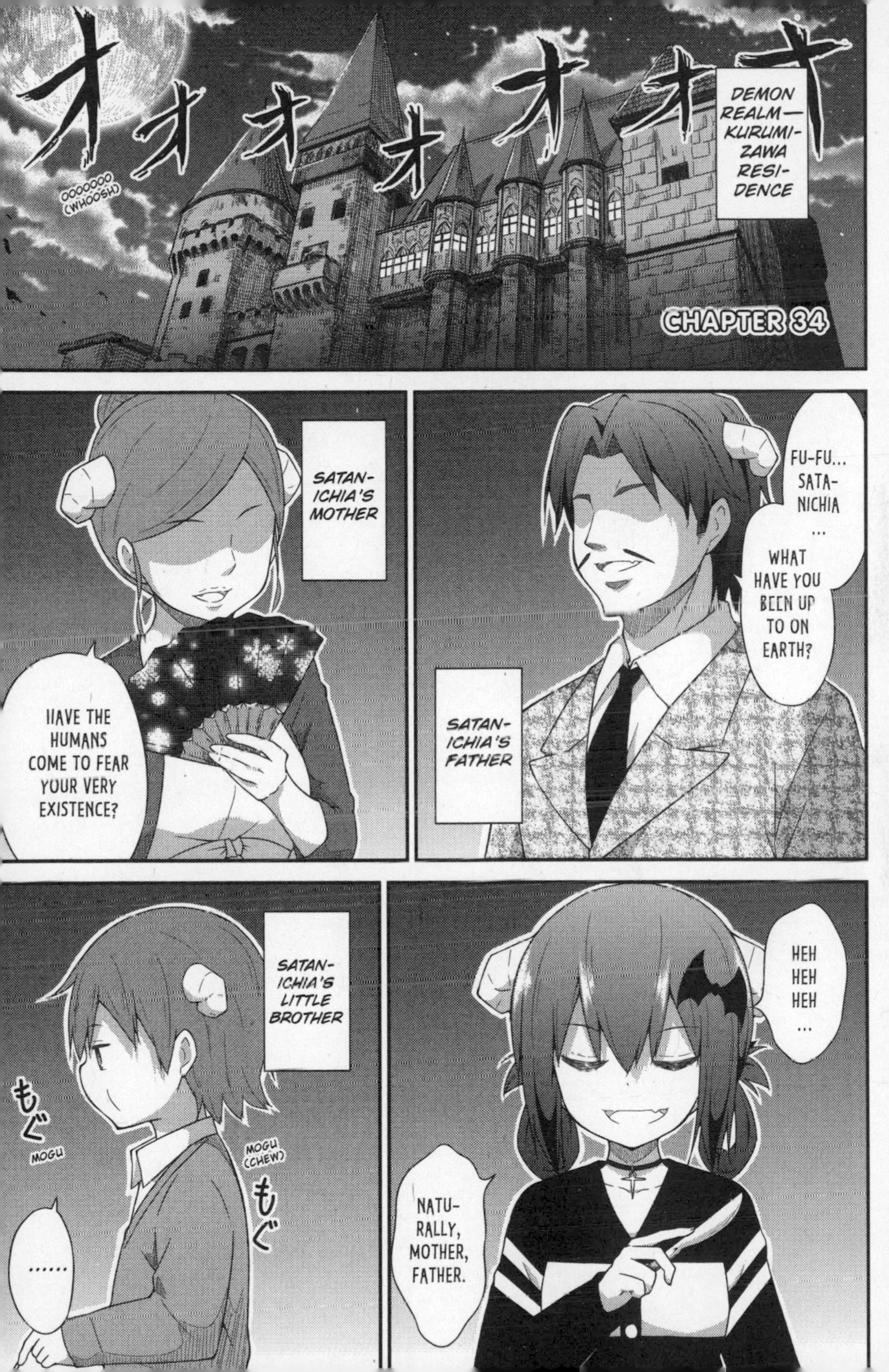
DEMON REALM—KURUMIZAWA RESIDENCE
オオオオオオ
OOOOOOO (WHOOSH)
CHAPTER 34
FU-FU... SATANICHIA... WHAT HAVE YOU BEEN UP TO ON EARTH?
SATANICHIA'S FATHER
SATANICHIA'S MOTHER
HAVE THE HUMANS COME TO FEAR YOUR VERY EXISTENCE?
HEH HEH HEH...
NATURALLY, MOTHER, FATHER.
SATANICHIA'S LITTLE BROTHER
もぐ
MOGU (CHEW)
もぐ
MOGU
......

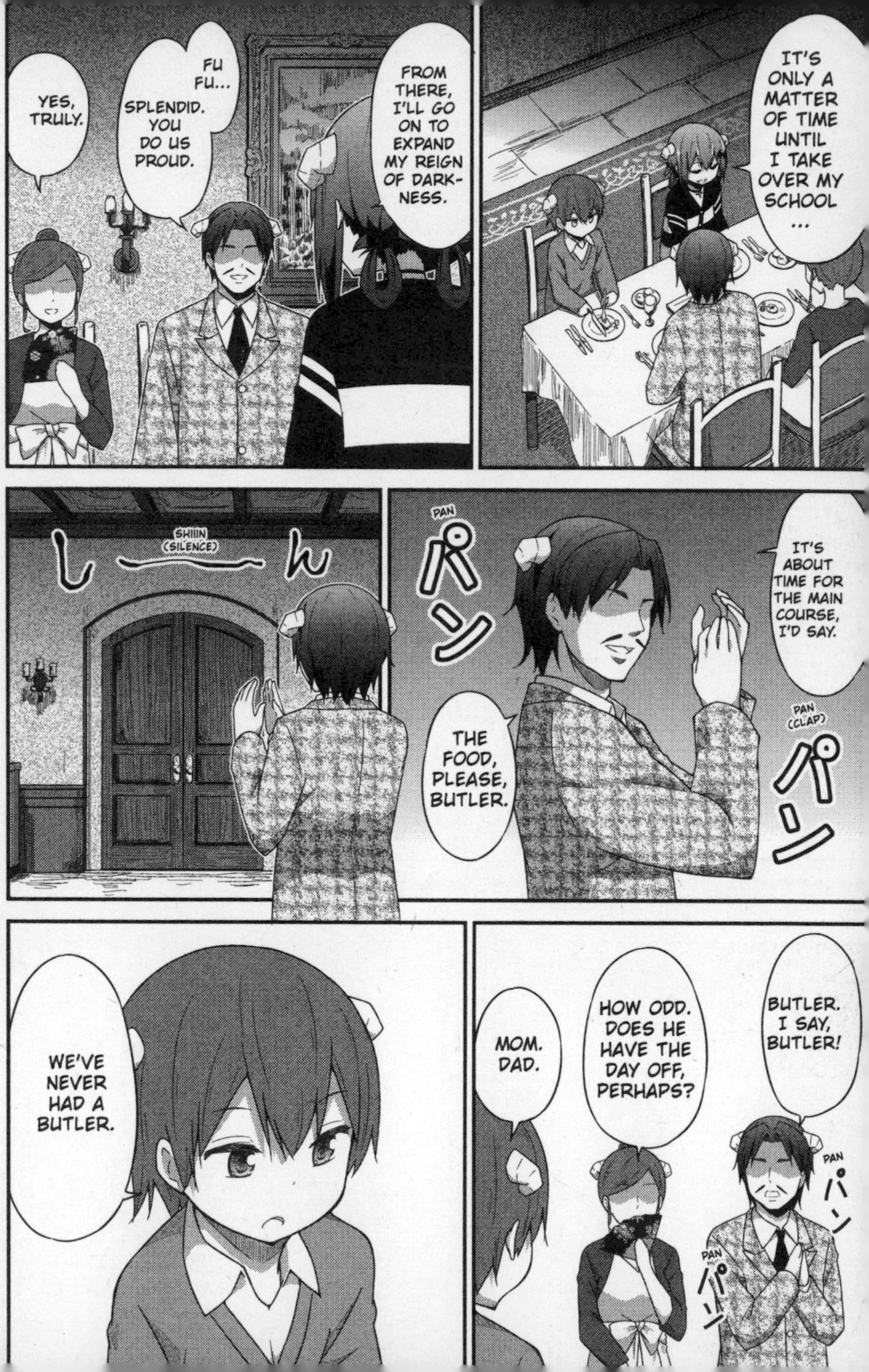
IT'S ONLY A MATTER OF TIME UNTIL I TAKE OVER MY SCHOOL ...
FROM THERE, I'LL GO ON TO EXPAND MY REIGN OF DARK-NESS.
FU FU... SPLENDID. YOU DO US PROUD.
YES, TRULY.
IT'S ABOUT TIME FOR THE MAIN COURSE, I'D SAY.
PAN (CLAP)
パン
PAN
パン
THE FOOD, PLEASE, BUTLER.
SHIIIN (SILENCE)
しーーん
BUTLER. I SAY, BUTLER!
PAN
パン
PAN
パン
HOW ODD. DOES HE HAVE THE DAY OFF, PERHAPS?
MOM. DAD.
WE'VE NEVER HAD A BUTLER.

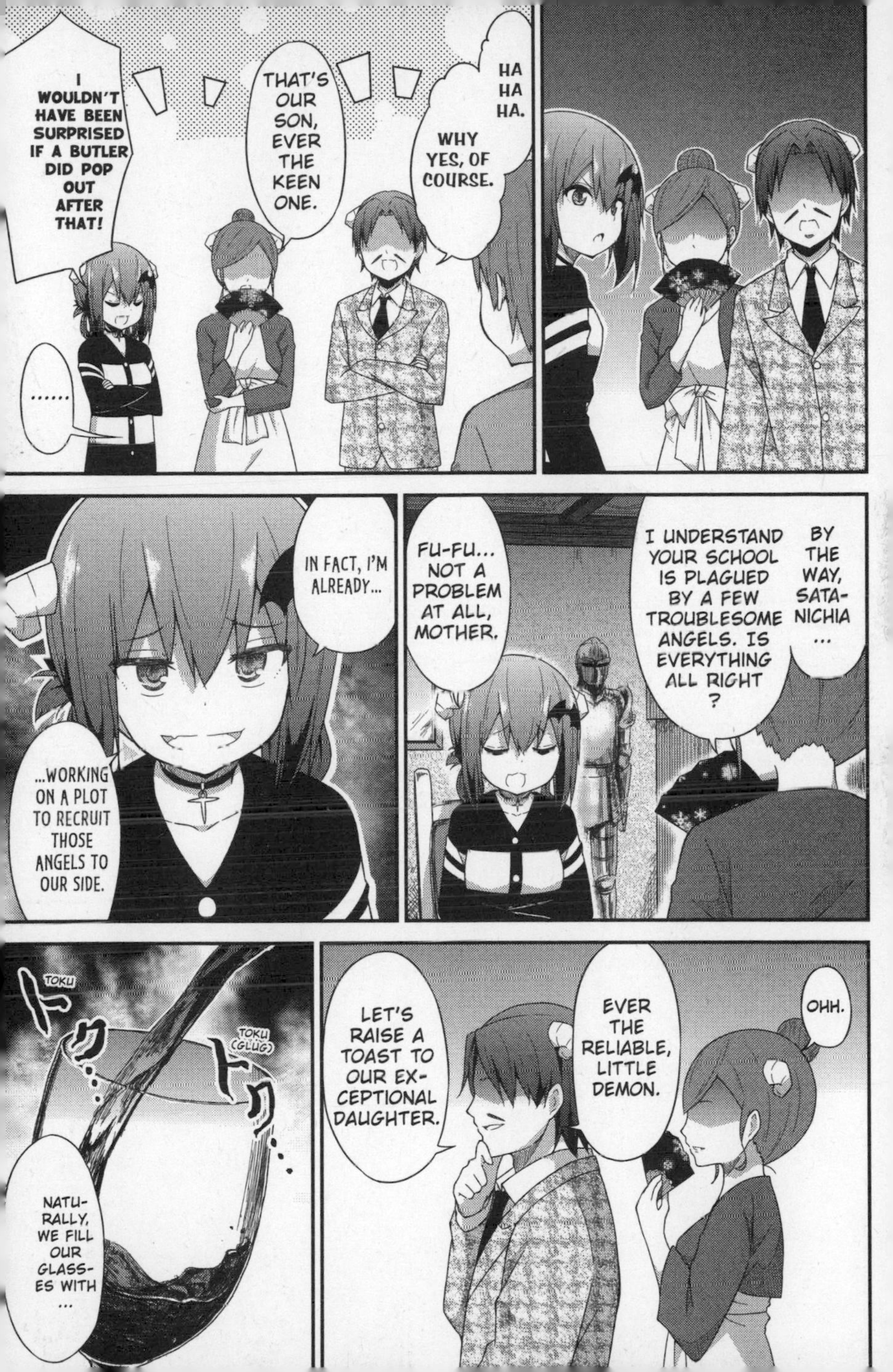
HA HA HA.
WHY YES, OF COURSE.
THAT'S OUR SON, EVER THE KEEN ONE.
I WOULDN'T HAVE BEEN SURPRISED IF A BUTLER DID POP OUT AFTER THAT!
......
BY THE WAY, SATANICHIA...
I UNDERSTAND YOUR SCHOOL IS PLAGUED BY A FEW TROUBLESOME ANGELS. IS EVERYTHING ALL RIGHT?
FU-FU... NOT A PROBLEM AT ALL, MOTHER.
IN FACT, I'M ALREADY...
...WORKING ON A PLOT TO RECRUIT THOSE ANGELS TO OUR SIDE.
OHH.
EVER THE RELIABLE, LITTLE DEMON.
LET'S RAISE A TOAST TO OUR EXCEPTIONAL DAUGHTER.
TOKU
TOKU (GLUG)
NATURALLY, WE FILL OUR GLASSES WITH ...

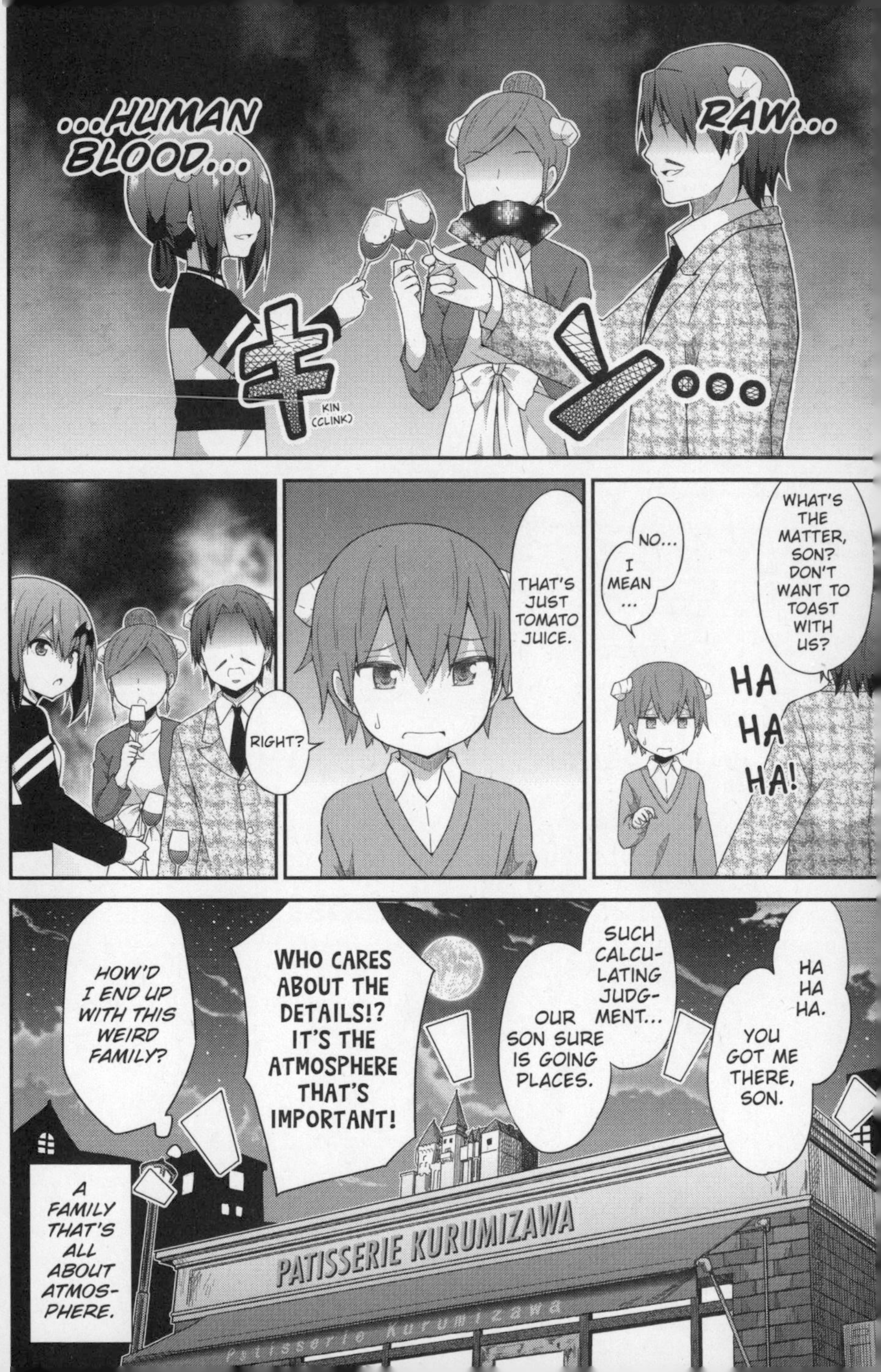
RAW...
...HUMAN BLOOD...
KIN (CLINK)
WHAT'S THE MATTER, SON? DON'T WANT TO TOAST WITH US?
HA HA HA!
NO... I MEAN ...
THAT'S JUST TOMATO JUICE.
RIGHT?
HA HA HA.
YOU GOT ME THERE, SON.
SUCH CALCULATING JUDGMENT...
OUR SON SURE IS GOING PLACES.
WHO CARES ABOUT THE DETAILS!? IT'S THE ATMOSPHERE THAT'S IMPORTANT!
HOW'D I END UP WITH THIS WEIRD FAMILY?
PATISSERIE KURUMIZAWA
A FAMILY THAT'S ALL ABOUT ATMOSPHERE.

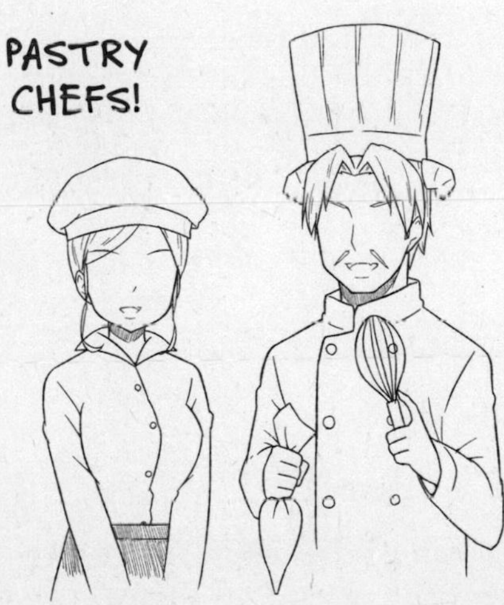
PASTRY
CHEFS!

Gabriel Dropout

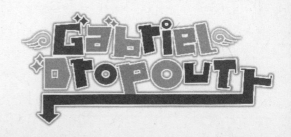

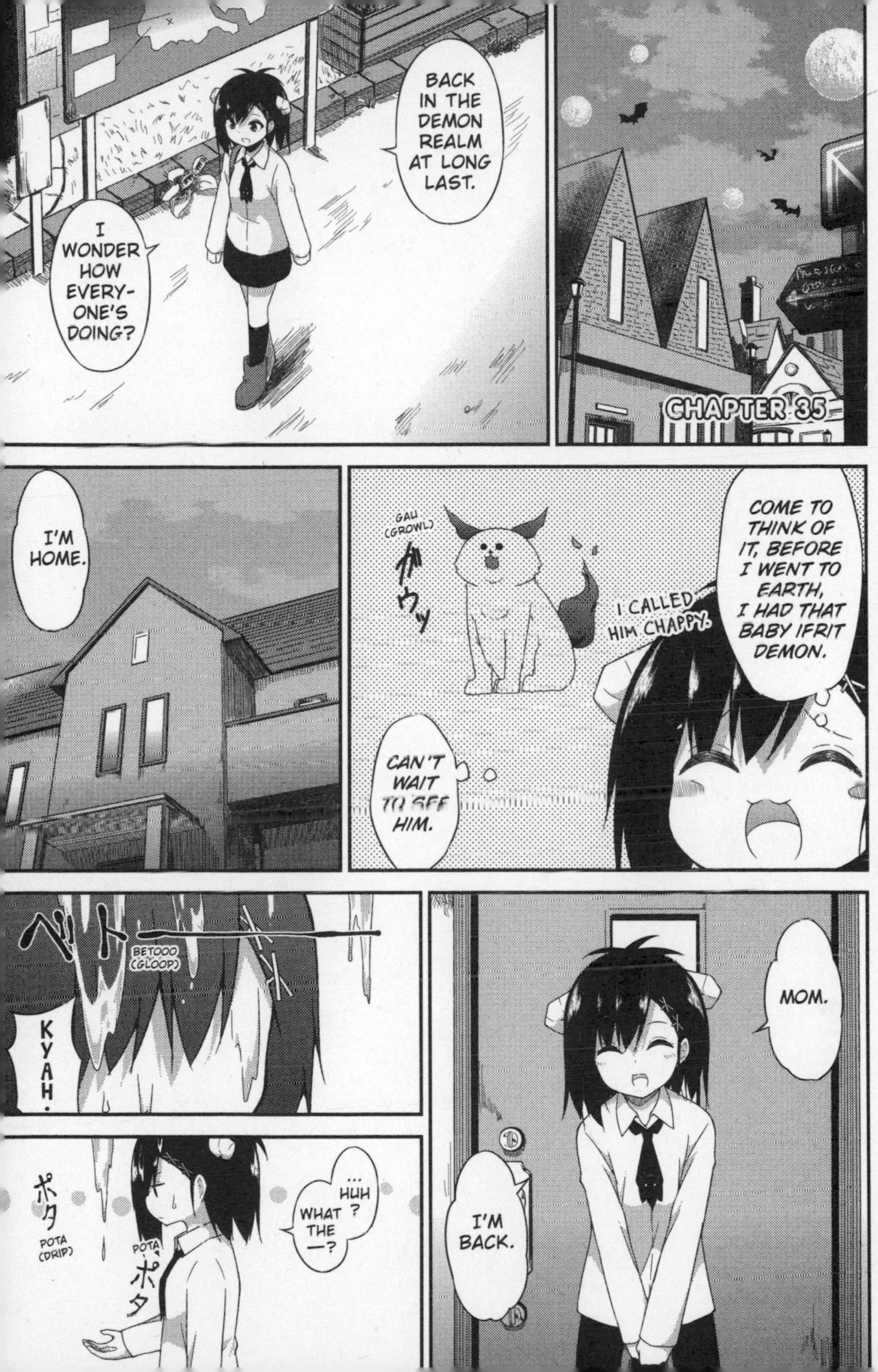
CHAPTER 35
BACK IN THE DEMON REALM AT LONG LAST.
I WONDER HOW EVERYONE'S DOING?
COME TO THINK OF IT, BEFORE I WENT TO EARTH, I HAD THAT BABY IFRIT DEMON.
I CALLED HIM CHAPPY.
ガウッ
GAU (GROWL)
CAN'T WAIT TO SEE HIM.
I'M HOME.
MOM.
I'M BACK.
ベトー
BETOOO (GLOOP)
KYAH.
ポタ
POTA (DRIP)
POTA
ポタ
...HUH? WHAT THE—?

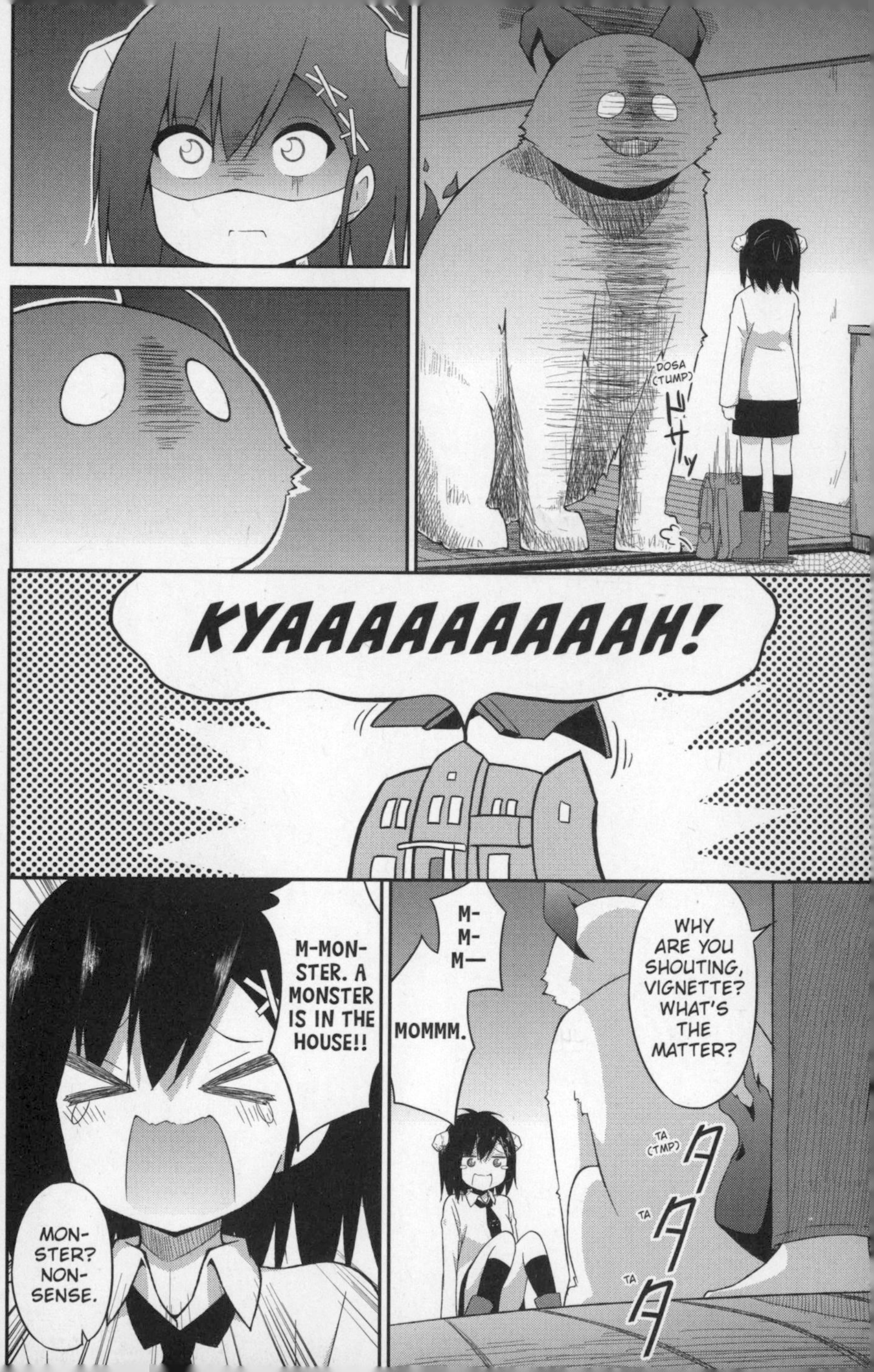

DOSA (TUMP)
ドサッ
KYAAAAAAAAAAH!
WHY ARE YOU SHOUTING, VIGNETTE? WHAT'S THE MATTER?
M-M-M—
MOMMM.
TA (TMP)
TA
TA
タタタ
M-MON-STER. A MONSTER IS IN THE HOUSE!!
MON-STER? NON-SENSE.

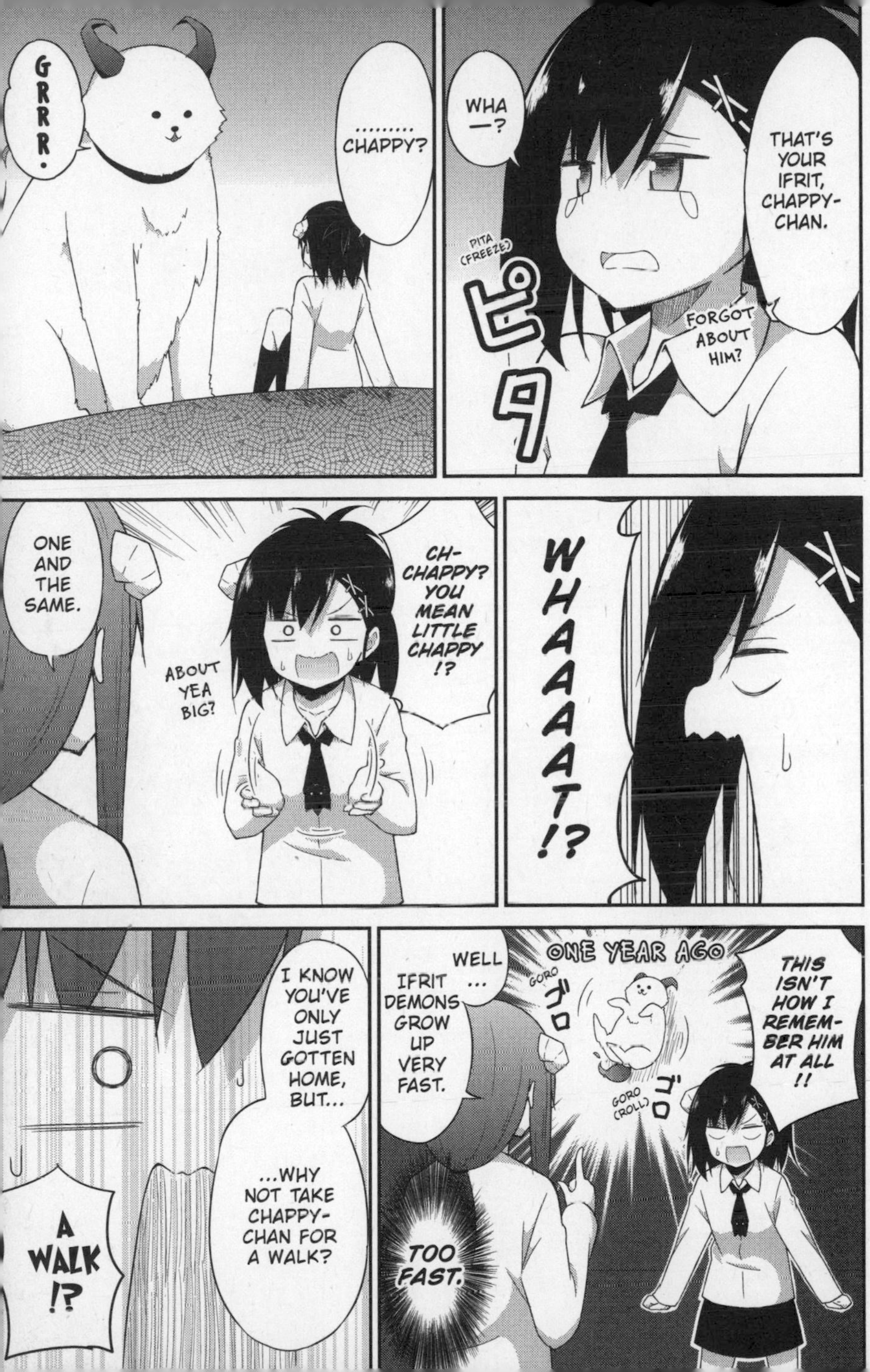
THAT'S YOUR IFRIT, CHAPPY-CHAN.
WHA—?
PITA (FREEZE)
ピタ
FORGOT ABOUT HIM?
....
CHAPPY?
GRRR.
WHAAAAAT!?
CH-CHAPPY? YOU MEAN LITTLE CHAPPY!?
ABOUT YEA BIG?
ONE AND THE SAME.
THIS ISN'T HOW I REMEMBER HIM AT ALL!!
ONE YEAR AGO
GORO
ゴロ
WELL...
IFRIT DEMONS GROW UP VERY FAST.
GORO (ROLL)
ゴロ
TOO FAST.
I KNOW YOU'VE ONLY JUST GOTTEN HOME, BUT...
...WHY NOT TAKE CHAPPY-CHAN FOR A WALK?
A WALK!?

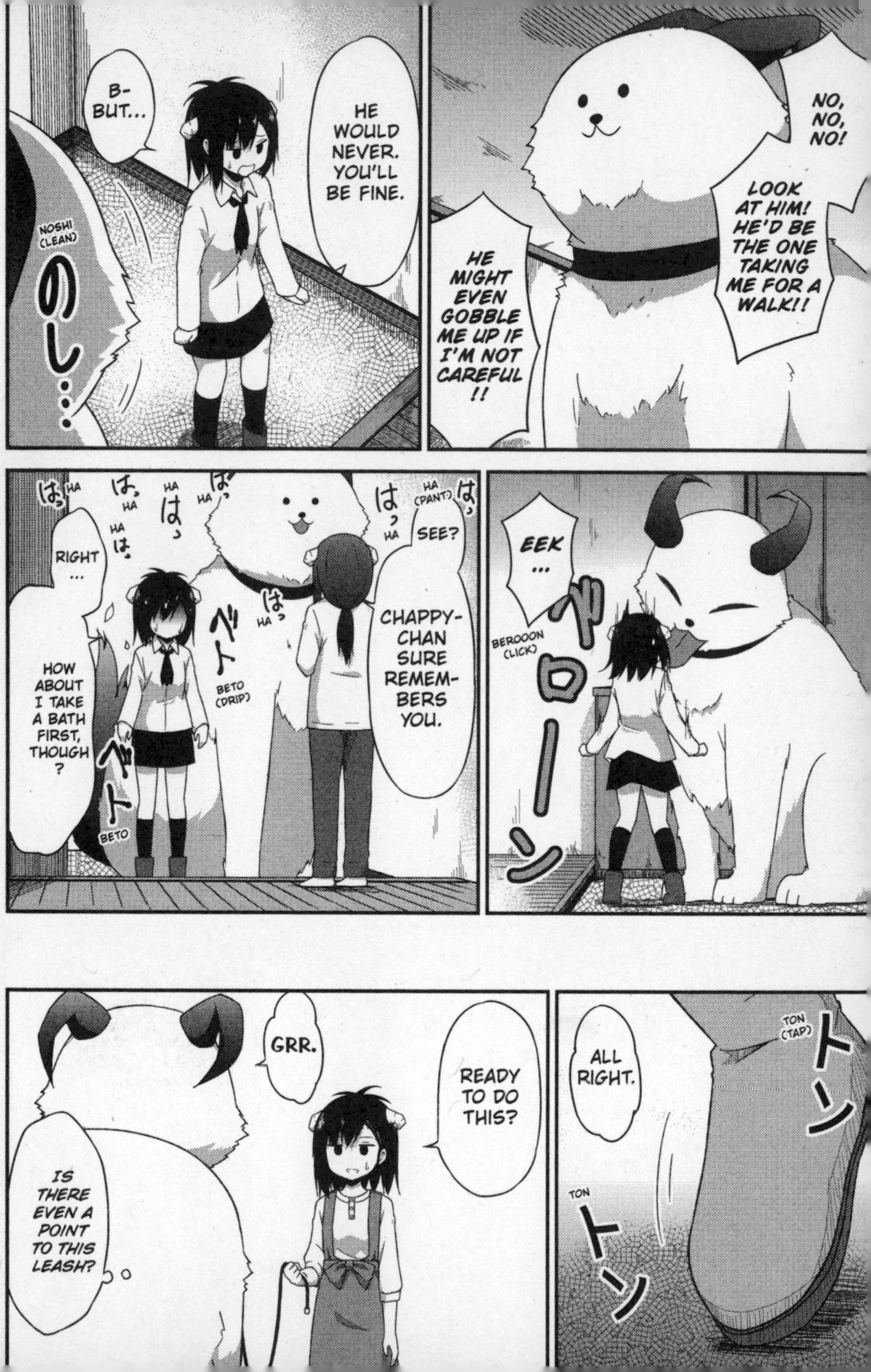

NO, NO, NO!
LOOK AT HIM! HE'D BE THE ONE TAKING ME FOR A WALK!!
HE MIGHT EVEN GOBBLE ME UP IF I'M NOT CAREFUL!!
HE WOULD NEVER. YOU'LL BE FINE.
B-BUT...
NOSHI (CLEAN)
のし…
EEK...
ベローン
BEROOON (LICK)
は、
は、 HA (PANT)
SEE?
CHAPPY-CHAN SURE REMEMBERS YOU.
はっ HA
はっ HA
はっ HA
は、 HA
は、 HA
はっ HA
RIGHT...
HOW ABOUT I TAKE A BATH FIRST, THOUGH?
ベト
BETO (DRIP)
ベト
BETO
ALL RIGHT.
トン
TON (TAP)
トン
TON
READY TO DO THIS?
GRR.
IS THERE EVEN A POINT TO THIS LEASH?

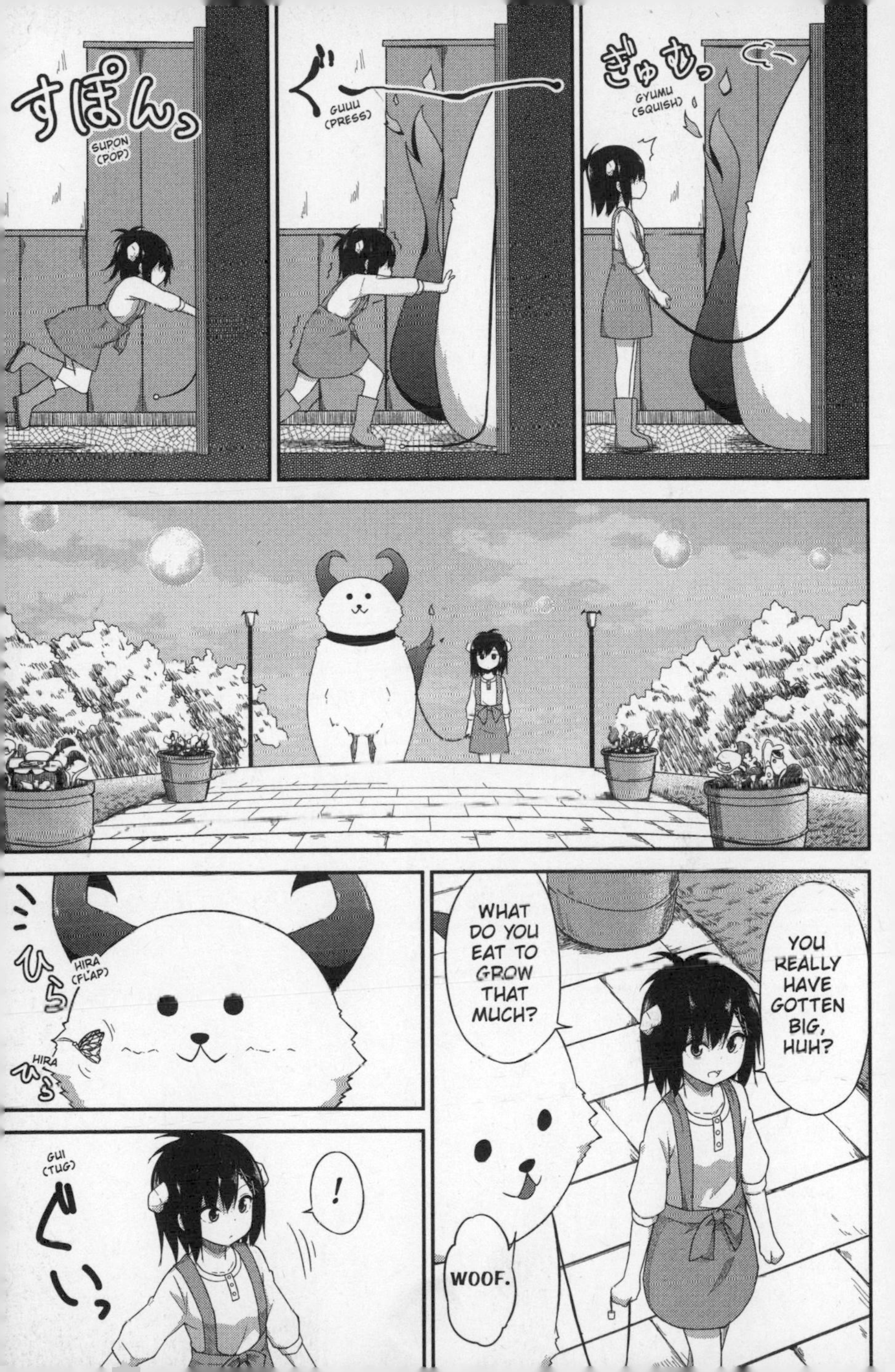
ぎゅむっ
GYUMU (SQUISH)
ぐーー
GUUU (PRESS)
すぽんっ
SUPON (POP)
YOU REALLY HAVE GOTTEN BIG, HUH?
WHAT DO YOU EAT TO GROW THAT MUCH?
WOOF.
ひら
HIRA (FLAP)
ひら
HIRA
ぐいっ
GUI (TUG)
!

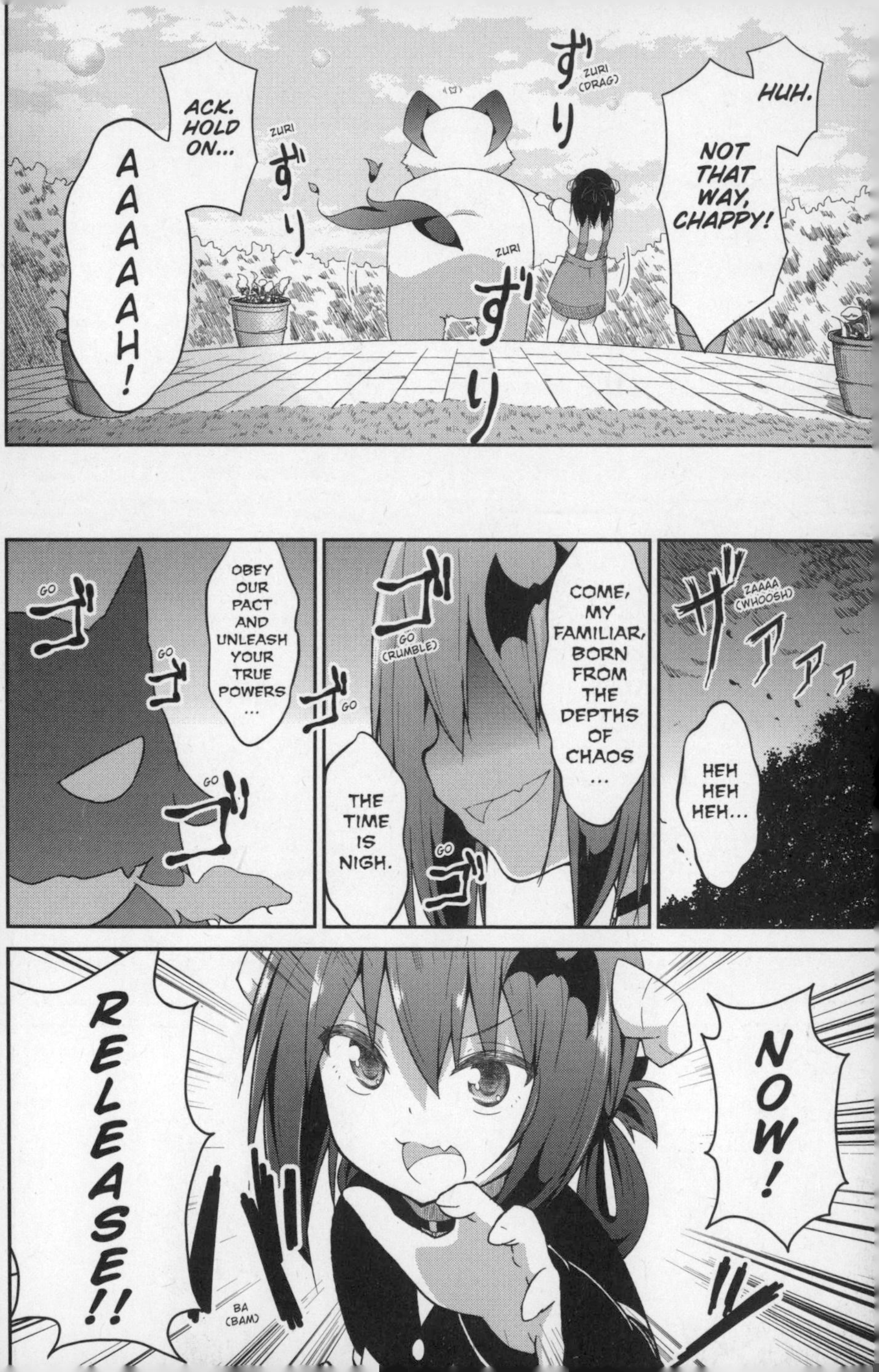
HUH.
NOT THAT WAY, CHAPPY!
ZURI (DRAG)
ZURI
ZURI
ACK. HOLD ON...
AAAAAAH!
ZAAAA (WHOOSH)
HEH HEH HEH...
COME, MY FAMILIAR, BORN FROM THE DEPTHS OF CHAOS...
GO (RUMBLE)
GO
THE TIME IS NIGH.
GO
OBEY OUR PACT AND UNLEASH YOUR TRUE POWERS...
GO
GO
GO
NOW!
RELEASE!!
BA (BAM)

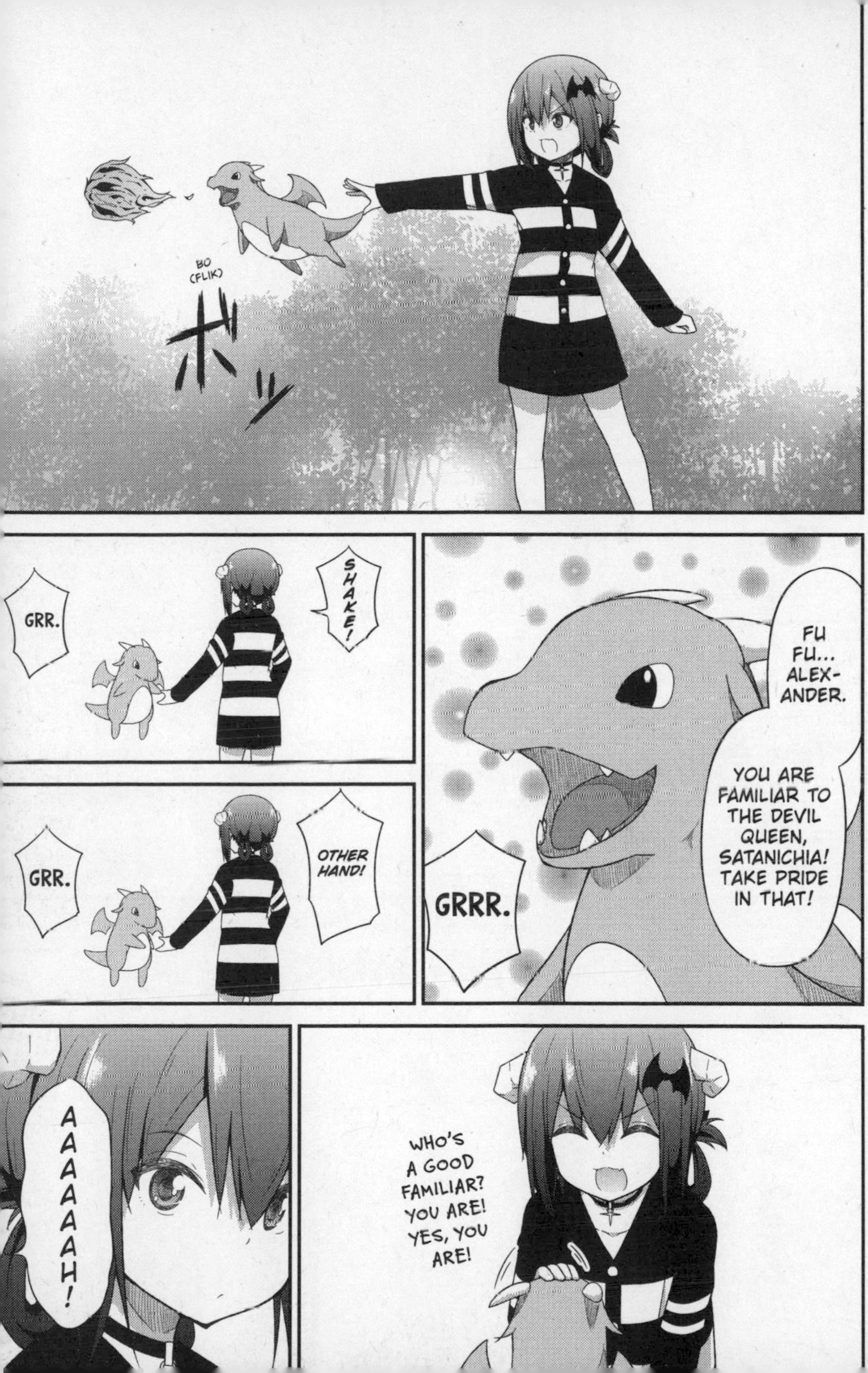
BO
(FLIK)
ボッ
FU FU... ALEXANDER.
YOU ARE FAMILIAR TO THE DEVIL QUEEN, SATANICHIA! TAKE PRIDE IN THAT!
GRRR.
SHAKE!
GRR.
OTHER HAND!
GRR.
WHO'S A GOOD FAMILIAR? YOU ARE! YES, YOU ARE!
AAAAAAH!

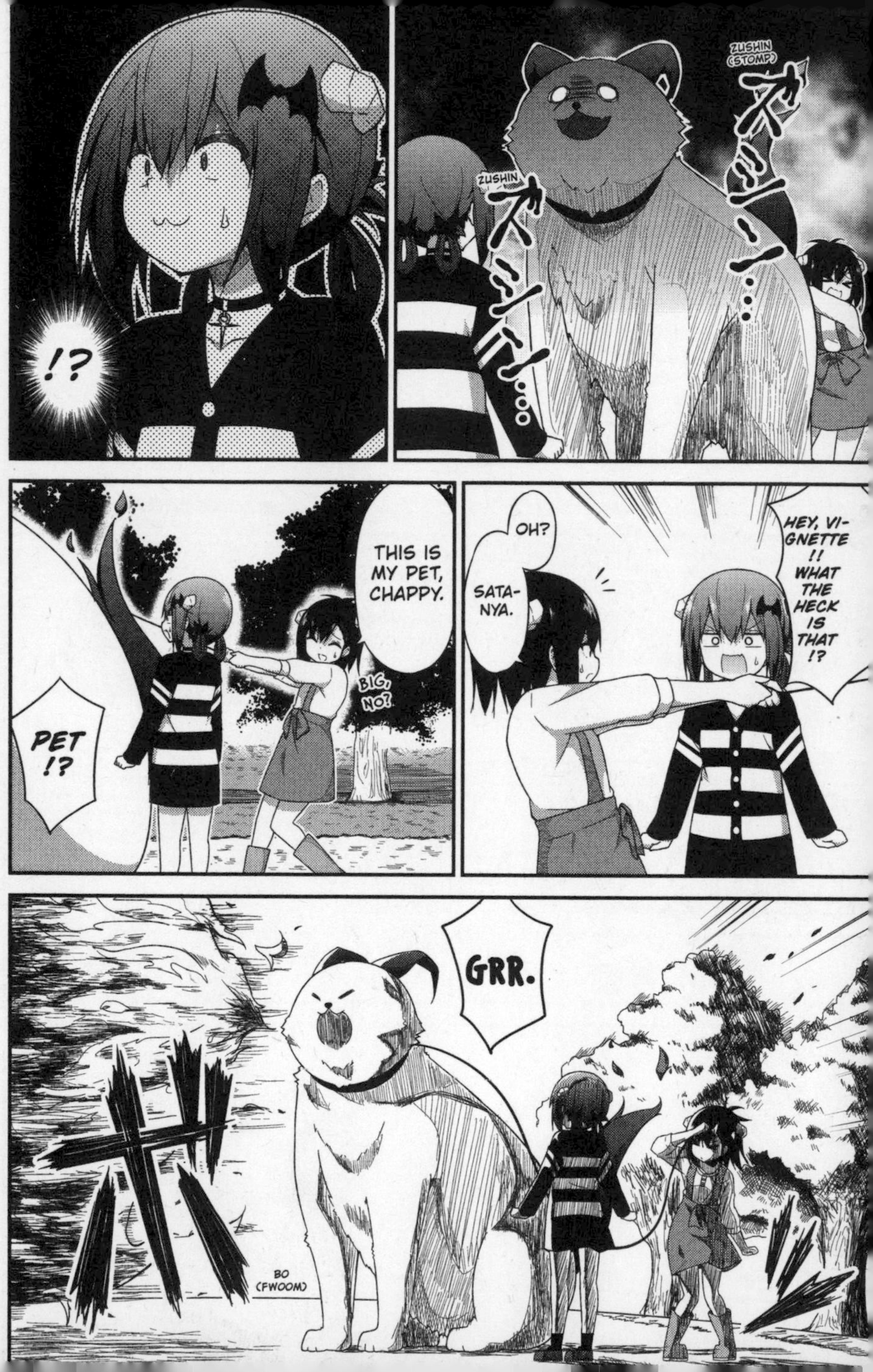
ZUSHIN (STOMP)
ZUSHIN
!?
HEY, VI-GNETTE!! WHAT THE HECK IS THAT!?
OH?
SATA-NYA.
THIS IS MY PET, CHAPPY.
BIG, NO?
PET!?
GRR.
BO (FWOOM)

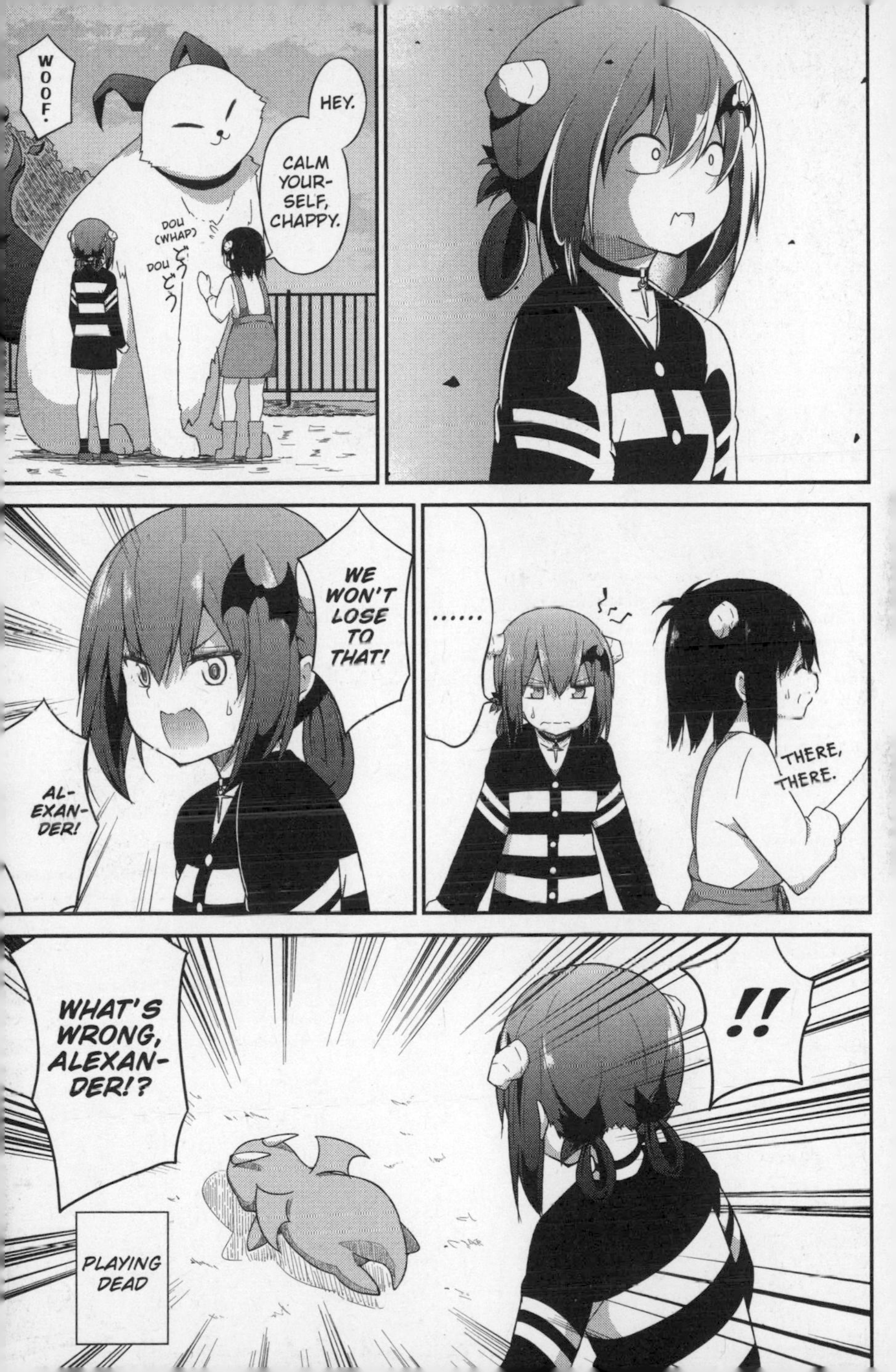
HEY.
CALM YOUR-SELF, CHAPPY.
DOU (WHAP) どう
DOU どう
WOOF.
......
THERE, THERE.
WE WON'T LOSE TO THAT!
AL-EXAN-DER!
!!
WHAT'S WRONG, ALEXAN-DER!?
PLAYING DEAD

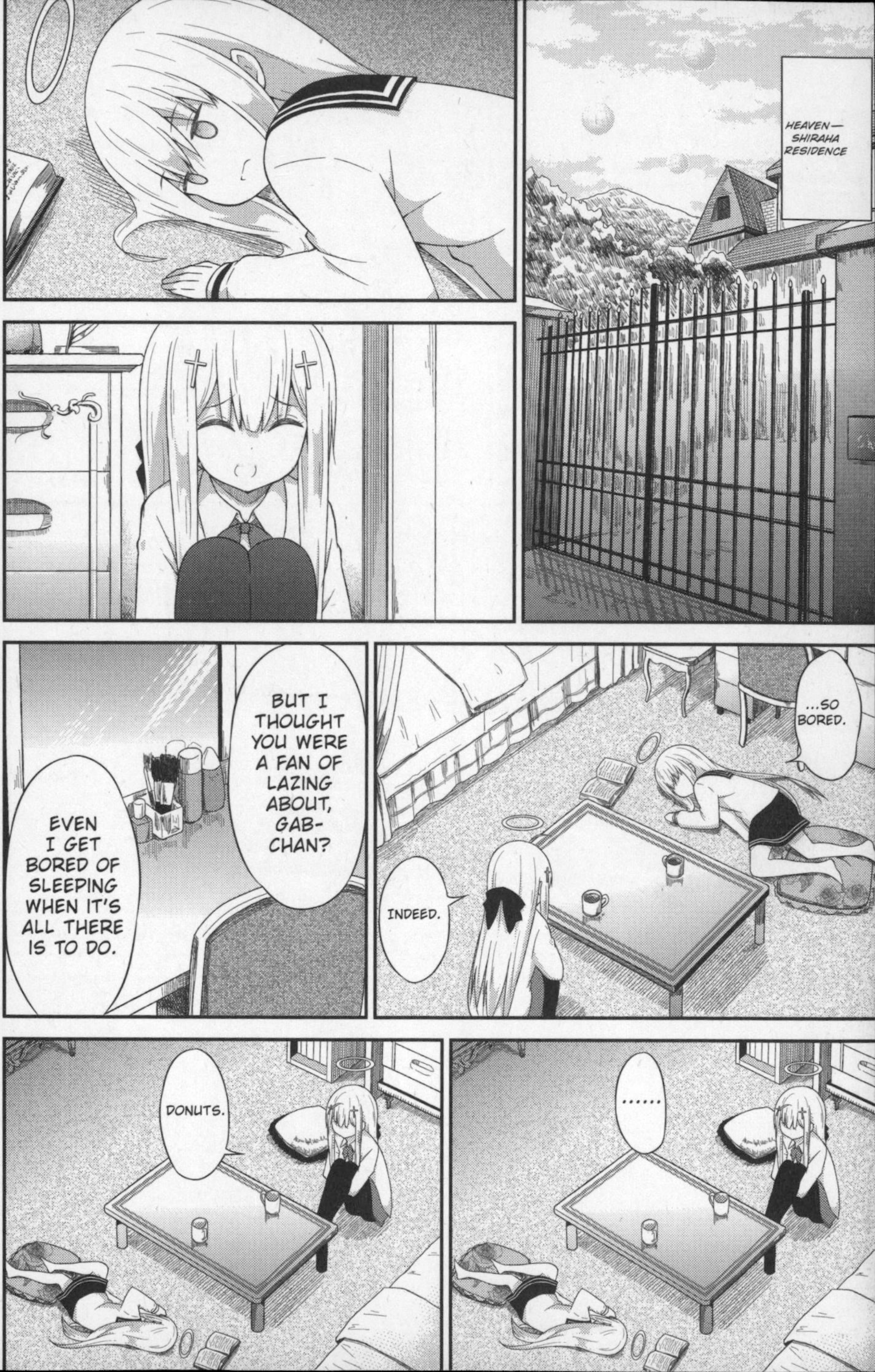
HEAVEN—SHIRAHA RESIDENCE
...SO BORED.
INDEED.
BUT I THOUGHT YOU WERE A FAN OF LAZING ABOUT, GAB-CHAN?
EVEN I GET BORED OF SLEEPING WHEN IT'S ALL THERE IS TO DO.
......
DONUTS.

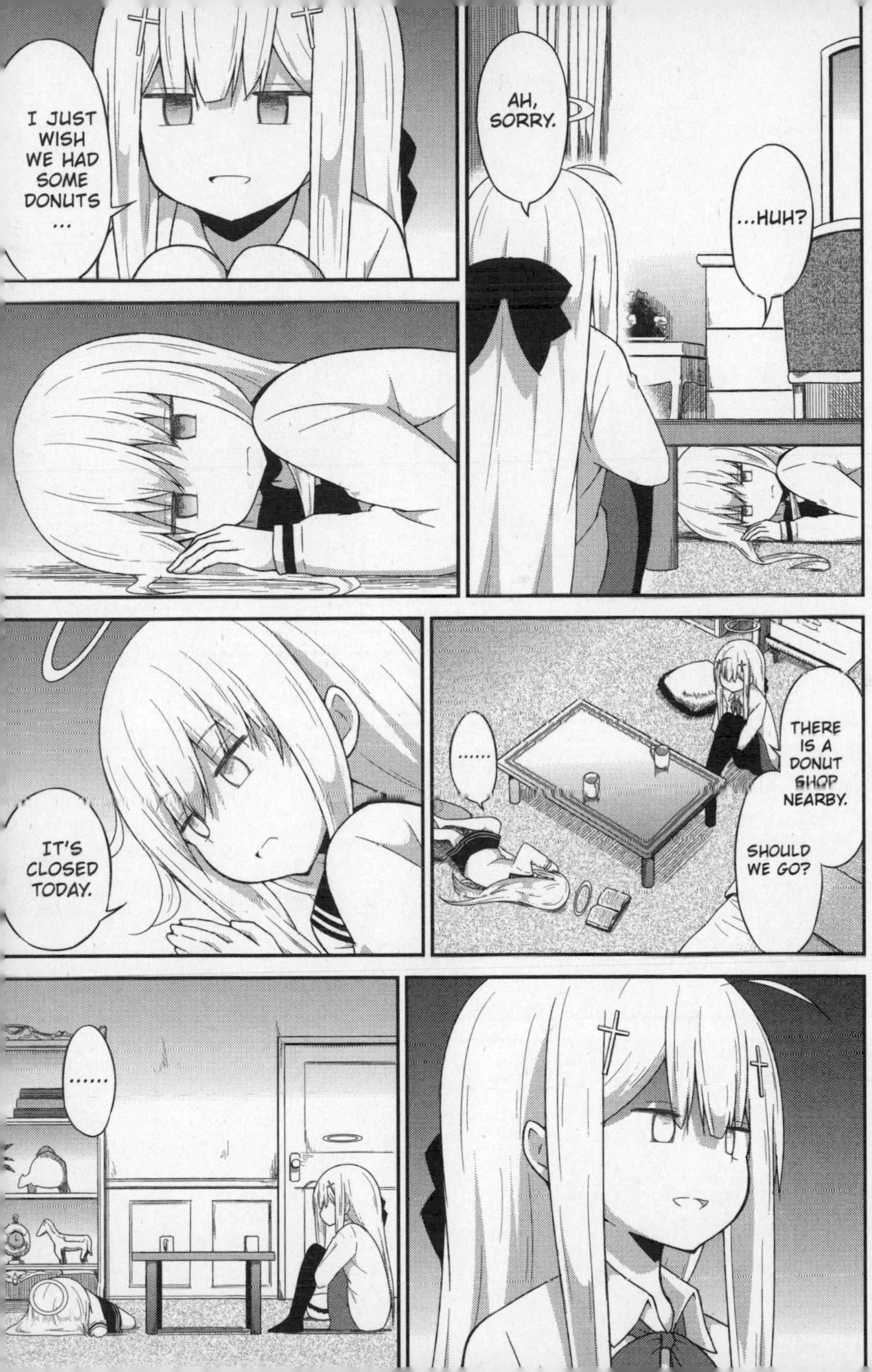
AH, SORRY.
...HUH?
I JUST WISH WE HAD SOME DONUTS ...
THERE IS A DONUT SHOP NEARBY.
SHOULD WE GO?
......
IT'S CLOSED TODAY.
......

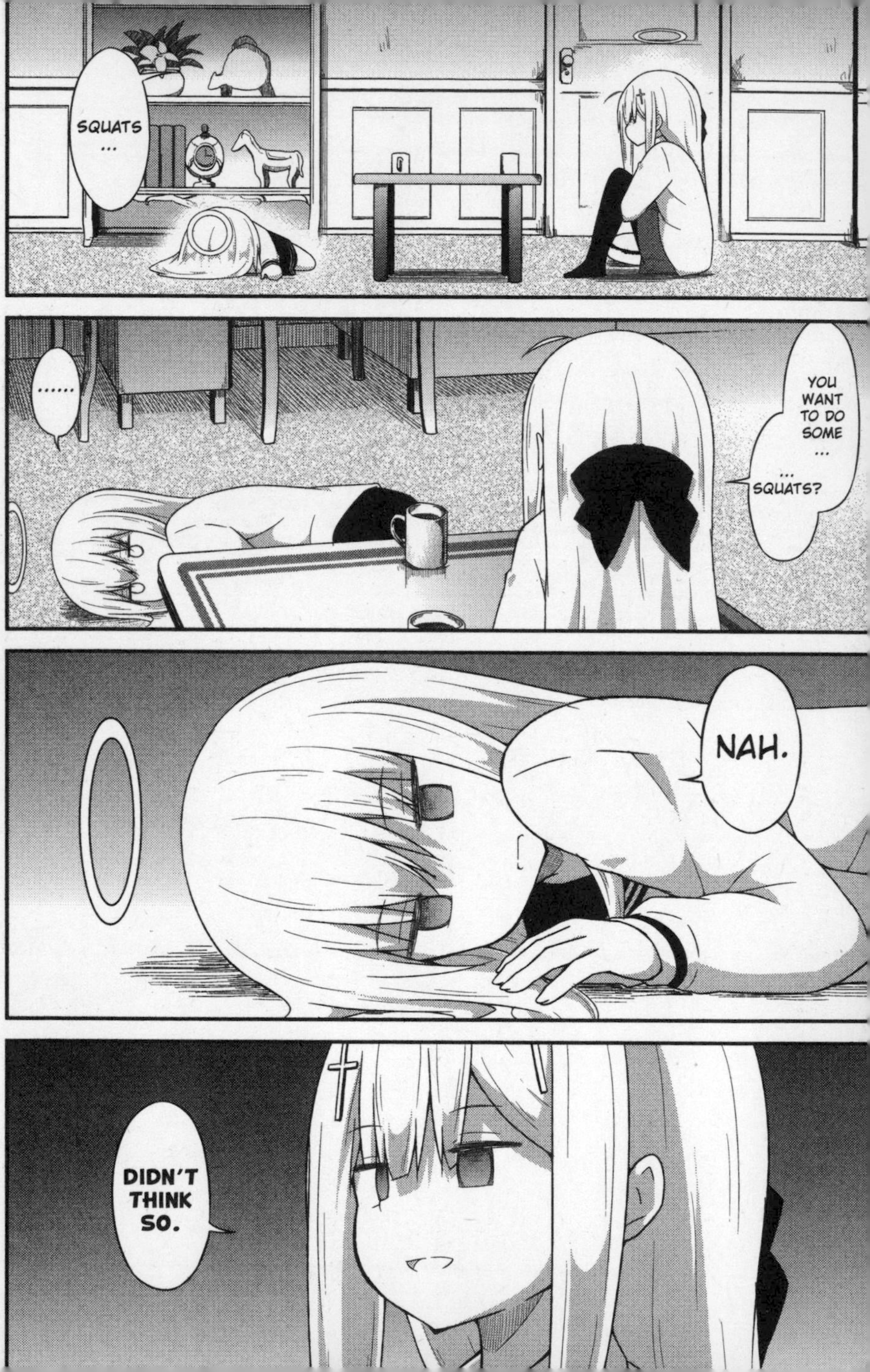
SQUATS ...
YOU WANT TO DO SOME ... ... SQUATS?
......
NAH.
DIDN'T THINK SO.

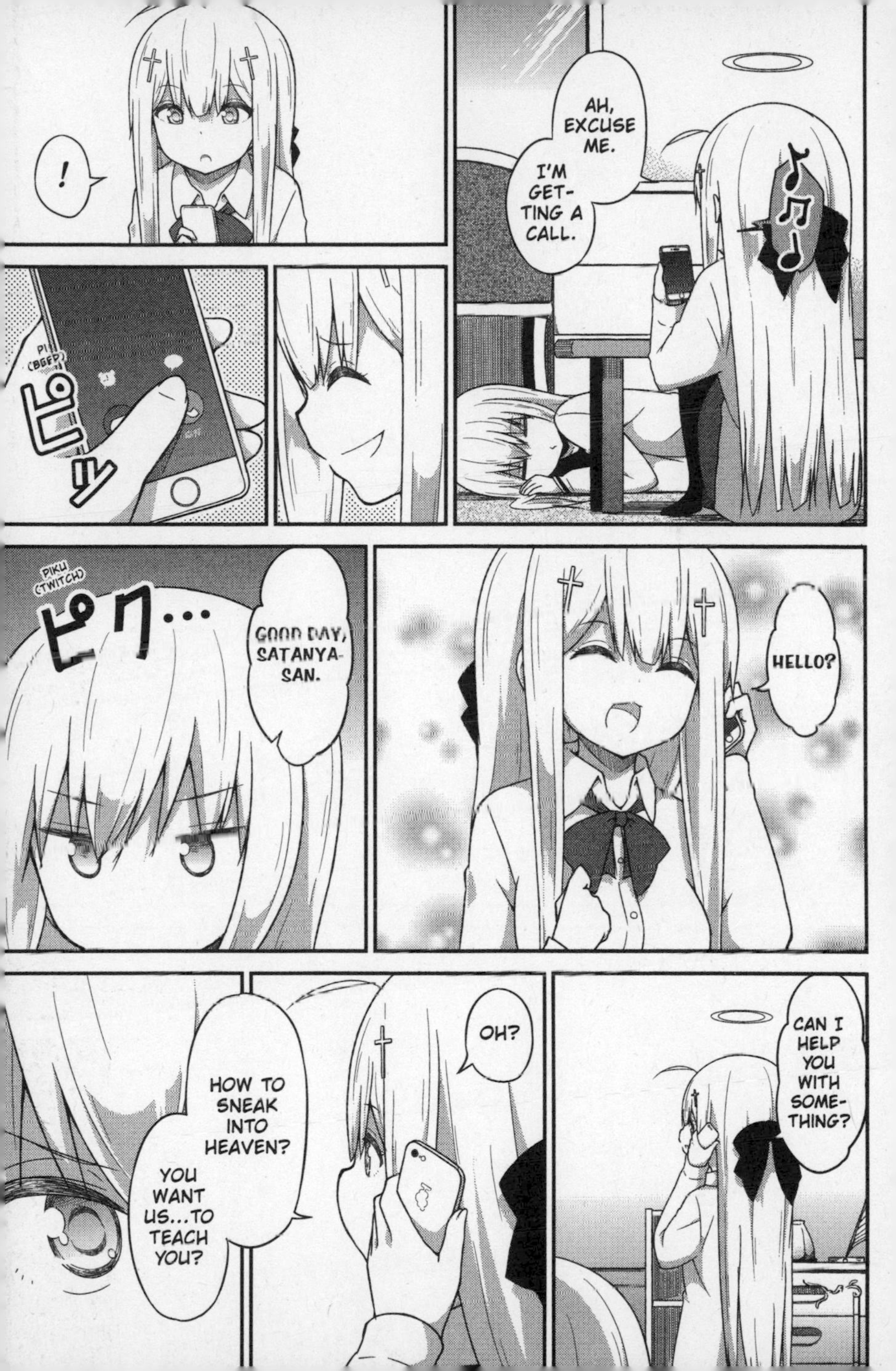
AH, EXCUSE ME.
I'M GET-TING A CALL.
!
PI (BEEP)
ピッ
HELLO?
GOOD DAY, SATANYA-SAN.
PIKU (TWITCH)
ピク…
CAN I HELP YOU WITH SOME-THING?
OH?
HOW TO SNEAK INTO HEAVEN?
YOU WANT US...TO TEACH YOU?

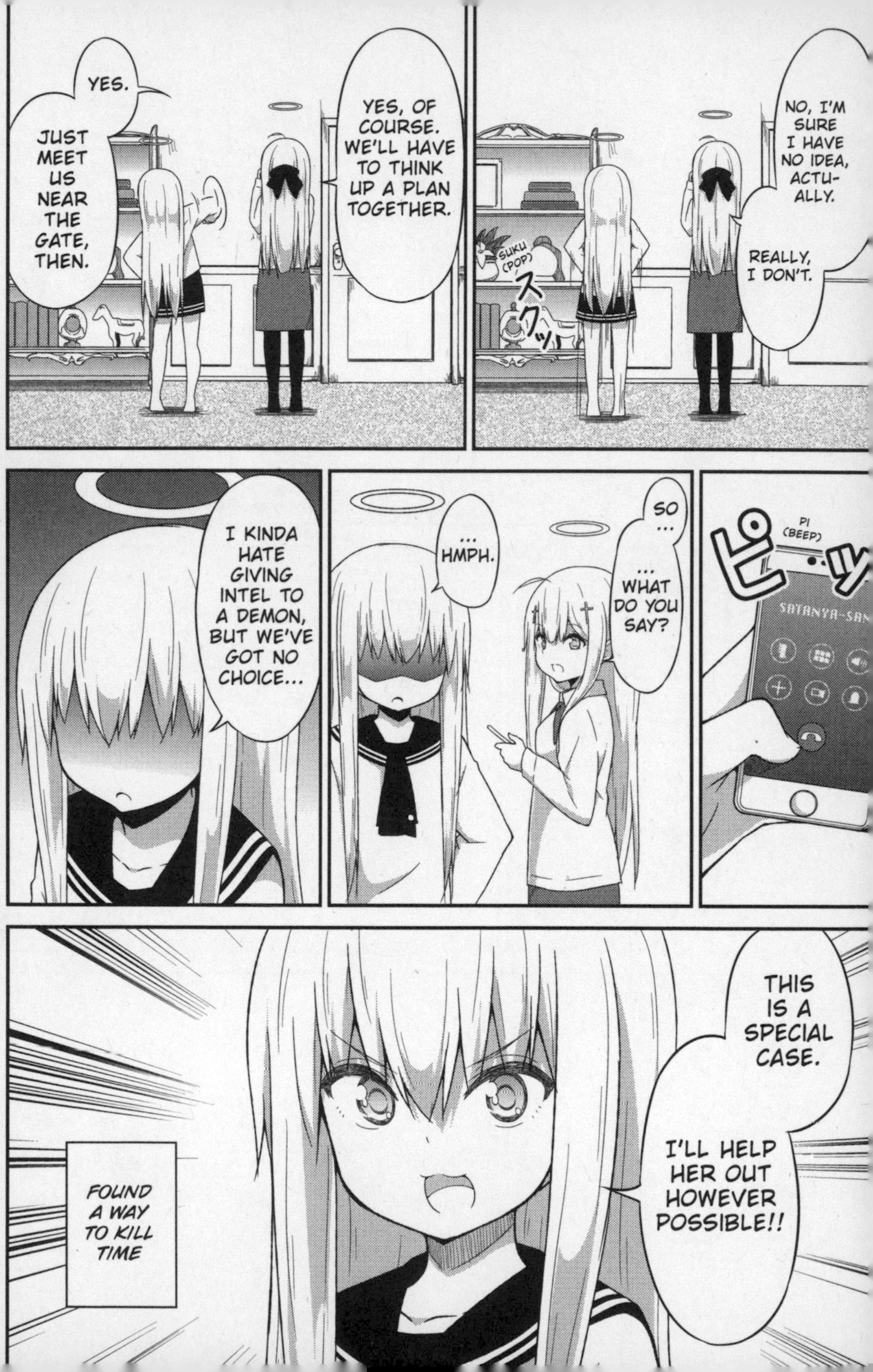
NO, I'M SURE I HAVE NO IDEA, ACTUALLY.
REALLY, I DON'T.
SUKU (POP)
スクッ
YES, OF COURSE. WE'LL HAVE TO THINK UP A PLAN TOGETHER.
YES.
JUST MEET US NEAR THE GATE, THEN.
PI (BEEP)
ピッ
SATANYA-SA
SO ...
... WHAT DO YOU SAY?
... HMPH.
I KINDA HATE GIVING INTEL TO A DEMON, BUT WE'VE GOT NO CHOICE...
THIS IS A SPECIAL CASE.
I'LL HELP HER OUT HOWEVER POSSIBLE!!
FOUND A WAY TO KILL TIME

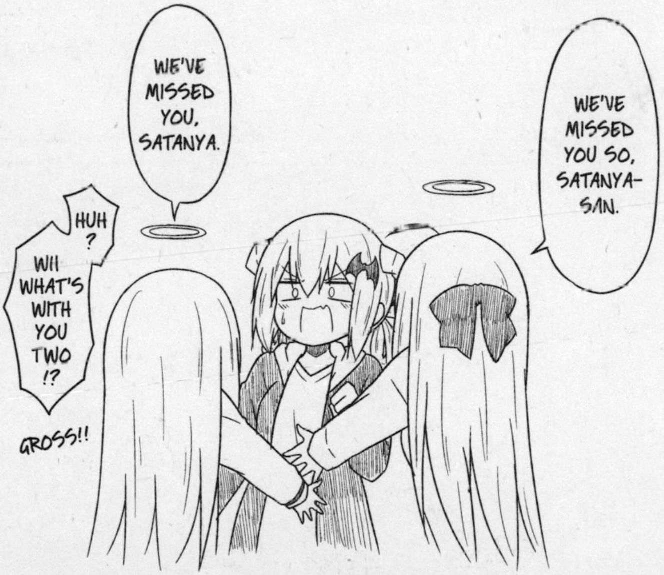
WE'VE MISSED YOU SO, SATANYA-SAN.
WE'VE MISSED YOU, SATANYA.
HUH?
WII WHAT'S WITH YOU TWO!?
GROSS!!

Gabriel Dropout

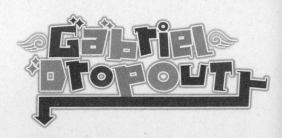

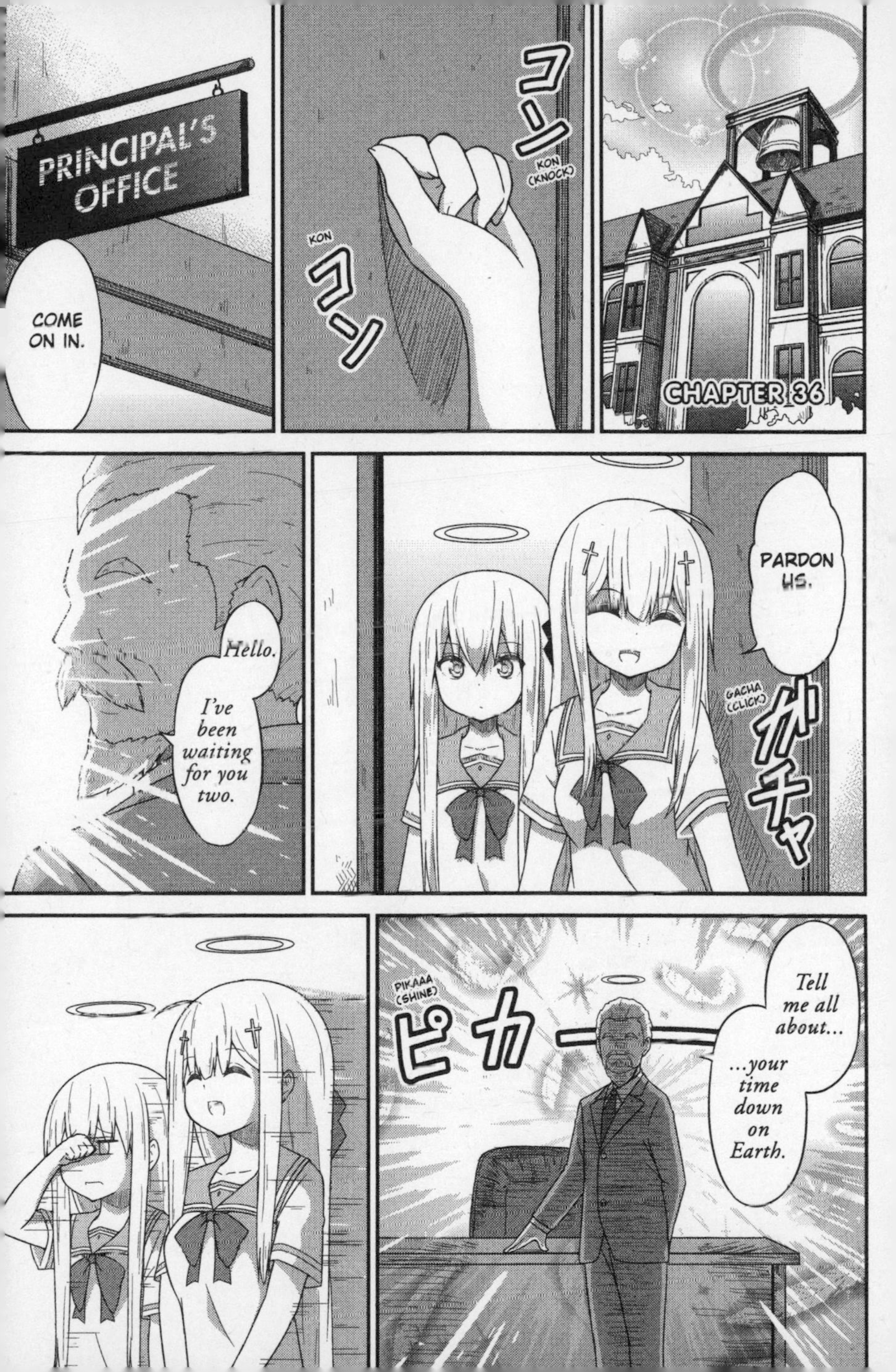
CHAPTER 36
コン
KON (KNOCK)
KON
コン
PRINCIPAL'S OFFICE
COME ON IN.
PARDON US.
GACHA (CLICK)
ガチャ
Hello.
I've been waiting for you two.
Tell me all about...
...your time down on Earth.
PIKAAA (SHINE)
ピカー

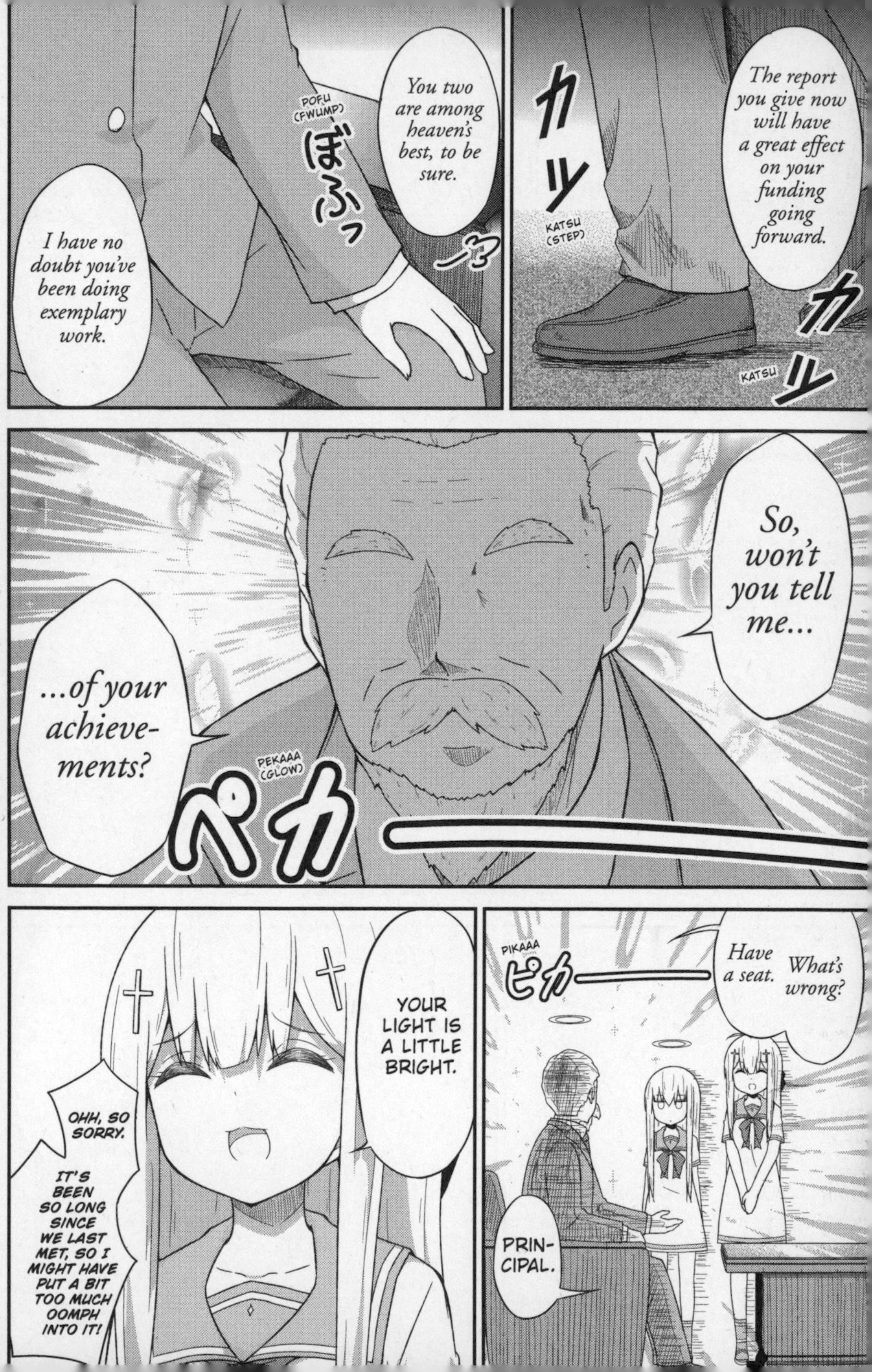
KATSU (STEP)
カッ
The report you give now will have a great effect on your funding going forward.
KATSU
カッ
POFU (FWUMP)
ぼふっ
You two are among heaven's best, to be sure.
I have no doubt you've been doing exemplary work.
So, won't you tell me...
...of your achieve-ments?
PEKAAA (GLOW)
ペカー
What's wrong?
Have a seat.
PIKAAA
ピカー
PRIN-CIPAL.
YOUR LIGHT IS A LITTLE BRIGHT.
OHH, SO SORRY.
IT'S BEEN SO LONG SINCE WE LAST MET, SO I MIGHT HAVE PUT A BIT TOO MUCH OOMPH INTO IT!

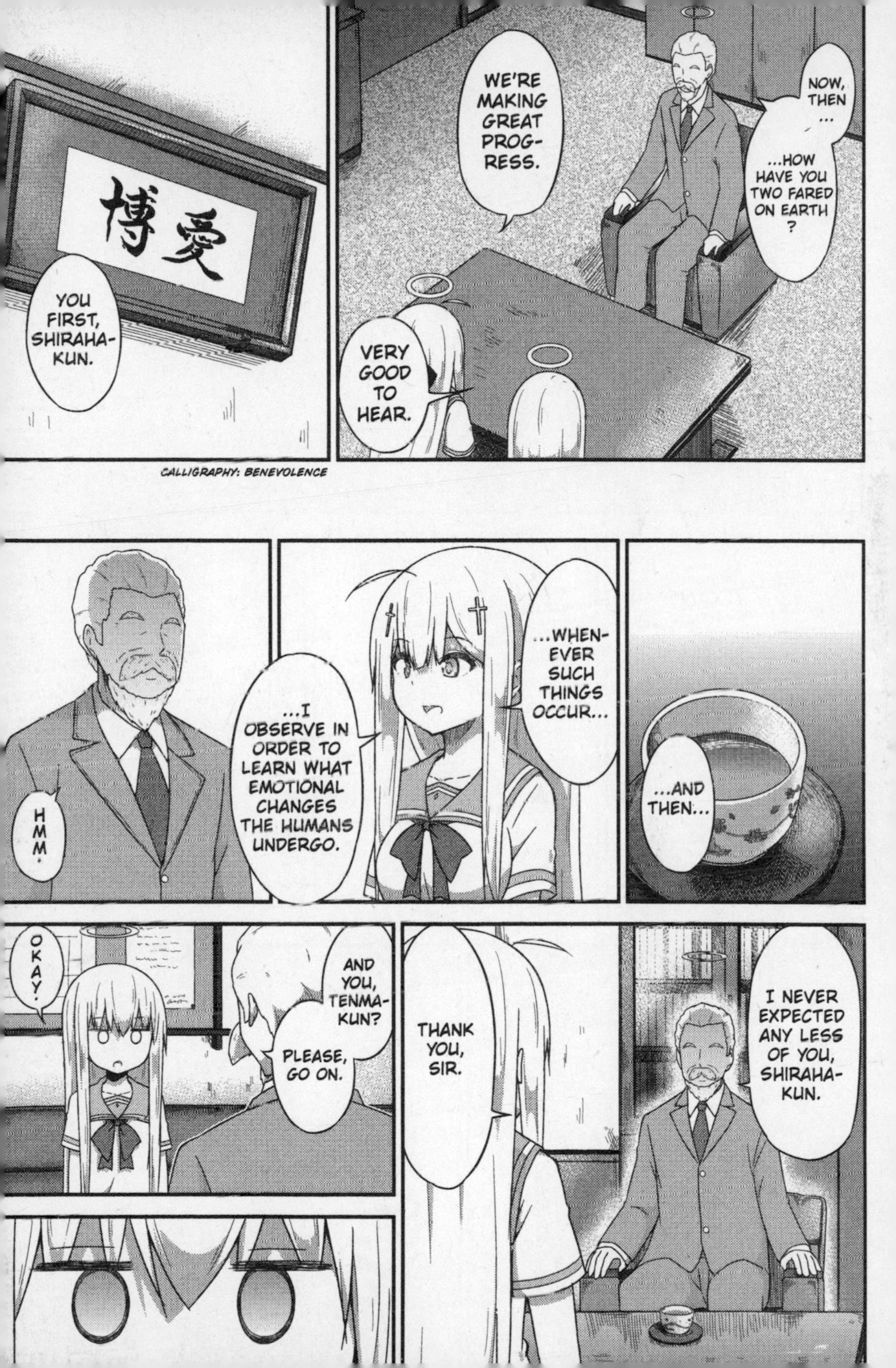
NOW, THEN ...
...HOW HAVE YOU TWO FARED ON EARTH?
WE'RE MAKING GREAT PROGRESS.
VERY GOOD TO HEAR.
博愛
YOU FIRST, SHIRAHA-KUN.
CALLIGRAPHY: BENEVOLENCE
...AND THEN...
...WHENEVER SUCH THINGS OCCUR...
...I OBSERVE IN ORDER TO LEARN WHAT EMOTIONAL CHANGES THE HUMANS UNDERGO.
HMM.
I NEVER EXPECTED ANY LESS OF YOU, SHIRAHA-KUN.
THANK YOU, SIR.
AND YOU, TENMA-KUN?
PLEASE, GO ON.
OKAY.

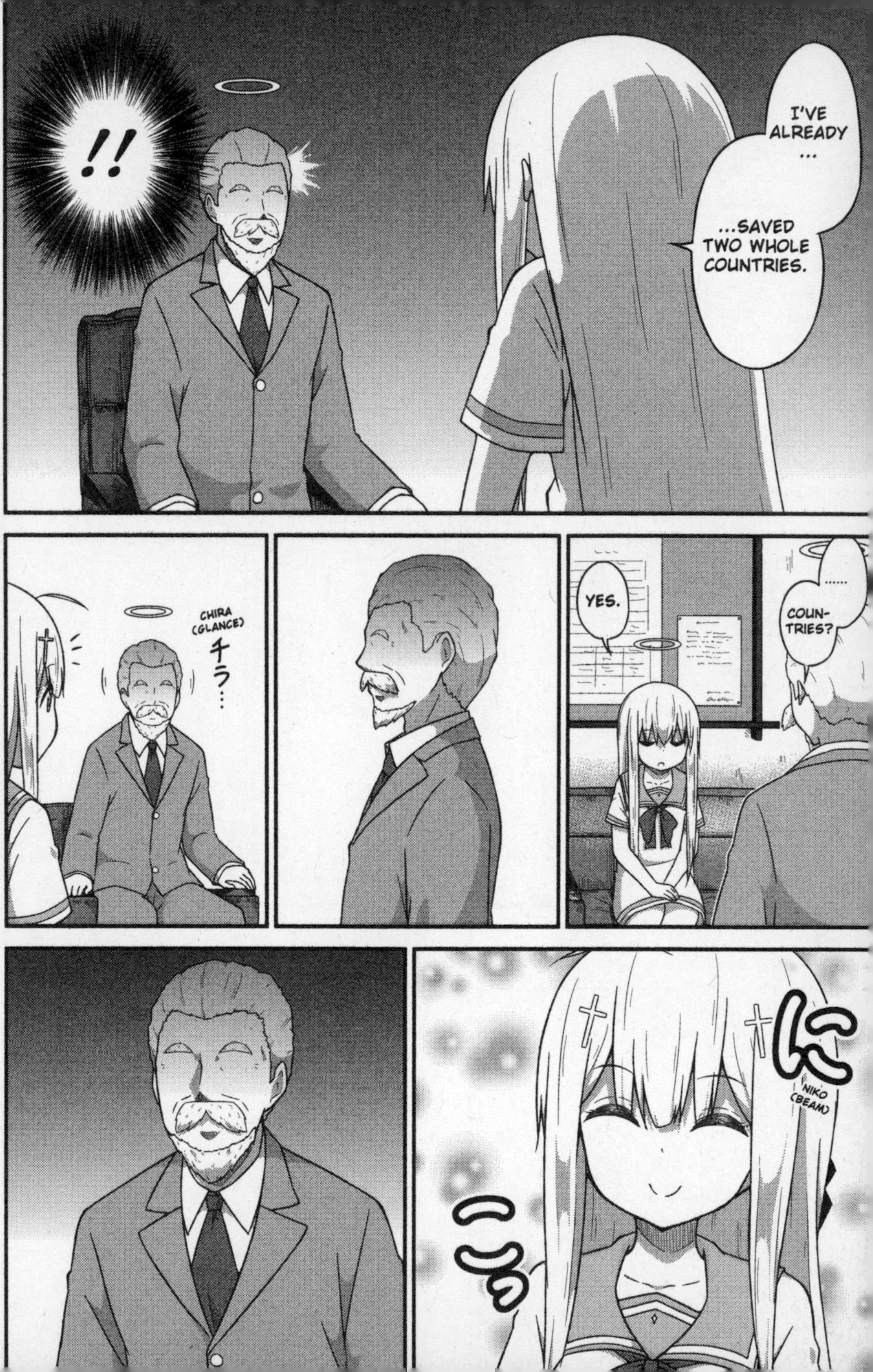
I'VE ALREADY ...
...SAVED TWO WHOLE COUNTRIES.
!!
......
COUN-TRIES?
YES.
チラ…
CHIRA (GLANCE)
にこっ
NIKO (BEAM)

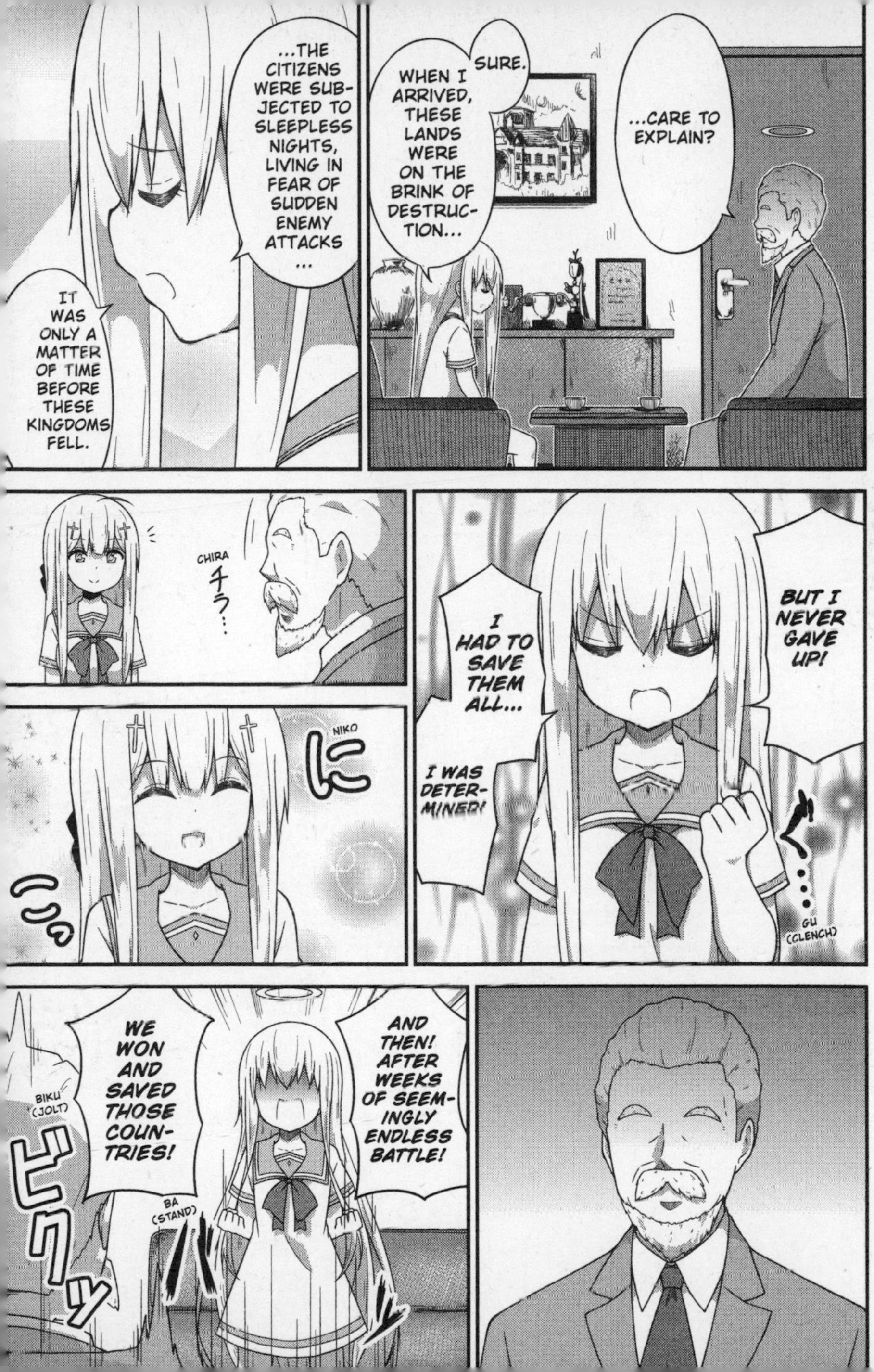
...CARE TO EXPLAIN?
SURE.
WHEN I ARRIVED, THESE LANDS WERE ON THE BRINK OF DESTRUCTION...
...THE CITIZENS WERE SUBJECTED TO SLEEPLESS NIGHTS, LIVING IN FEAR OF SUDDEN ENEMY ATTACKS...
IT WAS ONLY A MATTER OF TIME BEFORE THESE KINGDOMS FELL.
BUT I NEVER GAVE UP!
I HAD TO SAVE THEM ALL...
I WAS DETERMINED!
GU (CLENCH)
CHIRA
チラ…
NIKO
にこっ
AND THEN! AFTER WEEKS OF SEEMINGLY ENDLESS BATTLE!
WE WON AND SAVED THOSE COUNTRIES!
BA (STAND)
BIKU (JOLT)
ビクッ

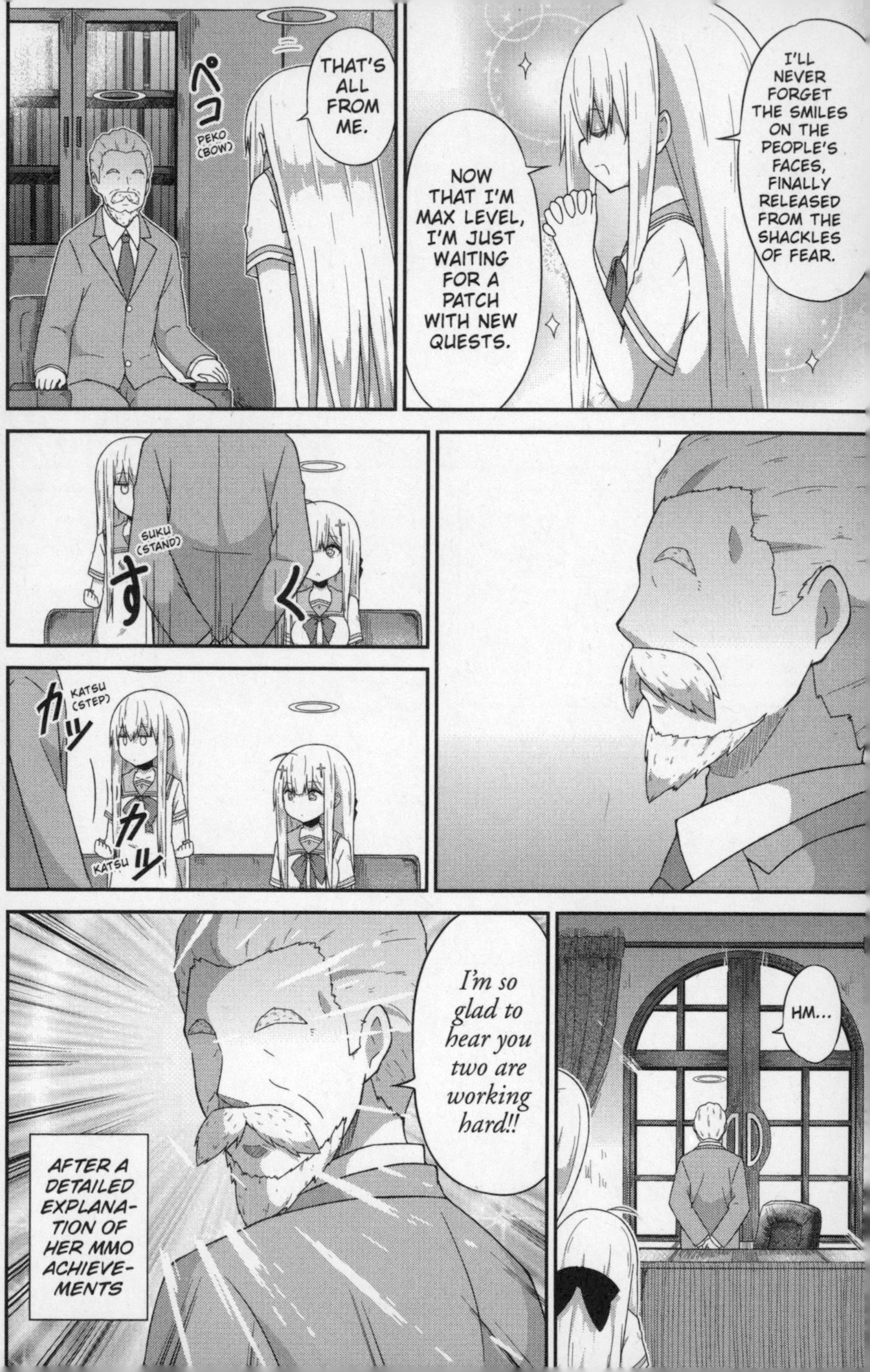
I'LL NEVER FORGET THE SMILES ON THE PEOPLE'S FACES, FINALLY RELEASED FROM THE SHACKLES OF FEAR.
NOW THAT I'M MAX LEVEL, I'M JUST WAITING FOR A PATCH WITH NEW QUESTS.
THAT'S ALL FROM ME.
ペコ
PEKO (BOW)
すく
SUKU (STAND)
カッ
KATSU (STEP)
カッ
KATSU
HM...
I'm so glad to hear you two are working hard!!
AFTER A DETAILED EXPLANATION OF HER MMO ACHIEVEMENTS

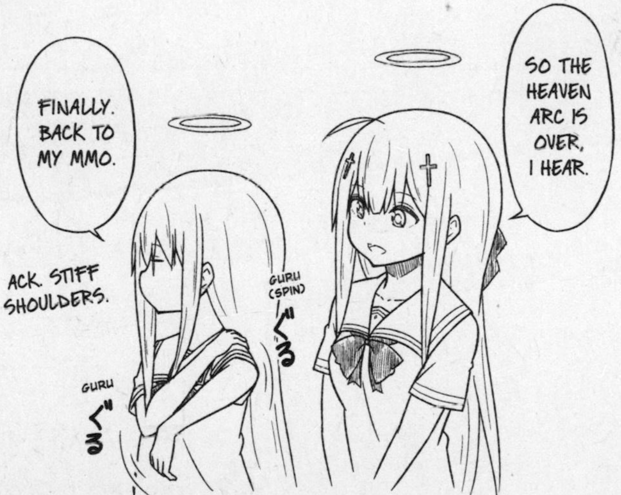
SO THE HEAVEN ARC IS OVER, I HEAR.
FINALLY. BACK TO MY MMO.
GURU (SPIN)
ACK. STIFF SHOULDERS.
GURU

Gabriel DropOut

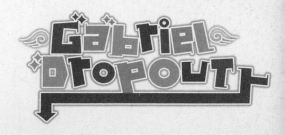

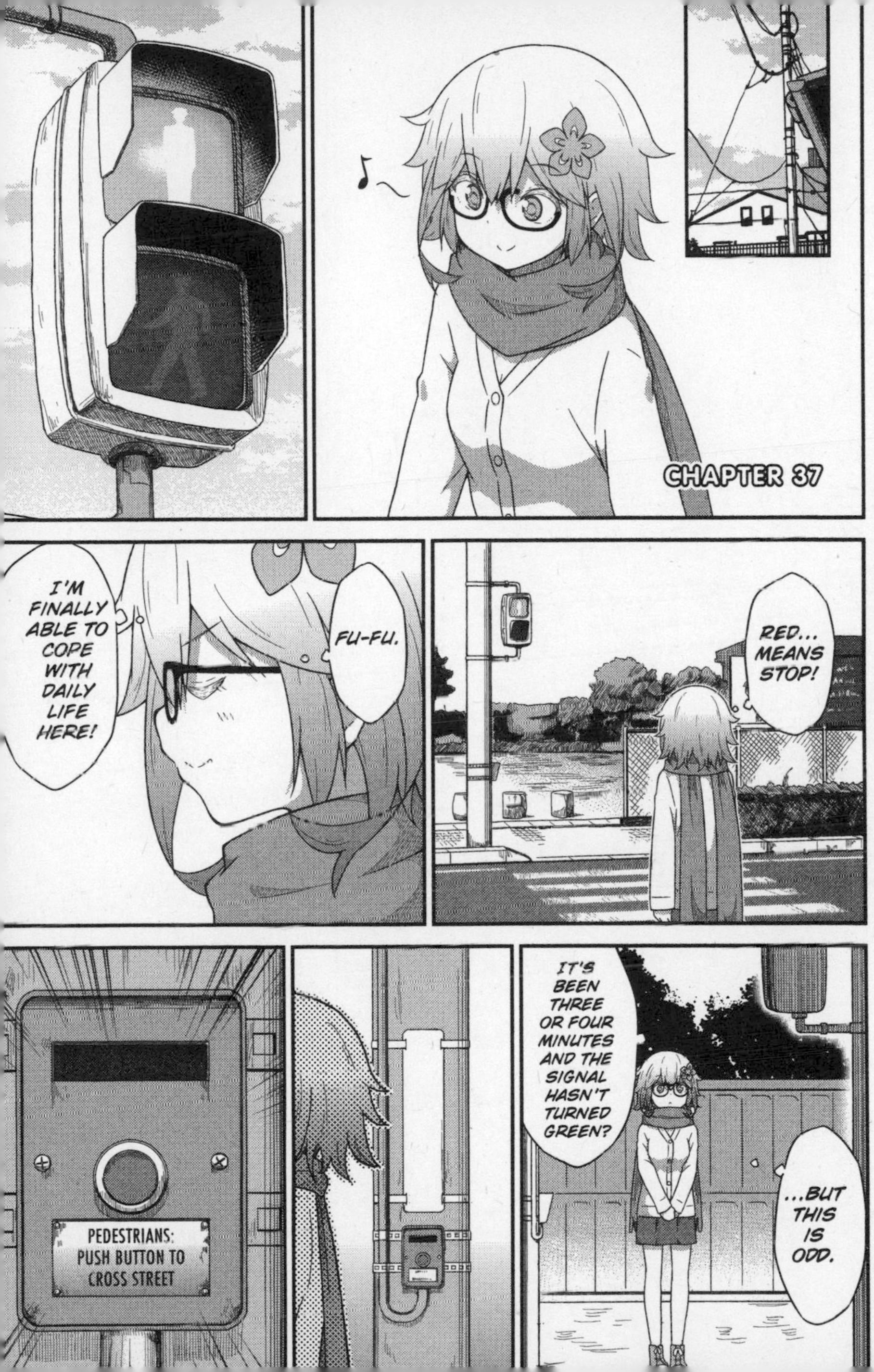
♪~
CHAPTER 37
RED... MEANS STOP!
FU-FU.
I'M FINALLY ABLE TO COPE WITH DAILY LIFE HERE!
IT'S BEEN THREE OR FOUR MINUTES AND THE SIGNAL HASN'T TURNED GREEN?
...BUT THIS IS ODD.
PEDESTRIANS: PUSH BUTTON TO CROSS STREET

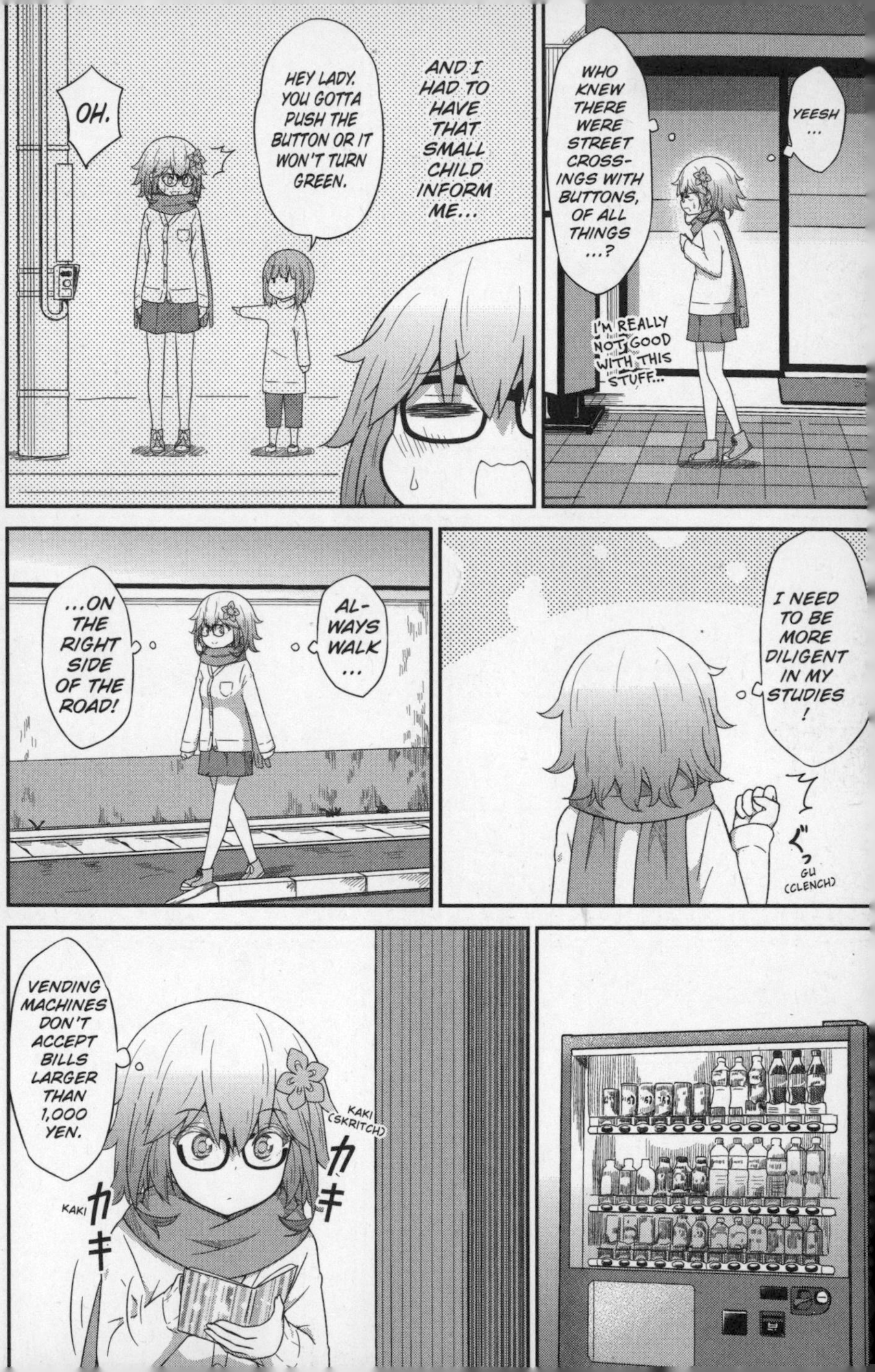
YEESH...
WHO KNEW THERE WERE STREET CROSS-INGS WITH BUTTONS, OF ALL THINGS...?
I'M REALLY NOT GOOD WITH THIS STUFF...
AND I HAD TO HAVE THAT SMALL CHILD INFORM ME...
HEY LADY. YOU GOTTA PUSH THE BUTTON OR IT WON'T TURN GREEN.
OH.
I NEED TO BE MORE DILIGENT IN MY STUDIES!
ぐっ GU (CLENCH)
AL-WAYS WALK...
...ON THE RIGHT SIDE OF THE ROAD!
VENDING MACHINES DON'T ACCEPT BILLS LARGER THAN 1,000 YEN.
カキ KAKI (SKRITCH)
カキ KAKI

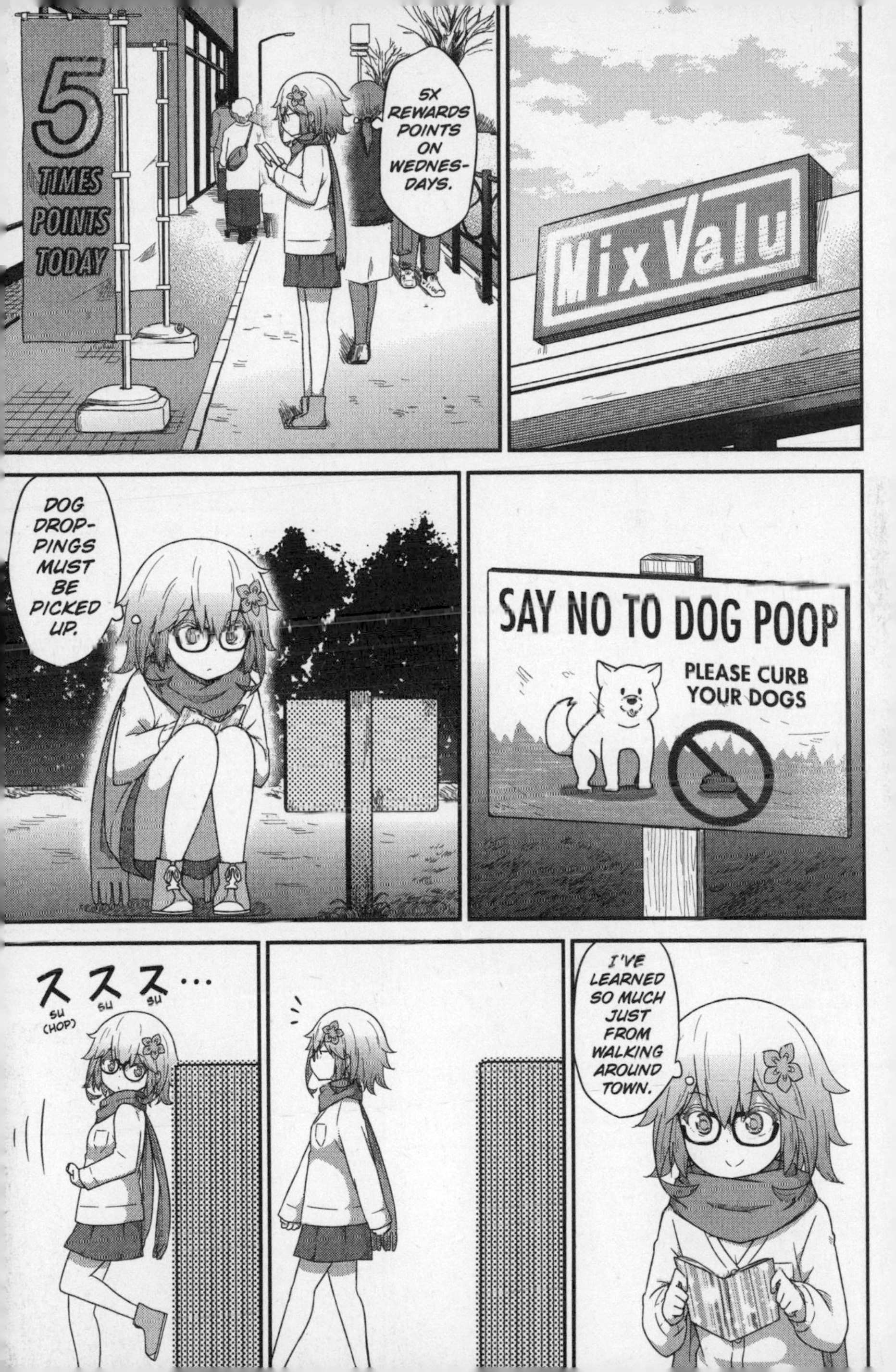

Mix Valu
5 TIMES POINTS TODAY
5X REWARDS POINTS ON WEDNES-DAYS.
SAY NO TO DOG POOP
PLEASE CURB YOUR DOGS
DOG DROP-PINGS MUST BE PICKED UP.
I'VE LEARNED SO MUCH JUST FROM WALKING AROUND TOWN.
ススス…
SU (HOP) SU SU

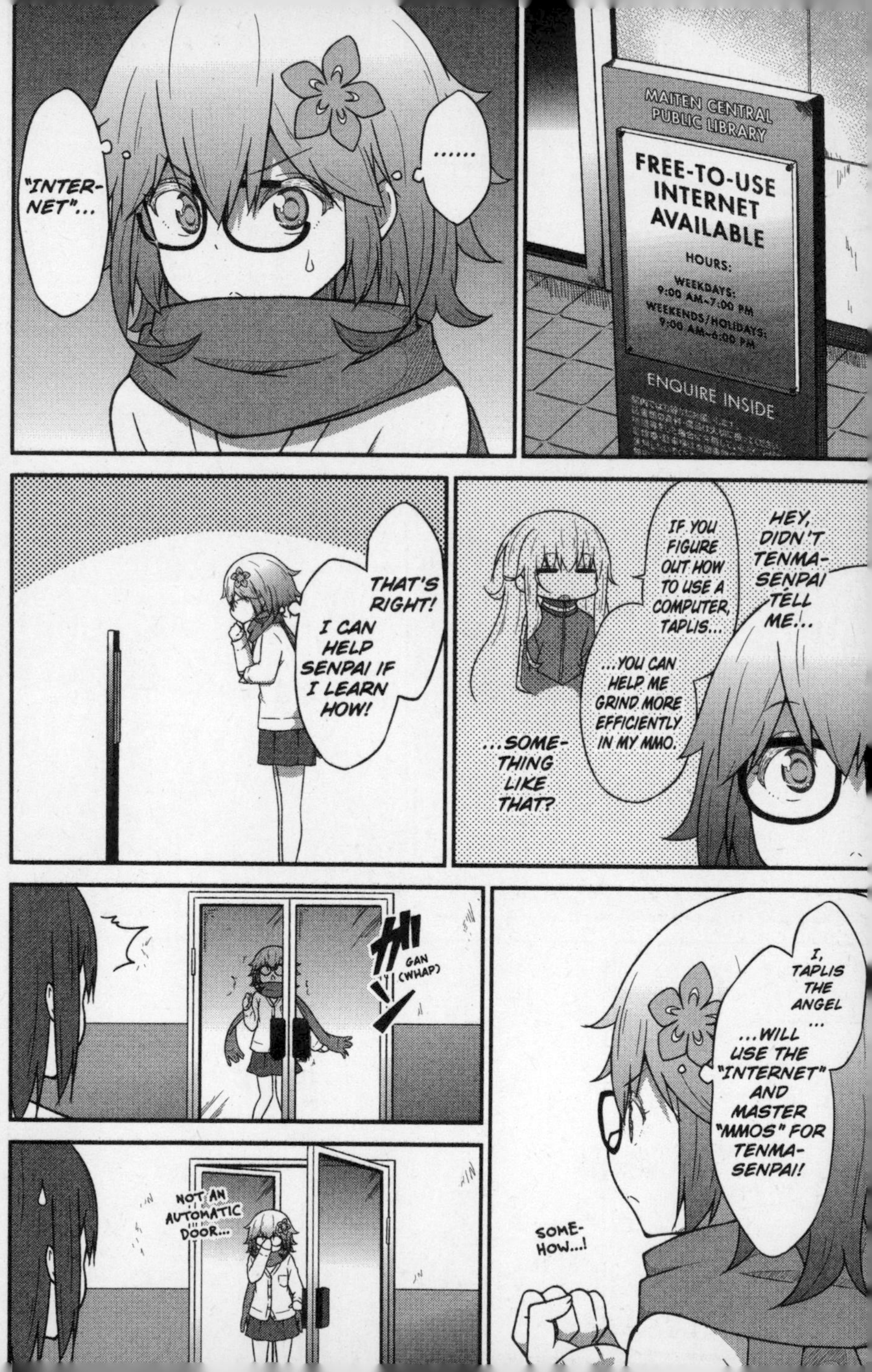
MAITEN CENTRAL PUBLIC LIBRARY
FREE-TO-USE INTERNET AVAILABLE
HOURS:
WEEKDAYS: 9:00 AM~7:00 PM
WEEKENDS/HOLIDAYS: 9:00 AM~6:00 PM
ENQUIRE INSIDE
......
"INTER-NET"...
HEY, DIDN'T TENMA-SENPAI TELL ME...
IF YOU FIGURE OUT HOW TO USE A COMPUTER, TAPLIS...
...YOU CAN HELP ME GRIND MORE EFFICIENTLY IN MY MMO.
...SOME-THING LIKE THAT?
THAT'S RIGHT! I CAN HELP SENPAI IF I LEARN HOW!
I, TAPLIS THE ANGEL...
...WILL USE THE "INTERNET" AND MASTER "MMOS" FOR TENMA-SENPAI!
SOME-HOW...!
GAN (WHAP)
NOT AN AUTOMATIC DOOR...

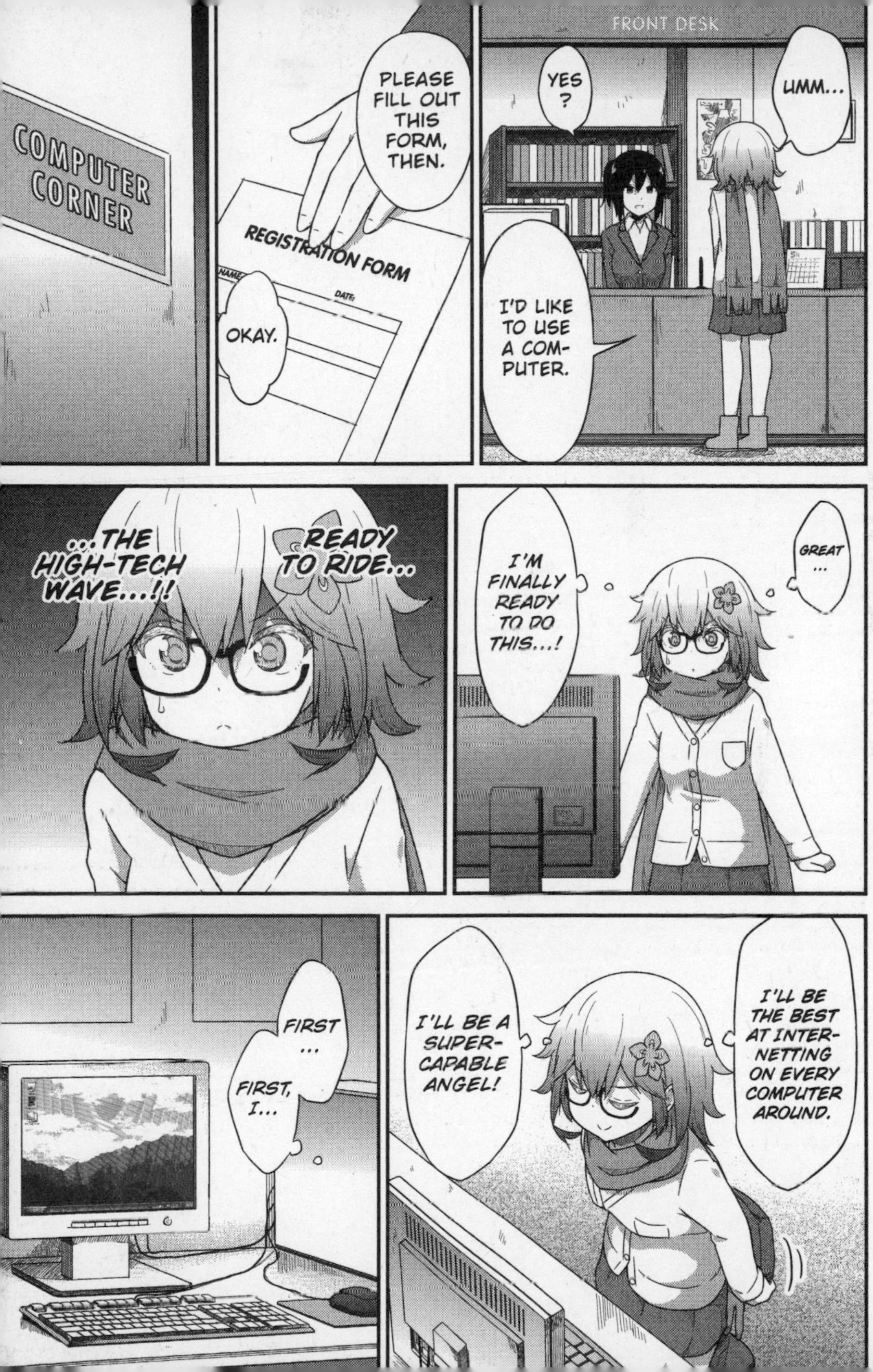
FRONT DESK
UMM...
YES?
I'D LIKE TO USE A COMPUTER.
PLEASE FILL OUT THIS FORM, THEN.
REGISTRATION FORM
NAME:
DATE:
OKAY.
COMPUTER CORNER
GREAT...
I'M FINALLY READY TO DO THIS...!
READY TO RIDE...
...THE HIGH-TECH WAVE...!!
I'LL BE THE BEST AT INTERNETTING ON EVERY COMPUTER AROUND.
I'LL BE A SUPER-CAPABLE ANGEL!
FIRST...
FIRST, I...

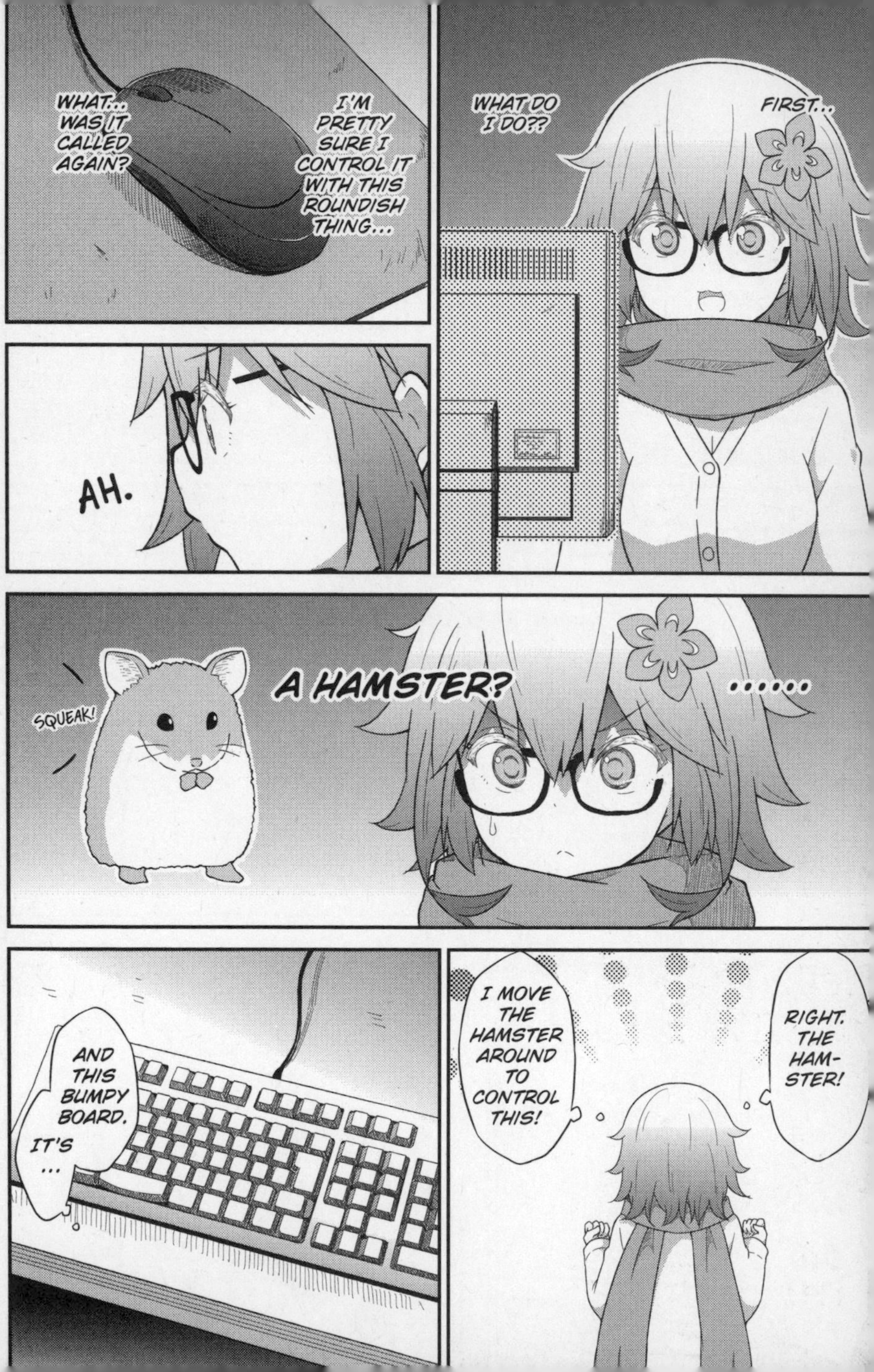

FIRST...
WHAT DO I DO??
I'M PRETTY SURE I CONTROL IT WITH THIS ROUNDISH THING...
WHAT... WAS IT CALLED AGAIN?
AH.
......
A HAMSTER?
SQUEAK!
RIGHT. THE HAM-STER!
I MOVE THE HAMSTER AROUND TO CONTROL THIS!
AND THIS BUMPY BOARD.
IT'S ...

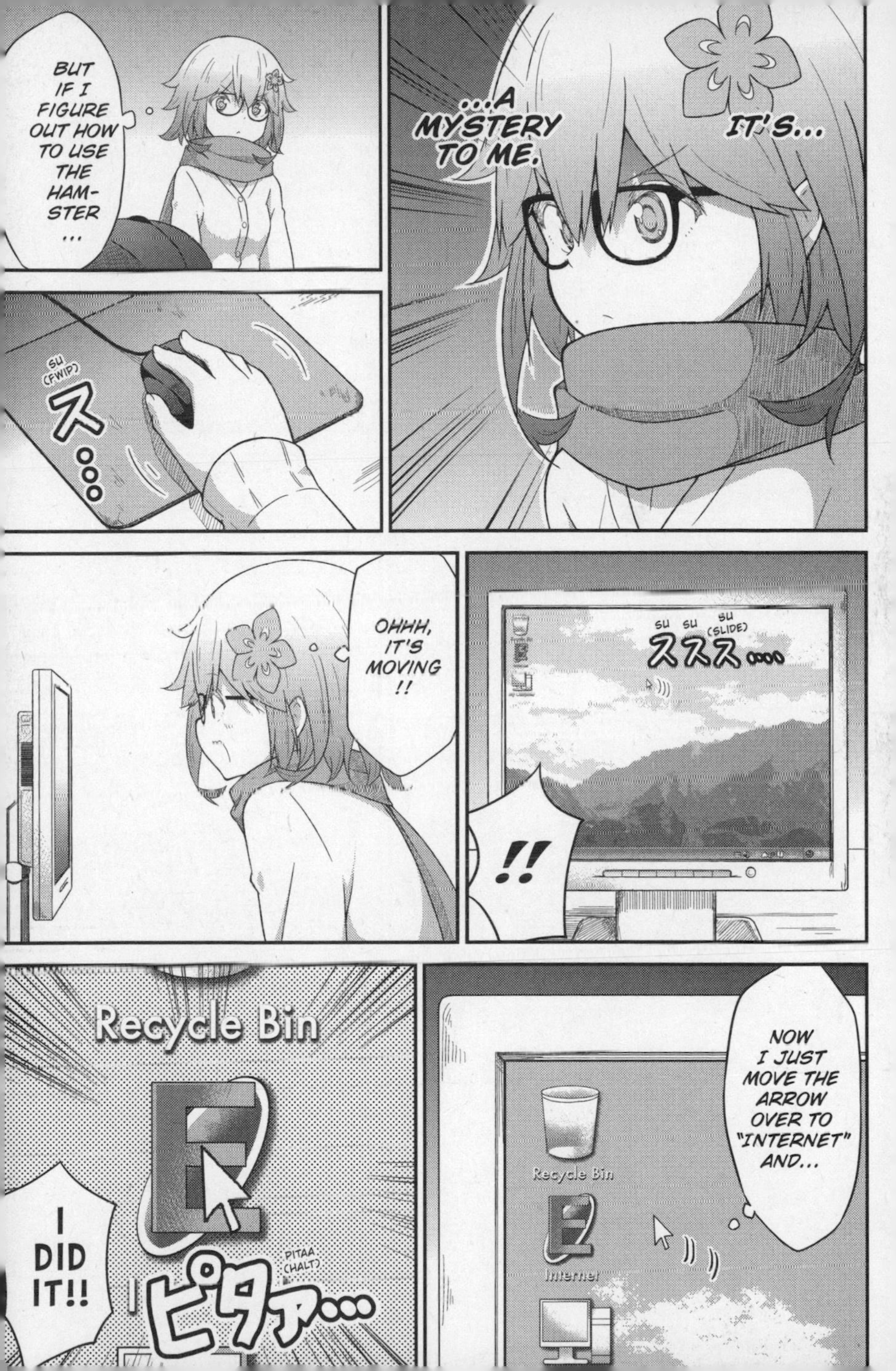
IT'S...
...A MYSTERY TO ME.
BUT IF I FIGURE OUT HOW TO USE THE HAM-STER...
SU (FWIP)
ス…
SU SU SU (SLIDE)
ススス…
!!
OHHH, IT'S MOVING!!
NOW I JUST MOVE THE ARROW OVER TO "INTERNET" AND...
Recycle Bin
Internet
Recycle Bin
PITAA (HALT)
ピタァ…
I DID IT!!!

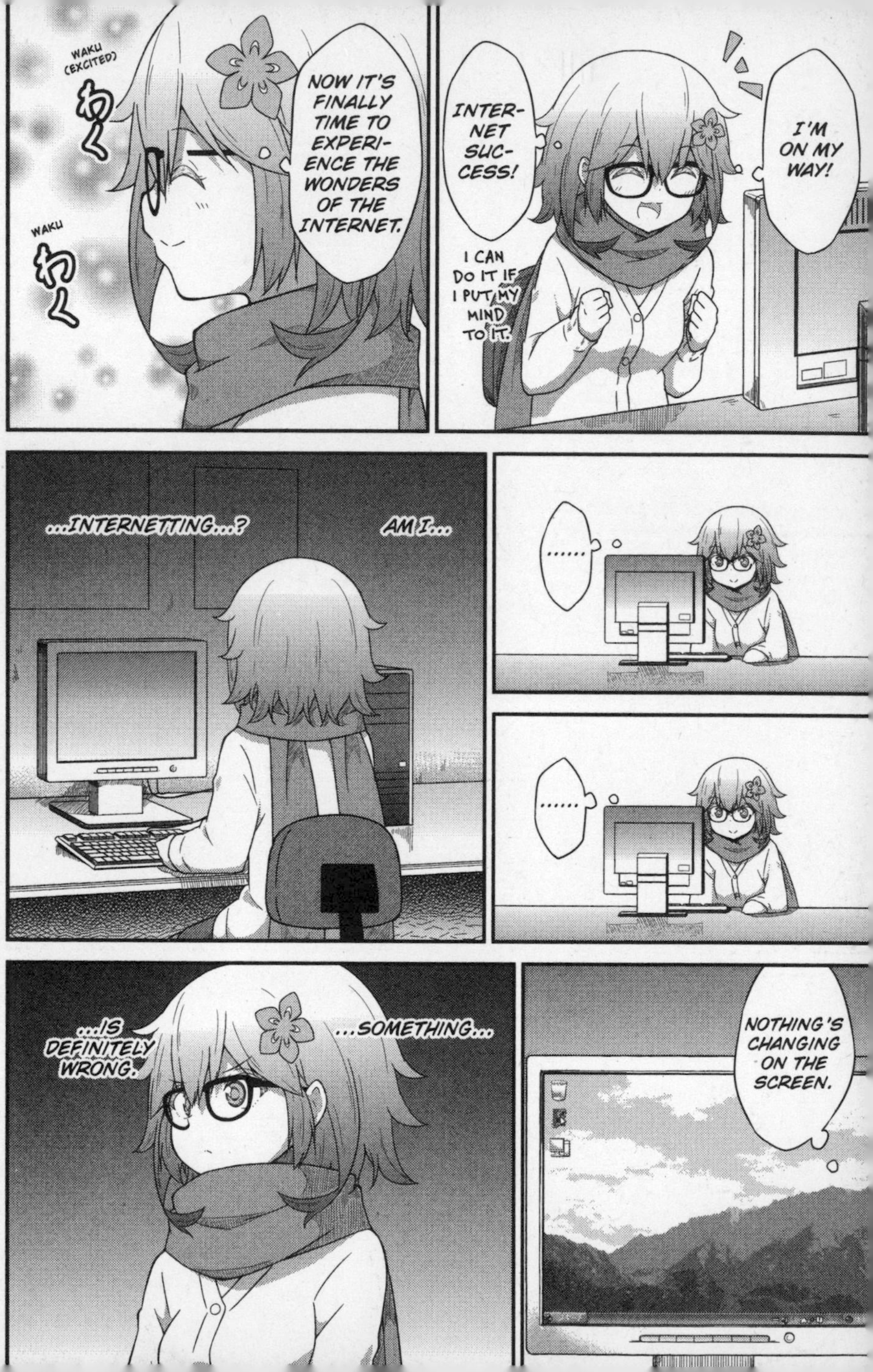
I'M ON MY WAY!
INTER-NET SUC-CESS!
I CAN DO IT IF I PUT MY MIND TO IT.
NOW IT'S FINALLY TIME TO EXPERI-ENCE THE WONDERS OF THE INTERNET.
WAKU (EXCITED)
わく
WAKU
わく
......
......
AM I...
...INTERNETTING...?
NOTHING'S CHANGING ON THE SCREEN.
...SOMETHING...
...IS DEFINITELY WRONG.

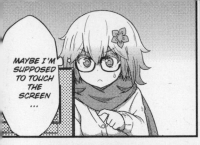

WHAT?
WHAT WENT WRONG?
HOW DO I MAKE THIS WORK!?
MAYBE I'M SUPPOSED TO TOUCH THE SCREEN ...
みょん
MYON (WARP)
みょん
MYON
!!
WAHHH!
I'M SO SORRY!!
DID I BREAK YOU!?
IS SOME-THING WRONG?
PYAH.
ドキ
DOKII (SHOCK)
UM, PAR-DON ME...
I THINK I MAY HAVE BROKEN THE SCREEN ...
DARA (SWEAT)
だら
DARA
だら
だら
DARA
THE... SCREEN?
...IT'S FINE.
I DON'T THINK IT'S BROKEN.
R-REALLY!?

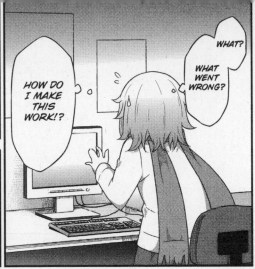

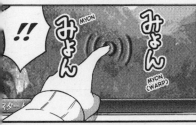

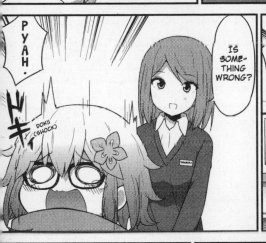

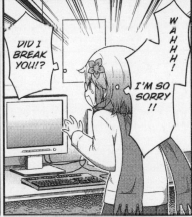

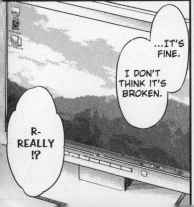

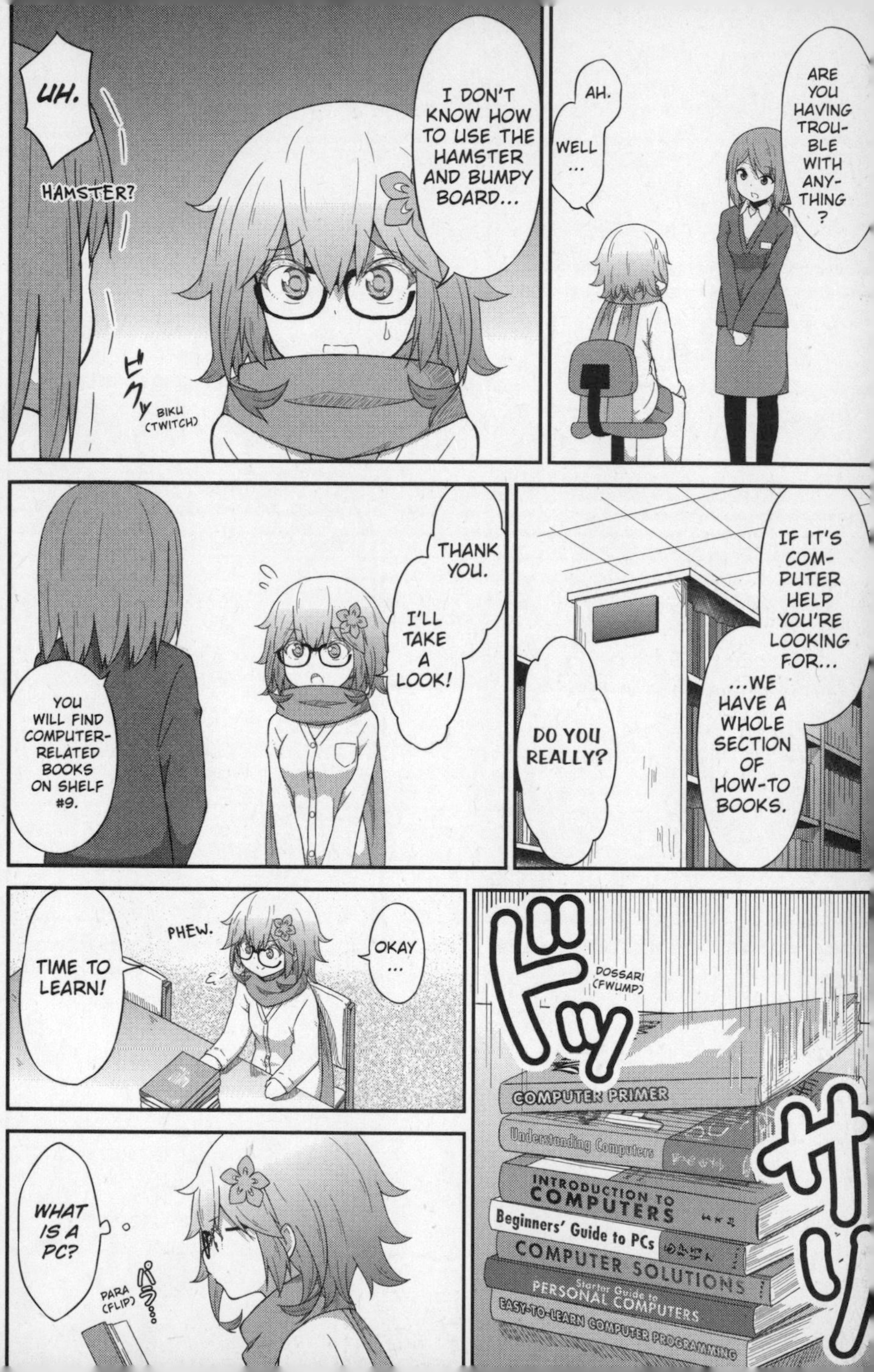
ARE YOU HAVING TROUBLE WITH ANYTHING?
AH.
WELL...
I DON'T KNOW HOW TO USE THE HAMSTER AND BUMPY BOARD...
UH.
HAMSTER?
ビクッ
BIKU (TWITCH)
IF IT'S COMPUTER HELP YOU'RE LOOKING FOR...
...WE HAVE A WHOLE SECTION OF HOW-TO BOOKS.
DO YOU REALLY?
THANK YOU.
I'LL TAKE A LOOK!
YOU WILL FIND COMPUTER-RELATED BOOKS ON SHELF #9.
ドッサリ
DOSSARI (FWUMP)
COMPUTER PRIMER
Understanding Computers
INTRODUCTION TO COMPUTERS
Beginners' Guide to PCs
COMPUTER SOLUTIONS
Starter Guide to PERSONAL COMPUTERS
EASY-TO-LEARN COMPUTER PROGRAMMING
OKAY...
PHEW.
TIME TO LEARN!
WHAT IS A PC?
パラ
PARA (FLIP)

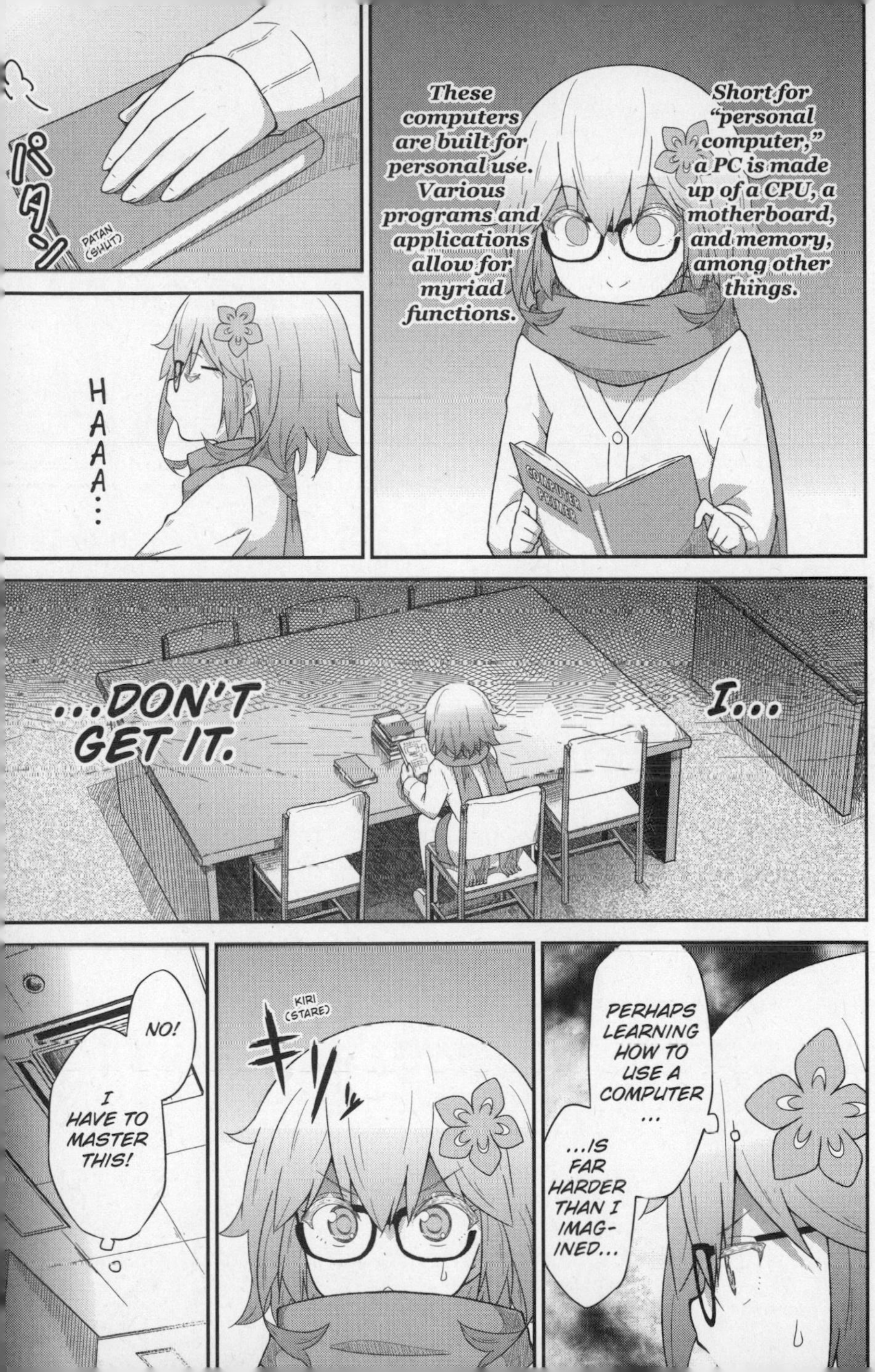
Short for "personal computer," a PC is made up of a CPU, a motherboard, and memory, among other things.
These computers are built for personal use. Various programs and applications allow for myriad functions.
PATAN (SHUT)
HAAAA...
I...
...DON'T GET IT.
PERHAPS LEARNING HOW TO USE A COMPUTER...
...IS FAR HARDER THAN I IMAG-INED...
KIRI (STARE)
NO!
I HAVE TO MASTER THIS!

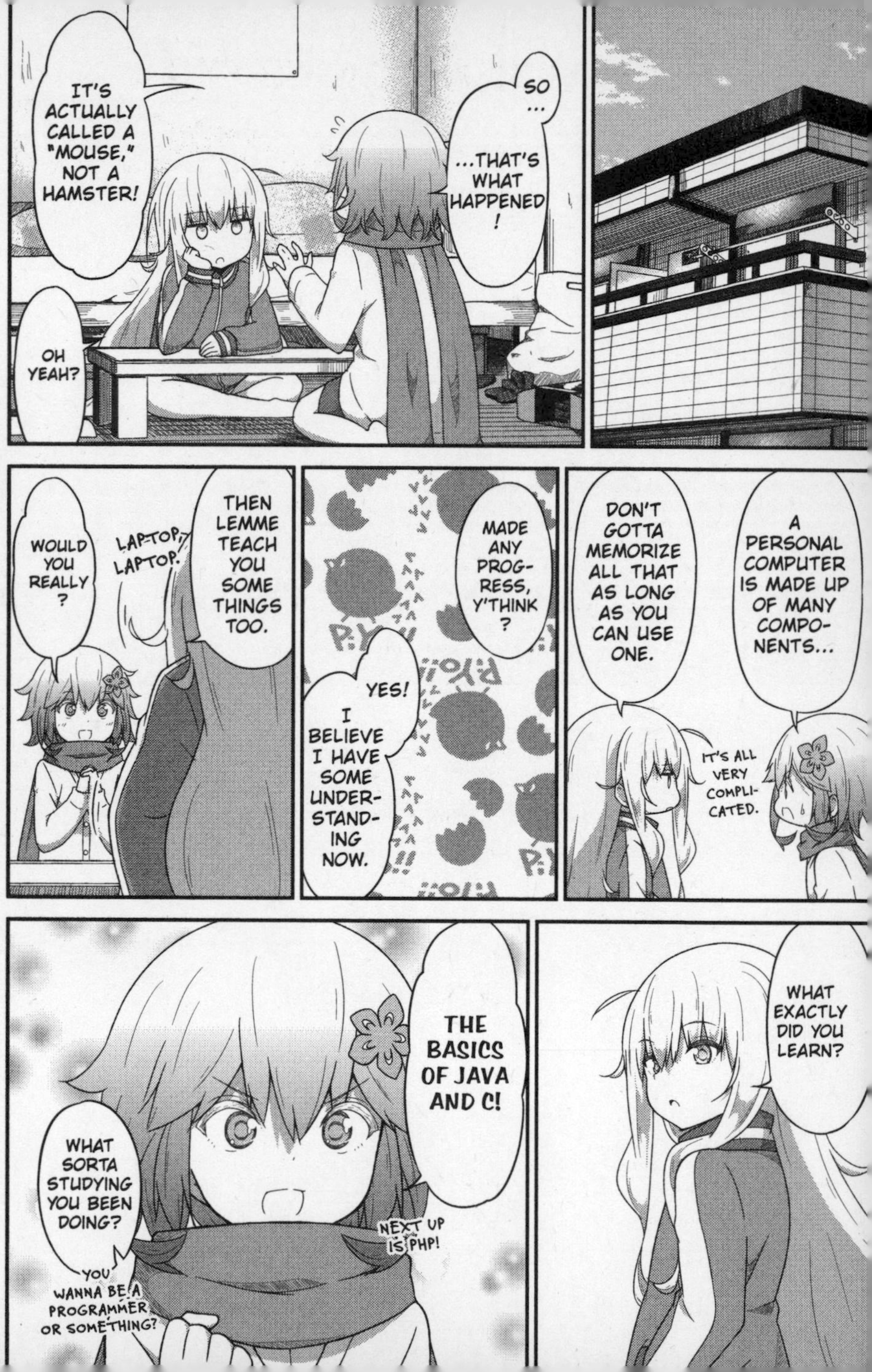
SO ...
...THAT'S WHAT HAPPENED!
IT'S ACTUALLY CALLED A "MOUSE," NOT A HAMSTER!
OH YEAH?
A PERSONAL COMPUTER IS MADE UP OF MANY COMPONENTS...
IT'S ALL VERY COMPLICATED.
DON'T GOTTA MEMORIZE ALL THAT AS LONG AS YOU CAN USE ONE.
MADE ANY PROGRESS, Y'THINK?
YES! I BELIEVE I HAVE SOME UNDERSTANDING NOW.
THEN LEMME TEACH YOU SOME THINGS TOO.
LAPTOP, LAPTOP.
WOULD YOU REALLY?
WHAT EXACTLY DID YOU LEARN?
THE BASICS OF JAVA AND C!
NEXT UP IS PHP!
WHAT SORTA STUDYING YOU BEEN DOING?
YOU WANNA BE A PROGRAMMER OR SOMETHING?

TRANSLATION NOTES

COMMON HONORIFICS

no honorific: Indicates familiarity or closeness; if used without permission or reason, addressing someone in this manner would constitute an insult.
-san: The Japanese equivalent of Mr./Mrs./Miss. If a situation calls for politeness, this is the fail-safe honorific.
-sama: Conveys great respect; may also indicate that the social status of the speaker is lower than that of the addressee.
-kun: Used most often when referring to boys, this indicates affection or familiarity. Occasionally used by older men among their peers, but it may also be used by anyone referring to a person of lower standing.
-chan: An affectionate honorific indicating familiarity used mostly in reference to girls; also used in reference to cute persons or animals of either gender.
-senpai: A suffix used to address upperclassmen or more experienced coworkers.
-sensei: A respectful term for teachers, artists, or high-level professionals.

GENERAL
One hundred yen is roughly equivalent to one US dollar.

PAGE 93
The **kendama** is a Japanese toy that features a ball tied to a wooden spike. The goal is to use the spike to catch the ball, which has a hole cut into the bottom of it.

Otedama is a game in which small bean bags are tossed into the air and juggled, similar to jacks.

Menko is a game similar to milk caps in which players throw cards onto a playing field in an attempt to flip other players' cards and claim them. Whoever flips the most cards or claims all of the cards wins the game.

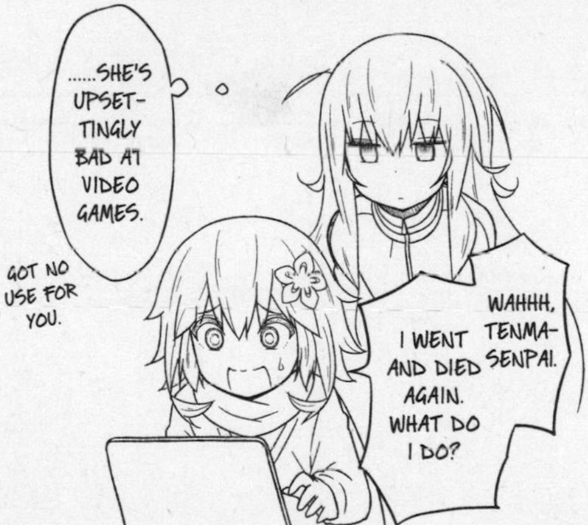
WAHHH, TENMA-SENPAI.
I WENT AND DIED AGAIN. WHAT DO I DO?
......SHE'S UPSET-TINGLY BAD AT VIDEO GAMES.
GOT NO USE FOR YOU.

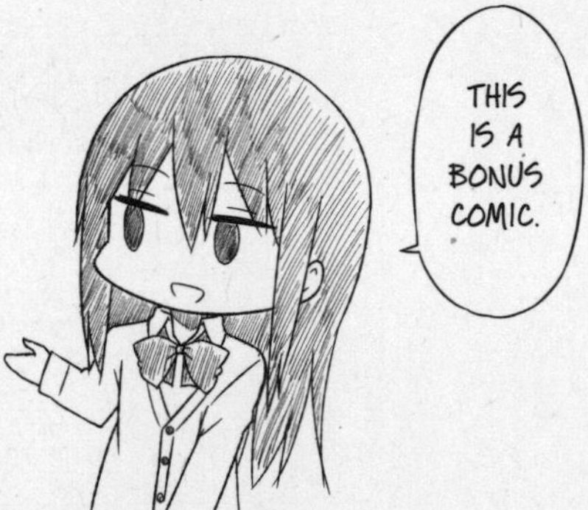
THIS IS A BONUS COMIC.

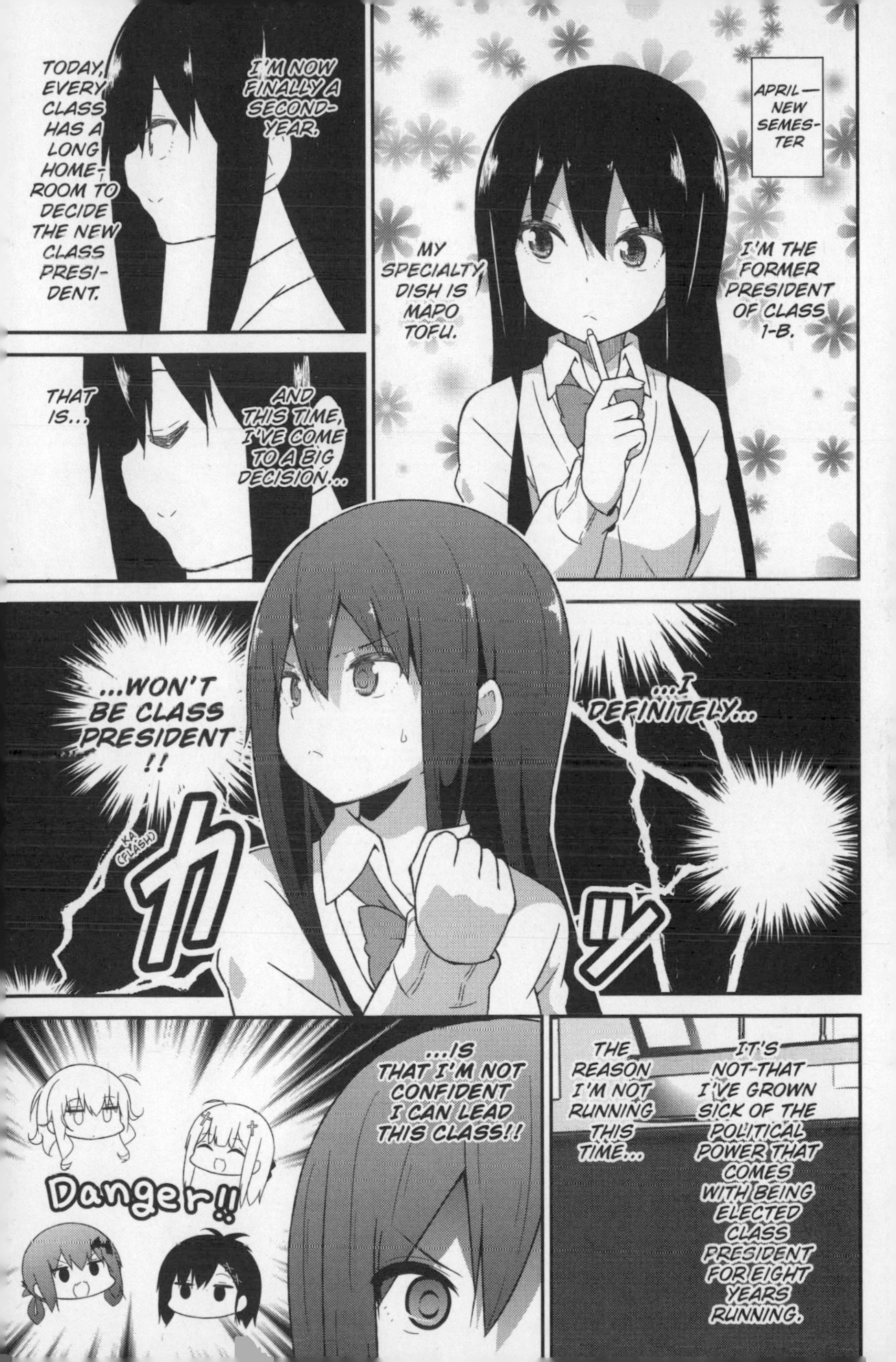
APRIL—NEW SEMESTER
I'M THE FORMER PRESIDENT OF CLASS 1-B.
MY SPECIALTY DISH IS MAPO TOFU.
I'M NOW FINALLY A SECOND-YEAR.
TODAY, EVERY CLASS HAS A LONG HOMEROOM TO DECIDE THE NEW CLASS PRESIDENT.
AND THIS TIME, I'VE COME TO A BIG DECISION...
THAT IS...
...I DEFINITELY...
...WON'T BE CLASS PRESIDENT!!
カッ
KA (FLASH)
IT'S NOT THAT I'VE GROWN SICK OF THE POLITICAL POWER THAT COMES WITH BEING ELECTED CLASS PRESIDENT FOR EIGHT YEARS RUNNING.
THE REASON I'M NOT RUNNING THIS TIME...
...IS THAT I'M NOT CONFIDENT I CAN LEAD THIS CLASS!!
Danger!!

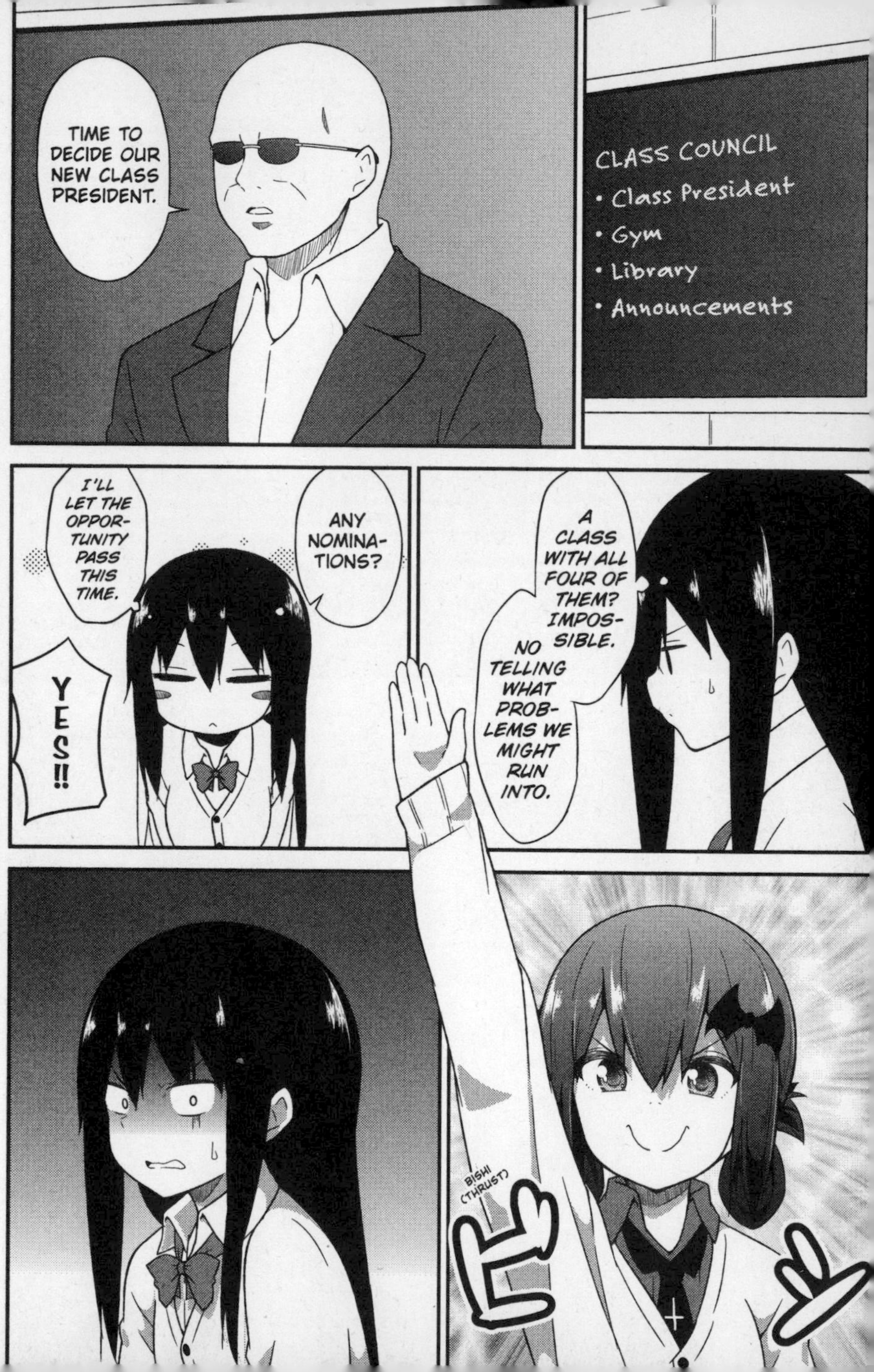
CLASS COUNCIL
• Class President
• Gym
• Library
• Announcements
TIME TO DECIDE OUR NEW CLASS PRESIDENT.
A CLASS WITH ALL FOUR OF THEM? IMPOSSIBLE.
NO TELLING WHAT PROBLEMS WE MIGHT RUN INTO.
ANY NOMINATIONS?
I'LL LET THE OPPORTUNITY PASS THIS TIME.
YES!!
BISHI (THRUST)

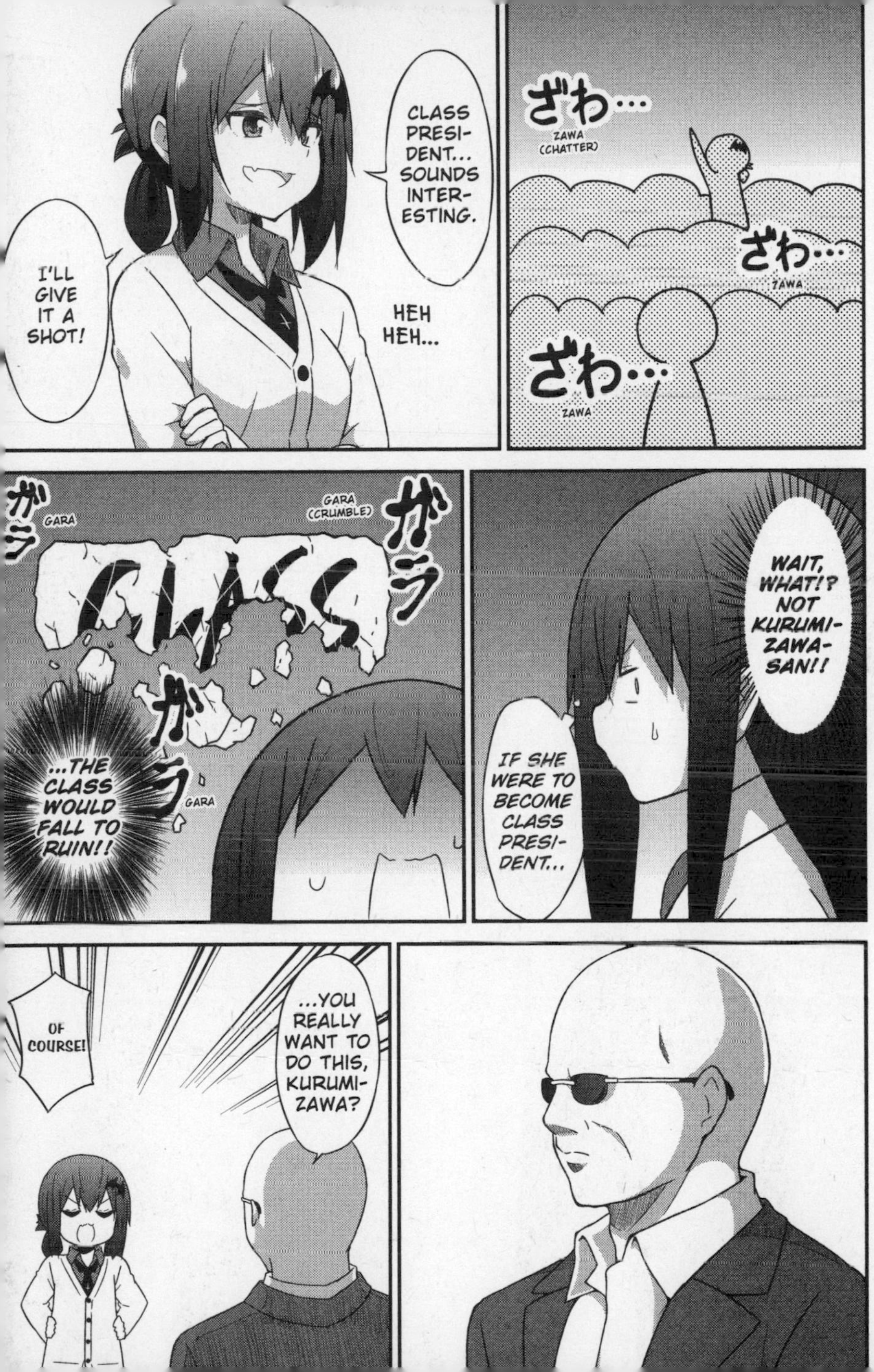
ざわ…
ZAWA (CHATTER)
ざわ…
ZAWA
ざわ…
ZAWA
CLASS PRESIDENT… SOUNDS INTERESTING.
HEH HEH…
I'LL GIVE IT A SHOT!
WAIT, WHAT!? NOT KURUMIZAWA-SAN!!
IF SHE WERE TO BECOME CLASS PRESIDENT…
ガラ
GARA (CRUMBLE)
CLASS
ガラ
GARA
ガラ
GARA
…THE CLASS WOULD FALL TO RUIN!!
…YOU REALLY WANT TO DO THIS, KURUMIZAWA?
OF COURSE!

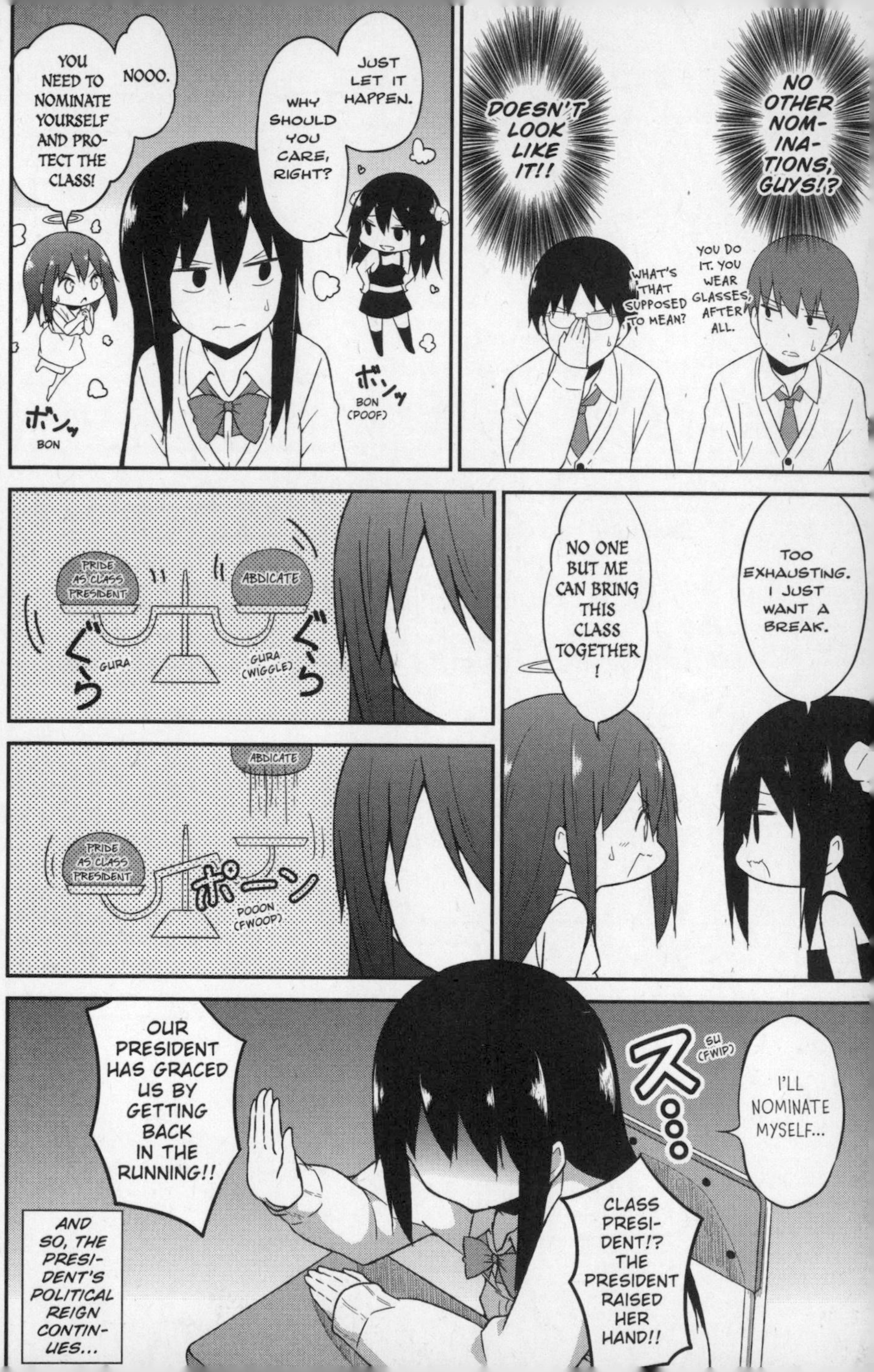

NO OTHER NOMINATIONS, GUYS!?
DOESN'T LOOK LIKE IT!!
YOU DO IT. YOU WEAR GLASSES, AFTER ALL.
WHAT'S THAT SUPPOSED TO MEAN?
JUST LET IT HAPPEN.
WHY SHOULD YOU CARE, RIGHT?
ボンッ
BON (POOF)
NOOO.
YOU NEED TO NOMINATE YOURSELF AND PROTECT THE CLASS!
ボンッ
BON
TOO EXHAUSTING. I JUST WANT A BREAK.
NO ONE BUT ME CAN BRING THIS CLASS TOGETHER!
ABDICATE
PRIDE AS CLASS PRESIDENT
ぐら
GURA (WIGGLE)
ぐら
GURA
ABDICATE
PRIDE AS CLASS PRESIDENT
ポーン
POOON (FWOOP)
I'LL NOMINATE MYSELF...
ス…
SU (FWIP)
CLASS PRESIDENT!? THE PRESIDENT RAISED HER HAND!!
OUR PRESIDENT HAS GRACED US BY GETTING BACK IN THE RUNNING!!
AND SO, THE PRESIDENT'S POLITICAL REIGN CONTINUES...

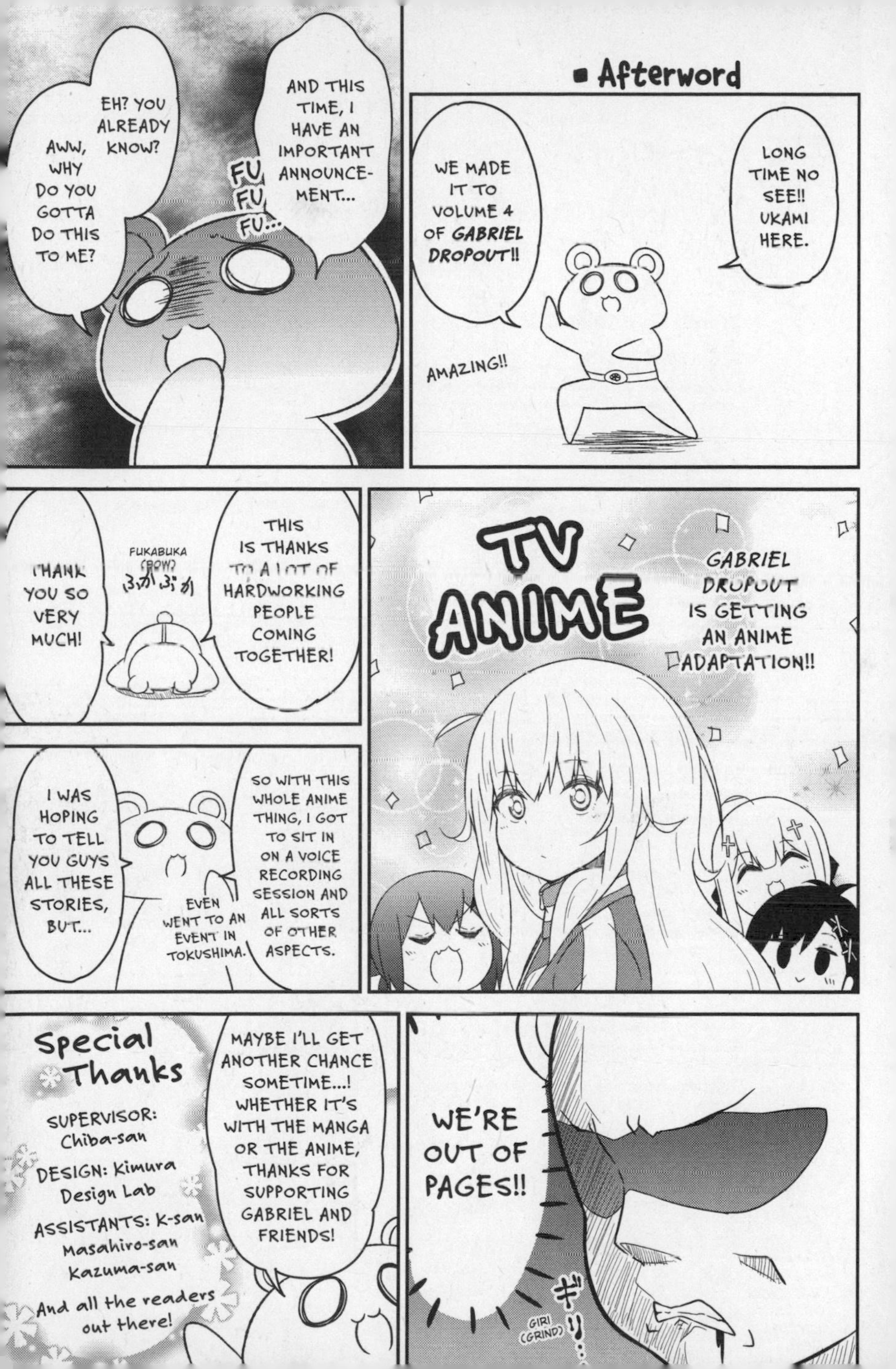
Afterword
LONG TIME NO SEE!! UKAMI HERE.
WE MADE IT TO VOLUME 4 OF GABRIEL DROPOUT!!
AMAZING!!
AND THIS TIME, I HAVE AN IMPORTANT ANNOUNCEMENT...
FU FU FU...
EH? YOU ALREADY KNOW?
AWW, WHY DO YOU GOTTA DO THIS TO ME?
TV ANIME
GABRIEL DROPOUT IS GETTING AN ANIME ADAPTATION!!
THIS IS THANKS TO A LOT OF HARDWORKING PEOPLE COMING TOGETHER!
FUKABUKA (BOW)
ふかぶか
THANK YOU SO VERY MUCH!
SO WITH THIS WHOLE ANIME THING, I GOT TO SIT IN ON A VOICE RECORDING SESSION AND ALL SORTS OF OTHER ASPECTS.
EVEN WENT TO AN EVENT IN TOKUSHIMA.
I WAS HOPING TO TELL YOU GUYS ALL THESE STORIES, BUT...
WE'RE OUT OF PAGES!!
GIRI (GRIND)
ギリ…
MAYBE I'LL GET ANOTHER CHANCE SOMETIME...! WHETHER IT'S WITH THE MANGA OR THE ANIME, THANKS FOR SUPPORTING GABRIEL AND FRIENDS!
Special Thanks
SUPERVISOR: Chiba-san
DESIGN: Kimura Design Lab
ASSISTANTS: K-san Masahiro-san Kazuma-san
And all the readers out there!

Gabriel DROPOUT 4

UKAMI

Translation: Caleb Cook / **Lettering: Rochelle Gancio**

Gabriel Dropout Vol. 4
©UKAMI 2017
 First published in Japan in 2017 by KADOKAWA CORPORATION, Tokyo.
English translation rights arranged with KADOKAWA CORPORATION, Tokyo through TUTTLE-MORI AGENCY, INC., Tokyo.

English translation © 2018 by Yen Press, LLC

Yen Press
1290 Avenue of the Americas
New York, NY 10104

Visit us!
/ yenpress.com
/ facebook.com/yenpress
/ twitter.com/yenpress
/ yenpress.tumblr.com
/ instagram.com/yenpress

First Yen Press Edition: July 2018

Yen Press is an imprint of Yen Press, LLC.
The Yen Press name and logo are trademarks of Yen Press, LLC.

Library of Congress Control Number: 2017945425

ISBNs: 978-1-9753-2656-2 (paperback)
       978-1-9753-8241-4 (ebook)

10 9 8 7 6 5 4 3 2 1

WOR

Printed in the United States of America